SCHOOL MANAGEMENT.

BY

ALFRED HOLBROOK,

PRINCIPAL OF NORMAL SCHOOL, LEBANON, OHIO; AUTHOR OF NORMAL METHODS OF TEACHING.

LEBANON, OHIO:

PUBLISHED BY JOSIAH HOLBROOK.

1871.

LECTURE ON SCHOOL MANAGEMENT.

Delivered at the Normal Institute, at Lebanon, Ohio, July 8, 1868.

BY ALFRED HOLBROOK.

LECTURE I.

QUALIFICATIONS OF TEACHERS.

The lecture this morning is introductory to the course on *School Management.*

I shall first discuss the

QUALIFICATIONS OF TEACHERS.

Under this head, I shall illustrate by examples the most important qualification, COMMON SENSE.

It is the popular *dictum* that if a man is fit for nothing else he will resort to teaching for a livelihood. But if he could find any other employment he would never teach. There are of course some exceptions to this popular opinion, and a few persons sensible enough, to esteem the teacher, but I am speaking of the feeling which, Fellow Teachers, sways the multitude, and which too far neutralizes your influence and perverts and debases your power. Do I speak too strongly, when I say, that a large majority, even of intelligent people, think that the Profession of Teaching receives all such persons as have tried other kinds of business and failed, or who are too lazy to work, and yet imagine with a little knowledge of Grammar and Arithmetic, enough to pass through the flint mill of a county examination, they can teach, if afterward they can only "find a school not taken up?" Yes, teach at some price!

Did you ever feel depressed, Teacher, when you presented yourself before a board of Directors, yes, degraded by the power of this prejudice which characterizes you as a nobody, so that you hardly dared demand decent wages for your services?

This being the state of popular sentiment, I nevertheless wish to show that the true position of the teacher, is one of the highest dignity, and one to which men of pure and earnest ambition can well aspire.

I hesitate not to affirm that the qualification necessary to give success in any calling, *common sense*, is demanded in larger measures in Teaching than in any other profession. Furthermore, I dare assert, that the really successful teacher, male or female, can succeed at any other business for which he or she feels a predilection. He who can succeed according to my standard, *moderately*, in Teaching, can succeed according to the worlds' standard, *eminently*, in almost any other business, to which he shall feel himself called. You see, I take this popular opinion by the throat, and I intend to hold it there, and am determined to put it down, so far as a firm purpose and a kind Providence will permit.

We, Teachers, will have to work for ourselves and with each other, against this wide-spread error, and the way we will do it, Teachers, is to make ourselves more worthy, more efficient; and then we shall not complain of a want of appreciation, or of low salaries.

I will now proceed to develop a few positions and relations in which teachers more than others require that inestimable article, COMMON SENSE.

The adaptation of means to ends is wisdom. Wisdom is nothing more nor less than common sense. The Teacher above all others requires this power.

I. *Common Sense will indicate itself, by adaptation to circumstances.*

There is no business which at its commencement requires so great versality of adaptation, as that of the Teacher.

I will give one or two examples, in proof. If a teacher who has been raised in a village, takes a school in the country, and carries his village airs with him, they will certainly militate against his success, and well enough, will it be said by the boys, if not by the girls, "He hasn't common sense."

If, on the other hand, he comes from the country and brings his rusticity with him to the village; his homespun costume, and his awkward manners, if not speedily doffed, will inevitably arouse a spirit of insubordination and contempt, which all the *book knowledge* in the world will neither control nor subdue. But *common sense* may do both, or rather it would have foreseen and forestalled the difficulty. You may say the difficulty is country breeding, but I say country breeding is the best kind of breeding; and the trouble is, want of common sense.

I will go a little further and take a college graduate, as an example. I knew such a one, who went to New Orleans, and won the position of Principal of the High School, with eight or ten able competitors in the race. His qualifications, so far as a knowledge of books was concerned, were superior to any of his antagonists, but in the matter of dress, he showed a niggardly spirit, and a disregard to the demands of his position; so much so, that with other slovenly attire he wore an old glazed-top cap that originally cost about seventy-five cents, and which was so badly dilapidated that his hair projected through the crown. He certainly showed a want of common sense; he hadn't enough of that article to carry on the business of teaching; and he lost his place, as was right and proper, he should.

Again, if a Teacher who has been educated in a High School, attempts to carry out the usages, and the methods in which he was trained, in the management of a common school, failure will be the result, of course.

Again, if you attempt to carry out the particular methods of instruction by which you have been trained here, expecting children of ten, twelve, or fifteen years of age to receive the same benefits you have received, in the same length of time, it will all prove a sad mistake, and will demonstrate a want of common sense, and such, I think, as can hardly exist in any one before me.

Again, in this school we have no rules; suppose you at tempt this plan in almost any other, you might make a fail ure; and you might have success, if you were witty enough. But in the majority of districts, the most witty—the best teachers would not attempt it. They might aspire to it, but would scarcely be willing to announce such a plan, on opening school, for the first time.

II. *Common Sense will indicate itself, in not overtasking or undertasking scholars by the amount of labor required of them.*

There is particular necessity for the exercise of this qualification, where there is so much to do, and so little time to do it in. Besides this, there are in the same class, say in Geography, those who have studied it for two or three years and those who have studied it only for two or three terms. Here is a difficulty, in so arranging the lessons that the most advanced will not slide into mischief for the want of sufficient study, while the less advanced will be discouraged by the impossibilities demanded of them. It requires not a little contrivance and watchfulness, in other words, active Common Sense to avoid or overcome these difficulties. You may say, "Cut the class into two," I say, "Don't do it." You have only a half hour, out of the six, at the most, to hear this recitation. You will need all of that. There is not time in fifteen, nor in twenty minutes, to interest a class. It requires half an hour at least, to manage a class in Geography with any degree of success. But I shall show, in some future lecture, how Common Sense will overcome this difficulty and many others.

III. *Common Sense will indicate itself, in not permitting the teacher to enact rules which he cannot see carried out.*

Some Directors, who may wish to employ you, will have a long list of written or printed rules for the government of their school, and will expect you to enforce them. I advise you not to promise any such thing. I would say that I would try to govern the school in the spirit of these rules, and to carry them out as well as I was able, but would not be willing to accept such a code, with the expectation that I should enforce them to the letter. To make the case a little plainer, suppose your Directors impose a rule, among others, prohibiting swearing. Your scholars are scattered over the district, some in town, and some in the country. If you had omniscience itself you could not prevent swearing. It would be utterly vain to try it, especially, if you had a rigid rule against it. Of course I would raise a voice of kindly admonition and earnest remonstrance against it, presenting the evils of indulgence on one side and the advantages of abstinence on the other. I would do almost anything to prevent it, save attempting to enforce a law which would only prove a provocation to the commission of the sin.

I will, after a while, show, how you may lead your scholars by united action of their own, to accomplish what is desired in this direction, without involving yourself in an impossibility or absurdity.

IV. *Common Sense will indicate itself by not imposing study, or confinement in the school room, as a punishment.*

Now, I wouldn't be surprised if there were a dozen or more curly-headed young men present who are ready to say, "I never would have studied at all, if I had not been kept after school and compelled to." The wonder, to my mind is, that they learned anything, with such management working against them. I wish to lay down this general principle that whatever is forced upon us, however good or bad, in itself, will become repulsive, the moment we discover the pressure; and the more stringent the coercion, the more hateful will be the requisition. Suppose you force candy on a child, how long will the child love candy? Let us take another example. Here is a young man who has arrived at the age of maturity, and is beginning to think about making arrangements for life. But his father who still claims authority over him, says, "John, I want you to attend to that business immediately." A certain young lady lives over the way, and John has been considering an alliance, with her for some time. But the father says, "I want you to arrange matters, and push it through. There is no use in dallying any longer. You have wasted time enough. If you can't close up the business before long, I shall help you." What is the result? John, if he has never been impudent before, will be so this time, and will reply. "Father, I can manage my own affairs." And the more the father will, the more John won't.

The soul thirsts for knowledge, and nothing yields such rich delight as its acquisition; but when forced, it is worse than uncoated pills crammed into the resisting child. Now, teachers, you may object, that my view of Common Sense s contrary to universal usage. All that I have to say is, "All the worse then for universal usage. It is time that it should be reformed by one of the plainest dictates of Common Sense."

V. *Another indication of Common Sense is, in not referring to personal defects.*

If, for instance, one of your pupils is cross-eyed and you should make any allusion to the fact; it would not only show a want of sense, but a want of heart, and you ought not to succeed; you are out of your place, if you are occupying the position of a teacher.

Do you understand me? One of your little boys, perhaps, is lame. It is not his fault but his sad misfortune. He suffers enough from the ever present calamity without being taunted with it, as if a crime. If it is not sensible, kind, or christian ever to refer to defects in pupils; it is sheer folly, and abominable wickedness to refer to any delinquencies in friends, parents, or other relations. I need not dwell here, surely; but suppose one of your pupils has a father in the state prison. Would it not be splendid policy, sometime, when you are provoked by his waywardness, to say "You are a chip off the old block, and ought to be in the state prison where your father is." Yet such things are done. Not precisely in such terms but in the same spirit. In my mind, such teachers are terribly defective, themselves, somewhere. They don't continue to curse the school room long, thank Heaven. They say "I don't like the business."

VI. *The next indication of Common Sense is in not riding a hobby.*

Take for example, Singing Geography. Teachers formerly came around with their big out-line maps and claimed to teach all that was necessary to be known about Geography in a week or two, in all the tunes from Old Mear to Fishers' Hornpipe, from Coronation to Money-Musk. The children remember the tunes and whistle them to the present time, perhaps. But what discipline or development was attained by singing,

" Connecticut, Hartford and New Haven,
Connecticut, Hartford and New Haven."

It does not take much Common Sense to discover that such hobgoblin performances don't do much, in favor either of knowledge or virtue.

Grammar and Mental Arithmetic are too often hobby-ridden. But of all, the last and worst ridden is "Object Lessons." In another connection I will show you that every good teacher from the Great Teacher, down, has found "objects" such as materials, machinery, apparatus, cabinets, incidents and accidents indispensable to his success in every department; but "Object Lessons" as object lessons in the rigmarole of the imported "Training Schools" is too great an offense to Common Sense to tickle the public love of humbuggery much longer.

Now turning the grindstone, and possibly the creaking of the gudgeon are necessary to the sharpening of the axe. "Teaching object lessons," is too much like applying the edge of the axe to the grindstone for the benefit of the turning and the creaking. Why, my father, Josiah Holbrook, had thousands of children in Boston and New York, engaged in collecting cabinets of common and uncommon things and studying natural science in a natural system, thirty years ago. He invented and introduced Holbrook's apparatus into thousands of schools and thus hundreds of thousands of children were taught science pratically and were led to develop their perceptive and reflective faculties, as well as their physical energies.

But object lessons have come from Europe since, and since Barnum took the lead in importing similar articles for a nine days' wonder.

Don't be alarmed, I have over a dozen object lesson books, and several sets of object lesson cards, in my posession, and think "I know whereof I affirm."

Do not suppose I wish to decry the use of objects of any

kind as means of illustration, instruction and development. In a future lecture I will endeavor to show that they are indisensable in greater variety and utility than many trained object-lesson teachers, ever dreamed of, to any effective course of instruction.

VII. *Common Sense will indicate itself in not talking too much.*

Excessive talking in the way of explaining, and lecturing, is a too common fault of good teachers, or of those who might be good teachers, if controlled by Common Sense in this particular. If you have the "gift of gab," hold on to it, and develop the power of expression in your pupils—hold on, I say, though it be with a double-purchase bit. You not only waste your own energies by so much talk, but repress and paralyze all ambition in your scholars. I say, hold on with a double bit, with a gag, and if that won't do, place a slip-noose around your neck and engage some one to tighten it for you when necessary. Do you know that a lazy teacher does nearly all that is done in his school? The lazier the teacher the more he talks. The more energetic and efficient the teacher, the less he talks, within certain limits, and the more cheerful work will he draw out his scholars.

If there is any preference, the teacher who asks the questions by the book, and marks the special words for his scholars to memorize for answers, is better than the lecturing teacher; for the former furnishes *something* for pupils to do. The teacher who consumes the time of his pupils in talk, will make them more stupid and lazy from day to day. The scholars may think and declare him a great teacher, a very learned man, but the result of his great learning used in this manner, will be, that his scholars will lose all ambition in study if they ever had any, and his school will diminish in numbers from term to term.

VIII. *Common Sense will exhibit itself in not being too zealous in sectarianism.*

Every teacher, more than any other man or woman, should be a living, working, consistent Christian. The spirit of a trusting believer should evince itself at all times; but to be a

Methodist, and simply a Methodist, a red-hot Methodist, and use all his influence to bring everybody's children into the Methodist Church, will not even promote Methodism. I do not speak of the Methodists because I think them zealots above all others; the Methodist Church if we judge by the extent of its usefulness, is one of the best. But the same may be said of Quakers, or Presbyterians, or zealots of any other denomination. I have spoken of the Evangelical Churches. If this course is bad and even here works against the teacher's interest, against the true interests of education, and religion; how much worse is it to work for skepticism, or Universalism, where Universalism is more feared than skepticism. So I say common sense will guide us in this matter. If I am a Methodist I will not use my influence to persuade my scholars to become Methodists; or if I am a Presbyterian or Baptist, I will not be disappointed and vexed because all my scholars do not become Presbyterians or Baptists; but if I have any influence, in this way, I will exercise it, so that the children will go with their parents, in the way of righteousness.

IX. *Again, Common Sense will indicate itself in not permitting you to work in bad air.*

The ceiling of most school-rooms is too low. The ceiling of this room is low enough—about eighteen feet; but your school-rooms are not more than two-thirds, or one-half as high as this, and sometimes, basement of churches are used, especially for select schools. Now, suppose, Teacher, you are six feet two inches, and your ceiling but seven feet from the floor, what kind of air will you necessarily breath in such a place? If, in violation of common sense, you occupy such a room you will lose your interest in your work, impair your health, be likely to break down with hemorrhage of the lungs, before a year has elapsed. Were I a physician, I would tell you, "If your countenance is florid now, if you are plump and fair, that you will be much more likely to suffer than if somewhat thin and bony," but in any case, whether plump or puny, fair or faded, pure air is cheap and plenty, and you are silly, yes, not over cleanly, if you will suffer yourself to breath the putrid exhalations which have been breathed over and over by each of your fifty pupils. Think how you would like to eat food that has gone through as many mouths, with this difference in its favor, that it was not poisoned in its transit.

X. *Again Common Sense will indicate itself in not working in dishonesty.*

The Teacher has some peculiar temptations to act dishonestly His scholars expect him to know more than others; they may think he ought to know almost everything. But if he lacks a proper knowledge of what he is to teach it will be discovered soon enough. You will find none but the veriest quack or the most hopeless ignoramus to claim that he knows everything. Such men as Newton and Agassiz are the ones who most frequently say, "I don't know." If when questions arise which you are unable to answer, you are accustomed to put the pupils off, by some evasion or other, you may be assured that they will ever have difficulties ready to spring upon you, and behind your back laugh at your simplicity. Now, the best way is to own up, and say "This is new to me, I will take time to examine it, and I hope, pupils, you will do the same, and we will call up the matter to-morrow. If I should forget it, you must not. Bring it up at the beginning of the recitation so that it may not be passed over."

XI. *Again, Common Sense, will indicate itself in not scolding.*

This is the last point I shall present in this lecture. I don't know that there is any need of discussing this point. So far as you are concerned I suppose you are well satisfied as to the virtues of scolding. If there are any, ladies and gentlemen, and any one of you thinks that a pupil can be benefited by scolding, let him raise his hand. On some fitting occasion I will try it on, and we will see how you like your own prescription. Suppose some day, I am very much provoked and agitated, and I yield to this habit; the next day before going to school, I would declare in the sight of Heaven, and a good conscience "whatever I do, or do not do to-day, I will not use a cross word to my scholars. I will lay my neck under their feet, but I will not scold."

These are some of the points in which common sense will indicate itself in the true teacher. And I am now perhaps justified in the position taken, that common sense is as much needed in our profession as in any other; nay more needed than in any other. Furthermore I wish to reiterate that any person who has common sense enough to succeed amid the difficulties and responsiblities of a common country school will succeed in any business to which he may desire to turn his attention. The successful common school teacher can accomplish anything under Heaven, that his good sense will permit him to aspire to. If he does not manage a school well, he ought not expect to succeed in any other profession, he may succeed possibly as a day laborer. He may not have as large powers of mind, as some others, but if he has mind enough, energy enough, perseverance, and moral character and influence enough to meet the difficulties arising from a common district school of fifty or sixty scholars, if he can make his school attractive, if he can harmonize all the discordant elements in the children and young people of his district, and gradually but certainly bring a good moral atmosphere into the neighborhood, he has power to accomplish a work that angels might aspire to. What good teacher will desire to do less?

LECTURE ON SCHOOL MANAGEMENT.

LECTURE II.

SECOND QUALIFICATION. KNOWLEDGE OF THE BRANCHES.

LADIES AND GENTLEMEN: I shall this morning consider the Knowledge of the Branches as the second qualification of the teacher, for School Management.

HOW TESTED.

You are aware that this, the only qualification tested by the County School Examiners, is the least important and least indicative of skill, in developing and controlling your pupils. A person may be eminently qualified in the knowledge of the branches, yes, profoundly erudite in *all* the branches, and yet lack aptness to teach, and be entirely destitute of power to manage either himself or others. Bookworms are not generally noted for business tact, a trait so necessary to success in school management.

You ask, How can examinations reach this most necessary qualification?

I answer, Let us have a town superintendency; in every town a superintendent, who will visit the schools and examine the teachers at their work. A county superintendency would do something, but each town needs a superintendent, as much as each school-house of a dozen rooms, in Cincinnati, needs a special superintendent, aside from the general superintendency of the entire school system of the city.

The Kind of Knowledge Necessary.

I have spoken of a knowledge of the branches as of the least importance, and yet it is indispensable. Furthermore, it is a crime, in my estimation, for a person to attempt to teach any branch he does not himself understand.

He must not only understand the branch, but must love it; not only for the satisfaction it yields him in studying it, but for the delight it enables him to impart to his pupils through its instrumentality.

You will grant that the teacher who does not understand Arithmetic himself will never lead his pupils to understand it; but I say the teacher who does not love Arithmetic is unfit to teach it; for, without such appreciation, he will not be likely to arouse any enthusiasm for that branch in the minds of those under his instruction.

You have seen the influence, I suppose, of teachers who had a dislike for Grammar. We see it here in our grammar classes, in almost every degree, amounting in some cases even to aversion and contempt. Yet it is frequently our privilege to overcome such prejudice and to hear our pupils say, "I never liked Grammar before. I did n't know that there was so much in it." You understand, then, that, in my opinion, unless you take satisfaction in investigating its principles, in mastering its difficulties, and in applying its utilities, you can never teach any branch well.

But, some one present objects, "I never could understand, I have no natural gift for Arithmetic, and I do n't see how I can ever like it; yet I will have to teach it, if I teach at all."

Now, my friend, I admit you may have no very remarkable ability in Mathematics. You may have a perfect dread of it; yet you can obtain a positive relish for it, and take real delight in teaching it. Do you ask, "How?"

I answer, The difficulty is not so much, after all, in natural inability as in acquired prejudice; and I will try to tell you how you can overcome both.

Make Arithmetic your leading study; give it your best hours, your most diligent and earnest attention; make it cost you something. Do not imagine the labor of a week, or of a month, will entirely overcome your inability or your prejudice. This can be done only by the most determined and persistent efforts, and by making each partial failure a stepping stone to a higher success.

But, just in proportion to your former aversion, just and in so far as it costs you labor and self-sacrifice to overcome the difficulties, just in the same proportion, if you pursue the plan proposed, will you eventually value Arithmetic, and delight in teaching it.

This blessed law, "What costs much is worth much, and what costs little is worth little," is incorporated in our mental and moral constitutions. I will give a few examples to illustrate it.

A Methodist Presiding Elder, residing in our town, in Northern Ohio, had an interesting family, except one child almost helpless and imbecile, requiring the constant care and attention of the mother. The boy was eight years old when I first knew him. It may well be supposed that this child had cost his mother more labor and anxiety than all the other six. The report came one day that the child was sick and likely to die. I felt thankful, and said so. He died; and do you suppose that mother was thankful that she was relieved of such a burden? such a constant and exhausting care? I have seen mothers grieve for their darlings so full of promise, snatched from their fond embrace, but never did I see mother grieve as this one. An extreme case, you say. So say I; and it illustrates my position all the better.

There is the old Nutmeg State, in which I was born, that had an immense income for educational purposes, by grant of Congress, enough to pay a fair tuition fee for every child in the State.

What was the result? Education was more backward, school privileges more neglected there than in any other Eastern State.

Massachusetts, on the other hand, never had a school fund, but taxed herself annually and adequately, and has always had the most efficient school system in America, perhaps in the world.

There, school privileges cost something, and were worth something.

But I have another example in mind, more directly in point. One of the best teachers in this State, who has attained to the first position in the State, was naturally less gifted in mathematics, I judge, than any one before me. I have been told that from Mental Arithmetic upward, through Written Arithmetic and Algebra, he wrote out the solutions as obtained from his teachers or fellow pupils, and preserved them for future use in teaching. I have heard him say that he never had but one teacher that had patience with his dullness. By dint of perseverance and a good purpose, however, he became noted for his skill and success in teaching Arithmetic. He succeeded marvelously in interesting slow minds, and in many cases where better and quicker mathematicians had failed. So, teachers, do not be discouraged. It matters little where your disqualification lies, whether in Arithmetic, Algebra, Grammar, or Latin; just where you think nature has done the least for you, there resolve to do the most for yourself; and in due time you will feel that you love no branch so well, and that in no other branch you have the same amount of power to inspire and bless your pupils.

THIRD QUALIFICATION. TEACHING POWER.

I pass now to another qualification in school management, the power of teaching.

As no school can be well managed which is not well taught, I shall dwell somewhat at length on this qualification. Correct management must be based on mutual respect of scholars and teachers; and permanent respect can be secured only as the teacher can benefit his pupils, and convince them of the fact.

ANALYSIS OF TEACHING POWER.

In order that you may better understand what I mean by the *Teaching Power*, I shall attempt what no one hitherto has done, so far as I know—an analysis of this power.

First Element in Teaching Power. Securing Attention.

The first element is the power of securing attention during recitation; the power of arresting and maintaining the persistent attention of every pupil in the class, not of the brightest and best only, but of the dullest and worst; those who before have been heedless, stupid, indolent, wayward, sensual, brutal, or devilish; children of butchers, tavern keepers, doggery men, and such like. It is a pupil of one of these kinds that you, teacher, will desire to win over. Always take the worst one in the class, and strive to arouse him, not by frowns and censure, but by your own magic skill and heartfelt goodness in his behalf. Why, that pupil can not withhold his attention, he can not avoid being interested when he once feels that you are interested in him. He has always before been the fool or the devil of the school; and now he is astonished to discover that, in your opinion, he is neither fool, brute, nor devil, but one whom you can regard with interest and consideration. Again, teacher, you will not be satisfied with holding the attention and interest of your pupils while in the class merely. Your power must go beyond the recitation seat. It must arouse such an eager attention and such an increasing interest as shall carry the pupil, as if spontaneously, to prepare himself for the next recitation. It does not require a *teacher* to interest a class during recitation; a mere *lecturer* can do that. I shall endeavor to show, in a subsequent lecture, how almost any teacher of fair abilities and honest purpose can accomplish what I have here indicated.

Second Element in Teaching Power. Power of Analysis.

Analysis is becoming a very vague term. In this case, however, it has a definite signification, viz.: a thorough and searching investigation of the subject you are teaching. Not such as you can obtain from any one book, but such only as can result from comparing many books, the latest and best on any given subject. Such an investigation, if you have the power of analysis I speak of, will make you, in a large measure, independent of books, for from each author's stand-point you will perceive the elements for which you are in search;

and reducing and harmonizing these perceptions, you will gain a more distinct and glowing conception than any author has himself had, perhaps. Not only so, but more correct; for error will be eliminated by the process, the elements will stand forth in all the beauty and power of their relations and uses.

Relations and uses, I say, for all useful knowledge is a knowledge of relations

First Example. The Watch.

For illustration, let us take a watch to pieces, as I suppose any one of you can, and notice the parts or elements, the plates, pillars, wheels, springs, etc., and learn their names carefully. Now, can we put them together so that the watch will keep time? Probably not. Why? We have not learned the relations of the parts to each other, and their respective uses in accomplishing the object of the watch. In fact, we might memorize all these relations and uses from a book and then be as great bunglers as before.

So, more than books or comparison of books is necessary, then, to accomplish that kind of analysis of any subject required by the true teaching power.

Second Example. Decimal Fractions.

I wish to show what analysis is by one more example. Most of you studied Decimal Fractions in the first place, as I did, I suppose. You thought Vulgar Fractions a very "hard" rule, and often, confused and perplexed by its intricacies, you were stalled in solving the examples; but when you came to Decimal Fractions you thought them very "easy," and wondered "why so easy a rule should come after such a hard one."

Now, all this was from want of analysis on the part of your teacher, who had neither analyzed nor arranged in his own mind the elements of either class of fractions. Had he done so, and presented them properly, you would have found Decimal Fractions much the most difficult subject, as it embraces all the principles of Common Fractions and others combined with them, thus increasing their complexity and the difficulty of managing them.

And even now it is possible, perhaps, that I might give this excellent class of teachers examples in Decimal Fractions which not one-half of you could write, to say nothing of performing other operations which might be required in their solutions or demonstrations.

But I trust your teachers in this institution, from the clear light of their own analysis, will not only make every principle and process perfectly transparent, but will impart to you the power of this analysis in every department of Arithmetic, that you may carry it into your own schools. I certainly would not have you go from here and teach as you and I were taught, merely skimming the surface, and never reaching the real difficulties nor appreciating the true beauties of any subject.

Third Element. Skill in Synthesis.

Synthesis is a Greek derivative, and signifies, etymologically, putting together. In this connection, however, it signifies the arrangement of the elements of a subject for the purpose of instruction. When there is *any* method recognized by the teacher or by the text-book, there will be one of two, viz.: the Logical and Dydactic, or Natural. These two methods will be explained and exemplified by the Teacher of Natural Sciences, at another time and place, and for this reason I will not elaborate the subject here. *

Fourth Element. Power of Distinct and Clear Apprehension.

This power results, almost necessarily, from the previous elements of the Teaching Power; yet they may be possessed in a high degree, and this in a low degree. This power depends on a lively imagination. Have you ever read Thomson's Seasons? If not, I beg you do so at the first convenient opportunity. You will see how, in describing some of the most common scenes, he makes them glow with life and beauty; and you idealize them in your imagination more vividly than

---

* This explanation is found in this Number of National Normal, p. 69.

you ever realized them in your experience. The teacher needs the poet's power, then. And you, teachers, must possess this clearness of apprehension and distinctness of conception, intensified by an excited imagination, before you can make any very deep or lasting impressions on the minds of your pupils.

It is a necessary part of our business, as teachers, to strive for an increase of this power of making vivid impressions, in order to arouse and sustain interest, as well as to stimulate the pupils to work for themselves.

Fourth Element of the Teaching Power. Facility of Expression.

This is vulgarly called "the gift of gab." The gift of gab and facility of expression, as an element of teaching power, are not identical. The one is a mere flow, a diarrhea oi words; the other is a clear and cogent form of expression. Words well chosen are "apples of gold in pictures of silver." Very few have this power as a natural gift, so it demands our attention here.

Facility of Expression consists in the ready use of accurately fitting words, suitably arranged in sentences; and, more than that, in the selection of the very best words our language affords for the most impressive utterance of living, burning thoughts.

I do not know that I can better impress my meaning than by giving this historic incident.

Fox and Pitt were Parliamentary leaders in the time of the Revolutionary war. Fox was a determined tory. Pitt, as all the world knows, was the staunch friend of the American colonies. Mr. Pitt, in reply to one of Mr. Fox's invectives, had carried the house by storm in favor of the colonies, and his measure passed almost by acclamation. Mr. Fox, meeting him soon after, and congratulating him on "the success of his oratorical effort," said, "Mr. Pitt, I have been attempting to discover the secret of the difference between your oratory and mine, and I think I have it." "Well, what is it?" "Why, while I always have *a* word, you always have *the* word."

I say, then, this is one of the elements that we must cultivate most assiduously for the highest success in our calling.

A teacher can never be too ready; he may be too profuse, but he can not have his words too well chosen, too forceful, or too accurate.

There is a man in a million that has the power of giving a new coinage to words. I knew one such, who, grasping words in the vise of thought, stamped them with his own imperial superscription, the royal impress of a new significancy, far surpassing what the same words possessed elsewhere.

Let us, then, strive to reach onward toward such a power. No person needs it so much, no person can make better use of it than the teacher.

Fifth Element. Facility of Illustration.

This being the rarest of all elements, as a natural endowment, thus far enumerated, and the one most generally neglected or abused, it needs the most attention and labor in its development, by careful and constant training of one's self and one's pupils. The almost universal neglect to which this element has been subjected has led, undoubtedly, to the other extreme, "object lessons."

Illustrations Classified.

For the purpose of aiding you in understanding the workings of this element of the teaching power, I shall divide illustrations into four classes, viz.: 1. Rhetorical; 2. Scientific; 3. Artistic; 4. Practical.

Classes Explained and Exemplified.

1. *Rhetorical*, as given by invention, or from association of ideas, in similes, metaphors, parables, allegories, anecdotes, stories, etc.

2. *Scientific*, as given by real objects and experiments, including specimens, apparatus, manipulations, cabinets, laboratories, etc.

Examples you will see in any institution where the Natural Sciences are properly taught. It is comparatively easy, with a good apparatus and with some suitable training in the use of it, to give this class of illustrations to your pupils; but, without apparatus or skillful training, to exhibit scientific experiments to your classes, and incite your pupils to make apparatus for themselves, requires a style of genius that few teachers possess. But this has been done, and with fine effect, by a few earnest, ingenious teachers.

3. *Artistic.* These are made with the crayon, pencil, graver, camera, chisel, etc., and are black-board illustrations, drawings, pictures, statues, wax figures, anatomical preparations, manikins, etc.

You see examples on any of our black-boards; of another variety in Nast's cartoons, given in the illustrated weeklies; of more elaborate character in parlors, art galleries, and anatomical museums.

4. *Practical.* I may give a practical illustration of the force of gravity by dropping this chalk on the floor; or of muscular energy, by throwing it through the open window.

The mechanic teaches his apprentice chiefly by this kind of illustration, in taking the tool into his own hand and doing skillfully what the boy is doing bunglingly. I suppose you are daily witnesses of practical illustrations of these several elements of teaching power, as exhibited by the various teachers of this institution.

Remarks on the Facility of Illustration.

To this arrangement and explanation of the different classes of illustration, I shall add a few general remarks on this element of teaching power, viz.: Facility of Illustration.

1. No lazy teacher, nor rote teacher, nor quack teacher will be likely to make use of this power, even if he should possess it as a natural endowment.

2. Illustrations have, for the most part, hitherto been used in the advanced classes of schools and colleges, whereas the least advanced classes most need such aids; and children require illustration of every kind immensely more than adults; but not in any such manner as will prevent independent effort on their own part, as "object lessons," to a large extent, do. In fact, object lessons are too much like stories for the

sake of the stories, rather than for the illustration of the subject matter.

A sermon made up entirely of random stories and miscellaneous anecdotes would be one kind of object lesson, and quite as useful as many others, now in vogue.

By the proper use of object illustrations I have known a child of quite ordinary capacity learn to read intelligently and intelligibly from a few lessons of ten minutes each ; while others of superior quickness were hammering away with their object-lesson teacher for weeks or months, and making no progress save as the teacher passed on in the order of her "object lesson book."

3. But, friends, what teacher was that, who possessed this power of illustration in such an unsurpassed degree, that I faint and fail before him?

It is my Lord and Savior Jesus Christ. Study the parables: observe the ingenuity and power of his object lessons. See, where the woman was before him "taken in the very act" and the effect of this object lesson on his unwilling pupils, unteachable as they were. With what inimitable skill does he ever meet the exigency, penetrating dullness, arousing stupidity, overcoming obstinacy, and turning subtility against itself, and winning his pupils both to hear and do his will. Let us together and apart entreat the Great Master, that he will vouchsafe to us, his humble disciples in the same divine art, more and more of that spiritual energy, that surpassing skill by which he so successfully taught the "hardest" of all schools, the unbelieving Jews, the most difficult of all branches, the Science of Salvation.

SEVENTH ELEMENT. TACT.

Now comes the ruling element, the sovereign power energizing and controlling all the rest. It is Tact.

Need enough of it, when we consider the forces to be met and vanquished. Arranged in order, they are stupidity, laziness, mischief, hoggishness, whispering, irregular attendance, hostility or contempt for any thing useful or decent. Seven divisions and each a host trained by long practice into almost invincible habit.

Now, come out my shepherd boy, not against Goliath, but against the armies of the Philistines. Here is a field for generalship.

What are you, teacher, with your simple weapons without the tact to forestall and baffle such an array; to supplant this old sensual dynasty, by a new and spiritual reign; to neutralize the activity of Wrong, by infusing the energy of Right; thus winning all these forces from self destruction to self preservation, to perennial life, harmony and vigor?

Not only is it necessary for you to cultivate thus all these elements in yourself, as a teacher, but to make diligent use of the last element, Tact, in imparting the same powers to your pupils. Which one of all these elements must not a successful business man possess? to say nothing of your embryo lawyers and ministers.

But you will probably see the time, teacher, when all your resources will seem exhausted, your energy, skill and struggling will appear futile. Then, I trust you will find the same Power that guided the stripling warrior, the same Counselor that the Master sought all night long in prayer, lives still, and that he will prove your willing, waiting, almighty Deliverer.

If young men come to this institution having some dissimilarity of character, I want them to be allowed to retain their individuality. I sympathize with all my heart in the remarks made concerning æsthetic culture. But if a young man comes here with the lion in him do not begin to pare his nails, or trim his mane, or tone his voice, or tame his spirit; but let his claws grow, let his teeth lengthen, let his mane thicken, let his eye brighten, let his thunder deepen, let his spirit wax till by his roaring he sends terror to all the haunts of wickedness, and dismay to all the dens of iniquity. There is just as much that is æsthetic in the lion as in the lap-dog. We want some majesty, some sublimity some grandeur, some glory, as well as beauty — *Bishop James* (at the opening of the Drew Theological Seminary.)

LECTURE ON SCHOOL MANAGEMENT.

LECTURE III.

FOURTH QUALIFICATION. GOVERNING POWER.

Preliminary Remarks.

The fourth qualification, and the most difficult of all to acquire is the Power of Governing.

It may well be considered that any plan of civil, school, or family government, which does not secure the hearty approval and cheerful co-operation of the large majority of the governed is essentially wrong, and can only work evil results; in the school and family, bad moral results, inevitably. This Governing Power, in any true sense, must rest ultimately on the principle of self-government; for what responsible agent can be satisfied with any control that is continually crossing his purposes, arousing opposition, and exciting conflict, in will, or act, or both?

That Governing Power which every truly successful teacher will exercise, or at least will aspire after, is that which will most enlist the generous sympathies and win the earnest support of his pupils. Such a government, with the most personal freedom to the governed, will secure the most thorough self-control, and self-mastery, for good and noble purposes, in school life; thus giving the pupil that training during school life which beyond comparison will be the most potent for his success in future life, whether considered from a civil, social, or religious stand-point.

In my last lecture I gave an analysis of the Teaching Power, thus affording you, teachers, an opportunity of testing yourselves by the light of the analysis, as possessing or not possessing the elements described and exemplified. But it is my design, in this lecture, to develop the nature of the Governing Power in an entirely different manner, viz.: by describing some of the most common forms in which it is exercised, at the present time, in our various schools and colleges. This course will enable me to characterize some of the sad perversions of authority, in school government and college rules, and to animadvert on the gross abuses and wide-spread evils which necessarily result from the false views and theories entertained by the majority of school-teachers and superintendents, College Professors and Presidents. This method of treating my subject, the Governing Power, will perhaps afford you some valuable aid in making out, each one for himself, an analysis of this all important Teacher's qualification. . shall call for these analyses, wrought out on paper, at the next lecture. You will please note in your written analysis the true elements of the Governing Power, their perversions, the abuses, and evils growing out of these perversions; also the false elements and their resulting evils. Determine, too, as far as you are able, the real principles underlying a good school government; and yet the false principles and their vicious results.

Government by Force.

The first plan of school government which I here introduce to your notice, I shall denominate the Force Method. I so call it, not that force excludes every other element, but because it predominates over all others, and is chiefly relied on by the teacher for securing order and propriety in deportment, as well as diligence and progress in study.

This is, I apprehend, by far the most prevalent form of school government now practiced in our General Educational System. Indeed, it is the only plan known, or, at most, considered of any efficiency, by multitudes of School Boards; though any individual Director or Trustee is always inclined to think, whenever force is applied to his child, that it ought to have been at some other time, or by some other method; and that the teacher is more blameworthy in his manner of administering the punishment than the child in committing the offense.

While few, if any, judicious teachers entirely discard the idea of coercion from their theory of School Management, this particular plan now under consideration strives to correct all evils, and stimulate all virtues by the same process, varied only in the degree of intensity to meet the demands of any given case.

If John has "played hookey," and the teacher finds it out, John knows what to expect.

If Joseph is tardy, without a note from his parent, (more commonly written by some older pupil,) he understands full well the nature of the penalty.

If James's uncontrollable love of fun gets the better of his fears, the Master's voice gives no uncertain sound, "Come up here, James, I 've got to ferule you again, I see."

If Willie's idleness has prevented his learning his spelling lesson, the same remedy is supposed to be the only effectual one, and the good teacher wonders why Willie, naturally so smart, can be so lazy; and really fears that he is growing worse and worse, in spite of all his faithful efforts to stimulate the boy to any kind of industry.

If Sarah is whispering, and repeated reproof has been found of no avail, the ferule must be used; this evil must be checked, or her example will render the school unmanageable.

If Miranda is detected playing tit-tat-too with her seatmate, when they ought to have been working out their Arithmetic examples, it is a sad instance of waywardness and deception, and the teacher is sorry, very sorry, that he feels compelled to punish such large girls, almost young ladies; but he must do his duty.

If a dozen or twenty of the large boys remain on the ice skating a half an hour after "school has taken up," the authority of the teacher must be vindicated, the rules of the school must be sustained, and, as undesirable a piece of business as it may be, the boys, in equity, must all be punished, every offender, severely punished. A new supply of hickories is sent for, and then a general *auto da fe*, unless the boys conclude they can whip the master—and then what?

But why enumerate further? This teacher is a good man, a professor of religion, reads the Bible and prays in his school, and is really esteemed where he is best known for his many manly qualities.

His scholars do not hate him; on the other hand, they rather respect him. Most of them give him credit for a good degree of faithful interest in their behalf. They admit among themselves, sometimes, "We do behave too bad, and I am going to try to do better, arn't you, Bill?" But every pupil is glad of an excuse to stay out of school a day or more. They all long for a holiday, and count the days to the end of the term. Any one is rejoiced if he can say that he doesn't expect to attend school next term; and he is not a little envied by the rest. Teachers, of how many of your own school experiences is this a true picture? If not true, very likely it is because it is too favorably drawn.

Another teacher of the same species, but of different variety, offers exemption from certain lessons as a reward for good behavior during a prescribed period, and occasionally a half-holiday to those who "bring all their recitations square up," for a certain length of time. In carrying out the same views he imposes extra lessons as a penalty for absence, tardiness, idleness, mischief, or any other infraction of the rules. These extra lessons, of course, are extorted by imprisonment, "in being kept after school," and by the use of rod or ferule, if necessary.

Now look at it, friends, for this is no fancy sketch, but the practice of thousands, and tens of thousands of schools, generally considered well conducted, all over the land, in cities, villages and country districts. In fact, it is virtually *the* plan by which most of our Union and Graded Schools are managed, and the requisite per cents obtained in examinations. Of course, the teacher who is the most inexorable in his demands, the most persistent in making a prison of his school, and a jailer of himself, is the one who prides himself on the highest per cents for his scholars.

But tell me, teachers, if ingenuity can devise a course of school management better calculated to make the school-room repulsive instead of attractive; the school duties irksome instead of pleasant; the teacher oppressive and hateful, instead of a joy and a pride. I say, is it possible to conceive a more direct and certain means for accomplishing such ends than those here given and so generally practiced?

Yes, it is; unfortunately, too many ot these teachers who pursue the plan of government by force, as above-described too often lay themselves liable to the charge of being partial, peevish, petulant, passionate, tyrannical and abusive.

Police System.

The next plan of school management that I shall bring to your notice is the Police System. This system exists in colleges, academies, and normal schools; while the Force System prevails more generally in both graded and ungraded schools, sustained by public funds.

As most academies and State Normal schools derive their *principals* and practices from colleges, their methods of government and instruction are but college methods modified; often for the worse. Colleges, then, being the chief seats and sources of the police system, I shall confine my attention to the workings of this system in this class of institutions where, from long usage, it ought to work well, if anywhere.

In the first place, the Police System, demands certificates of good moral character of its candidates for admission, thus assuming that all such candidates are untrustworthy and suspicious characters, and must establish the contrary by certificates; otherwise they are excluded, on the general assumption. Some colleges do not receive candidates, even on certificates, to full membership; but in addition, require the young man to demonstrate by a six weeks' or six months' probation that he is not a blackleg or a thief. And yet it is just this class, if any, that go through the period of probation without censure or particular suspicion.

How much better would it be to receive the young man cordially, bestowing on him full confidence that he comes with a good purpose; and if anything is said with regard to his character and conduct, that it should be something like this:

"We take you to be a gentleman and give you our confidence as such. We ask no certificates. Your coming to this institution is a sufficient guarantee that you aim at improvement, and are willing to make a determined and continued effort in that direction. We intend to maintain this opinion of you, and have no fear that you will ever compel us to abandon it. Indeed, it will require a persistent course of wrong doing to convince us that our present opinion is not well founded; and this, we are assured, is impossible in your case. No one act, scarcely, will do it. We are all human beings, prone to err, and liable, the best of us, to do wrong. You will not expect perfection of us, and surely we ought not to demand it of you. You will always find in us an earnest purpose to promote your interests and your personal comfort, to aid you in carrying out your designs. We shall also interest ourselves in trying to help you to correct any errors or faults that may develop themselves, on closer acquaintance, in your methods of study, self management, or otherwise. We hope you will always feel that we can be confided in as safe counselors and as personal friends, immeasurably more anxious to keep you out of any difficulty than, as captious judges, to condemn and crush you for errors, faults, or offenses, of any kind whatever."

But the young man being received as a suspicious character, and realizing that he is watched, and conceiving, perhaps, that his movements are dogged by some one of the professors, into whose particular care he is intrusted; or gathering, sooner or later, the idea that the President or proctor entertains a special dislike for him, from the general or special lectures of which he well imagines himself the special object, he places himself, as a matter of self-defense and self-protection, in direct antagonism with the authority of the college; and finding this the dominant feeling with a large class of the most influential students, he is ready to avail himself of every opportunity to defeat any measure of the faculty, or to join in plots and intrigues to annoy any officer or teacher particularly odious to him or his clique, even while he admits, perhaps, that the regulations, restraints and precautionary measures are necessary for the well-being of the institution. Why, who could do otherwise? What man, woman, or child is not indignant at being suspected, watched, dogged? How is it possible that any friendly feelings can exist between such parties?

I have said nothing here of the practice of employing students as spies or detectives, as it now continues but in few colleges, so far as I know.

But then, when the same spirit of espionage prevails in every class room, and every recitation is a process of inquisition, to detect shirks and shams, and to mark them, how can a pupil feel otherwise than that he is in the hands of enemies? How can he but consider it smart to outwit the professors, and that any plan he can adopt to get through a recitation and escape open censure or the fatal number of demerit marks is honorable, and a fit subject of exultation among his fellow students? The less honest labor he bestows on his studies the smarter he conceives himself to be, and the more he brags of his success in playing off on the faculty. Hence come the whole list of college expedients, ponies, concealment of written exercises under the coat sleeve, *extemporizing*, etc., etc College boys will think that I am green; I don't know half of their tricks and contrivances. Well, I admit it; I also admit that animated by such a spirit, they succeed to a large extent in avoiding all noble, earnest effort, in evading all thorough self-discipline, in suppressing every aspiration for a pure and manly development, in defeating every laudable purpose which college life ought to foster and consummate.

But I hold the college management responsible for all such abuses. The whole theory and plan is wrong from beginning to end, from center to circumference. What! any system right or to be tolerated which trains any one of its subjects to deceit, evasion, shirking, meanness, and excites all the manly forces of any individual to their own perversion and extinction?

You wish me, no doubt, to propose a better system. I intend to do so in due time. But there is one other consideration that should not be omitted in this picture. Who can not see that if any student resists, surmounts such influences both from the faculty, in arousing opposition and conflict; and from his fellow-students in exciting sympathy and conspiracy, that he must be an exceptional character, possessing too much or too little of the material that other men are made of, not thus to become the frequent receptacle of various vile epithets well known in college life, and unfit for ears polite, as well as the constant object of tricks and annoyances which might otherwise be directed towards the unpopular members of the faculty?

I do not wish to be understood as implying that all colleges, at the present time, practice the police system of government and instruction, exclusively; but that too many of these institutions rely on it to too great an extent; whereas it ought to be entirely abandoned by every organization and by every person that professes or desires to train the young to noble and virtuous action.

I am perfectly well aware that poohs, and sneers, and snuffs will be the only reply that many a college man will deign to offer to such positions. I have been fortified by such arguments these many years, and possibly more energized in my endeavors to discover a remedy for the evils which, no one of them pretends to deny, exist, more or less, in all colleges, and oftentimes to the extent of open rebellion and threatened disorganization.

But there are two *fundamental errors* in the College Management, one in the plan of instruction, the other in the plan of government. Both can easily be generalized into one.

Colleges, for the most part, hold the acquisition of knowledge as their principal element in education, and the attainment of scholarship as their highest aim. Thus college education begins, continues, and ends in self.

Whereas, a true system of education has the development of power as its principal element and constant aim. What

3

power? The power to do good; more definitely, that power which will give the individual the highest success and largest usefulness in that profession or calling to which he shall prefer to devote himself. This end being kept in view, in every recitation, in every drill, and in the preparation for every class duty or public exercise affords a stimulus incomparably more effective than the possibility of the highest scholastic attainment conceivable. And I do not hesitate to affirm that this object, viz.: the development of power, will accomplish thrice as much in any given time, for the majority of students, even in scholarship, as that of making scholarship the direct aim. Besides this radical error, there is also the police method of recitation already noticed, consisting chiefly of detecting errors and exposing shams, instead of giving full scope to mental activity, by encouraging independent and manly effort in investigation, generalization and free discussion; thus arousing a noble emulation in the right, instead of stimulating a mean rivalry in the wrong.

Another minor error in the police system of instruction is the offering of prizes. Who does not know, that only two or three in a class, who do not need the stimulus, are the only ones stimulated, while the majority are sensibly discouraged or entirely paralyzed by the influence of a prize? But prizes excite every mean passion in the rival aspirants, and almost compel them to practice various dishonest expedients in order to win.

The fundamental error in college government is, that virtue can be secured by detecting and repressing vice. This is monasticism, not christianity. Christ would have us fill our hearts so full of noble daring and aggressive action that there shall be no time, place or disposition left for sinful indulgence.

Teachers, let us heed our great Example, strive to imitate him in our glorious work, and, catching the inspiration ourselves, find how we can best impart it to our pupils; how can we most surely excite in them a spirit of glowing enterprise, that will do all that can possibly be done in the allotted time, for the mastery of any subject assigned, rather than tolerate a spirit of reluctance, complaining that the lessons are too hard or too long. The difference is that of mental health and disease, of moral life and death.

Any teacher, in any institution, that cannot arouse such a spirit of cheerful labor in a pupil, as will overcome his natural laziness, his love of mischief, and his tendency to animal indulgence, is so far as that pupil is concerned, a failure; imparting weakness instead of strength, willful virulence instead of manly self-control in every sensual gratification. And any institution, I care not how many and how commodious its buildings, how able and celebrated its Professors, I care not how extensive and well selected its libraries, how costly and well adapted its laboratories, how ample and well arranged its museums, how well stored and attractive its art galleries; I say any institution which can not excite in any pupil, a spirit of earnest industry and enthusiastic endeavor in legitimate pursuits, that will displace his lazy, shirking habits and evil tendencies, is educating that pupil in vice instead of virtue, for future evil instead of good, and to be a curse rather than a blessing to himself and his kind. Such an institution and such a pupil ought to be separated; and the sooner the better. How many colleges or academies or normal schools act on this principle?

Rather, is it not true, that a large proportion of the students, in nearly all the colleges, both male and female, take their chief pride in the least amount of labor they can grudgingly bestow in accomplishing the "tasks" or lessons assigned; while not a few make it their special boast among their associates that they study little, if at all; relying on subterfuges and shams of endless variety and exhaustless ingenuity to screen themselves from censure and disgrace?

Personal Influence Plan.

The next plan of School Government I shall present is that of *pure personal influence*.

But few, I apprehend, can succeed on this plan. It requires a combination of such physical, mental, moral and social endowments as very few possess.

It is so to govern that it is not known that there is any

government, and yet harmony prevails in all purposes and practices, resulting from the one all controlling, earnest, magic influence of your own heart, teacher.

Have *you* ever had a teacher, whose will manifested in the gentlest manner was the all-pervading power? If so, you have been remarkably fortunate. Or am I talking of an ideal, that never has been reached? Have you never had the idea of governing without governing, order and diligence being only the necessary resultants of harmonizing forces? This is my ideal of school government, of family government. It is the government of Heaven.

Such a government should exist in one's self as a man, a christian, a teacher. How? Because He hath loved me, and given Himself for me. How blessed the assurance, "I know that my Redeemer liveth." Continuing this line of thought, I will try to show how this personal influence system works in governing a school.

That christian who is governed by the fear that the transgressed law will bring penalty, either temporal or eternal, is but a beginner in the christian career. "The law is his schoolmaster," and bringing him to Christ. Now let us follow that same christian till he has attained a higher purpose and a nobler life. These lead out his soul in admiration and adoration, and elevate the man above wrong purposes and low indulgences. He is thus delivered from the bondage of fear and becomes a free man in love and obedience. Such are Christ's pupils.

But you are not all, I fear, trusting and praying christians and cannot fully realize the power and sweetness of the government in the school of Christ.

For such, I will give another illustration. There are laws on the statute book against burglary and horse stealing, but what do you care? It is immaterial to you, whether the penalty for these crimes is one year or ten in the penitentiary. In fact, I doubt whether there is a person here that knows what the penalty is for these crimes. It has scarcely ever occurred to one of you that there are such laws. You are free men and women so far as those laws are concerned, and a noble principle of right keeps you free from the fear of transgressing such laws and of the penalty annexed

So that the teacher who can pour his pure, loving spirit into the hearts of his pupils, and elevate them above all rules and regulations is my ideal, and the Personal Influence Plan of School Government is that plan above all others that I would aspire after.

Since, however, few of us will ever, in all probability, attain to the perfection of this system, it becomes common mortals, like ourselves, to adopt a plan better adapted to our own moderate powers, and reasonable expectations.

It is my purpose in this course of lectures to develop such a plan. That plan I shall denominate the Normal Method of School Management.

But far graver objections than these exist against the disciplinary system proper pursued in American colleges. The conclusion is inevitable that it tends directly to make the conduct of students, in their relations with the faculty, the reverse of manly and honorable. It is a legal presumption that a suspected man is innocent until the contrary is proved; but at Cambridge, at least, the contrary presumption generally obtains. It may even be said that a suspected student is supposed to lie until he proves that he speaks the truth. The result is as natural as it is deplorable. Espionage is met by cunning, and accusation by equivocation. Every graduate of the college must own that a thoroughly false system of morality is prevalent among undergraduates in their relations with the faculty; that young men, otherwise honorable, are too often to be found whose practice before a faculty meeting is, to use the mildest adjective, sharp, and who answer all remonstrances by declaring that it is lawful to fight the devil with fire. Students and instructors, in consequence, come to regard each other as natural enemies, and thus the governors and governed become thoroughly antagonistic bodies. And it is not generally until the lapse of time has softened old asperities that graduates begin to feel that affection for, and pride in, their college which ought from the beginning to be the strongest sentiment of college life.

The Nation. *Correspondence from U. S. Naval Academy.*

Physiological.—The latest and most readable text-books on Physiology are Huxley & Youman's, and Dalton's. The latter was reviewed in our last number.

Townsend's work on the Constitution, reviewed in this number, though a text-book, is an exceedingly *interesting* work. Every one, ladies and gentlemen, should possess the volume. It is another successful effort to release school books from the incubus of technicalities. We hail with glad welcome the spirit of attractiveness which publishers are now striving to cast over their new school publications.

LECTURE ON SCHOOL MANAGEMENT.

(COPYRIGHT SECURED.)

LECTURE IV.

FIFTH QUALIFICATION, LOVE OF THE WORK.

PRELIMINARY VIEWS.

I SHALL proceed to discuss the fifth qualification of the teacher, as characterizing and energizing his School Management. It is the last of the list of essentials, but so important do I deem it, that I shall devote two lectures to its consideration.

It is a proposition, clearer than an axiom to my mind, that no person ought to be intrusted with the responsibility of molding the character and destiny of children and youth, who does not realize the value of the material on which he works, and who does not see and feel the tremendous results for good or evil which must follow his labors.

Such being the fact, I hold it as a sad desecration of his office, if the teacher bestow anything less than his best efforts growing out of a high appreciation, an ardent love for his work; such a glowing heart devotion as can only spring from the consideration that he is the most highly favored, and yet the most solemnly responsible, of all human agents: being intrusted with the dearest interests known in human relations—the well being of so many in their most plastic period, the acting and re-acting, for weal or woe, on themselves, on each other, and on society, through all time; nay, through all eternity.

Oh! how absurd and abominable a thing is a teacher who looks no further than his school-room, or the per cents required in his school system for results, and confines his efforts to his daily success in "bringing up" the daily tasks; in grinding his little round of repressing disorder, of detecting and punishing the offenders. Better might the captain of an ocean steamer, in time of danger, direct his entire energies to the detection of gambling, drinking, and remissness of duty among his men, and leave the noble ship and the destiny of all on board to the mercy of winds, waves, and "breakers ahead."

There is a look-out for us, teachers, which none of us sufficiently consider, nor can fully appreciate. But, so far from an adequate love of the work, I think I am safe in affirming that there is not one teacher in five, taking all classes together, that has not a positive aversion for it, which many are not ashamed even to avow.

See that young man, compelled to earn his bread and cigars, looking around to find the easiest way of doing it. Too lazy for muscular toil, he conceives he can have an easy time "keeping school," if he can only get a county certificate. So he attends some Academy, or Union School, managed by one of the County Examiners, having learned that those who patronize the Examiners always "get through" the best. What love of the work incites him, or ever will? He abominates all work.

But, look again: another young man having determined to become a lawyer, and flattering himself that he can make a living more easily by his wits than by his hands, is obliged from time to time to replenish his shriveled purse by resorting to teaching. What love of the work has he?

I do not intend, here, to imply any positive culpability in using teaching to aid one's self in preparing for another profession. For, some of the best teachers I have ever known, were afterward among the most useful and honored in the pulpit and in the forum; and, I believe, that nearly all the leading men in the country at the present time were, at some period in their lives, successful teachers. Success in teaching gives almost certain promise of success in any other calling. Such men, no doubt, loved their work; well enough, at least, to excel in it.

But, again see that village miss, whose inordinate demands for "something to wear" entirely transcend the capabilities of her father's income. She resolves to do something for herself—too proud to go out to work, and thinking it unnecessary for a girl of her fine appearance to learn a trade, she determines to try for a certificate, but waits for an Examiner's Institute as the only practicable method of getting one. She has learned that the Examiner spends three or four weeks drilling his pupils on the special set of questions on which they are to be examined, and she is assured by circulars that "special facilities" will be given to the candidates who attend the County Institute. What a love for her work this girl carries to her school-room!

But, these are extreme cases, you say. Yes, extreme cases of folly and wickedness. But who is responsible for the waste of public money, for the squandering of the children's school time and school privileges, for this betrayal of the best interest of society? I am glad to be able to say, here, that I believe County Examiners, as a class, are honest public servants; more so than almost any other; but "one sinner" in such a position truly "destroyeth much good."

We will now turn to another class of teachers found crowding the profession, viz.: teachers pursuing the force method of school government. Is it a supposable case, that such a teacher can have any just appreciation of his work, of the nature of the material, or of the measureless, eternal interests committed to his daily charge? Is it not very easy for a teacher of this class to apply the epithets "brat," "imp of darkness," "numbskull," "hard-nut," etc., etc., while acting as jailer in pursuing what he considers the legitimate course of his business in forcing the delinquents to study, and compelling them to bring up their lessons neglected for mischief or lost by absence?

Can there be any true love of the work in the heart of a force-method teacher? He must be constituted of very strange materials if he can find any thing lovely in the evil passions which he is exciting by endeavoring to repress them; in the waywardness and meanness, in the obstinacy and malice, which for the most part are the necessary results of his own management, if not the direct reflection of his own character as exhibited to this class of pupils. No wonder that so many teachers slide into book agencies, insurance agencies, saw-mills and groceries. It's all right; they can enjoy themselves much better in any of these occupations and make more money besides.

But let us turn from these forbidding scenes, (I would that you could sav they exist only in my imagination) and discover, if possible, how the school-room, in some rare cases, is a paradise watered by the River of God; how the children *all* become as lovable as any human beings can be; how the work of teaching is every succeeding day an increasing delight, and the true teacher a man or woman who envies no mortal his position, his emoluments, or his fame.

REASONS FOR LOVING THE WORK.

I propose now to show, Ladies and Gentlemen, why we teachers should love our work, and I trust, these views will meet with a hearty approval from every person present.

REASON I. THE VALUE OF THE MATERIAL.

1. *The Susceptibility of Development.*

Not many days since, I saw an Irishman breaking stone on the South Lebanon turnpike. I hardly suppose the value of the material had much influence in stimulating his industry; other considerations might. But come with me down across the street, to Mr. Swartz's tombstone establishment. We shall find a dozen workmen sawing, chiseling, carving, or polishing sandstone, limestone, granite, or marble. Now, other things being equal, these laborers or artizans will be interested in proportion to the value of the blocks on which they are engaged. There is one sculptor there more skillful than the rest, to whom, I am informed, a mass of Parian marble is intrusted: just that kind on which Canova and Thorwaldsen achieved their immortality. What passer-by can fail to notice the zeal of this artist as he plies his chisel, and sympathize somewhat with his earnestness, as his design comes out to view, more and more, day by day? Yes, partake of his anxiety lest by some mischance he may not only defeat himself in completing his work, but ruin the costly block on which his best efforts have been so long and earnestly bestowed?

Does the idea of toil ever enter this workman's head? Does weariness ever interfere with the ardor of his application? May be. But he returns with increasing eagerness every day to the fuller development of the mental conception of grace, beauty, or sadness, which is being revealed from his material by the superior skill of his plastic hand. What common mechanic would dare to work on such material? Or, if he should, what owner would trust it to his bungling, uncertain hand?

If such ardor can be, and often has been, aroused in the elaborations of inanimate material, how much more must the true teacher, as the highest conceivable style of artist, glory in the intellectual and spiritual development of that priceless material which is committed to his charge and workmanship. But, I hear some of you say, or think, almost aloud: "I've seen enough of this kind of material, and have had trouble enough in trying to make something of it; but it seems to me that the harder I work and the more I try, the worse the children get, the more unmanageable and hateful. Why, there are some boys I've been obliged to keep after school almost every night for weeks together and punish frequently beside; and yet they seem to get worse and worse, in spite of every thing I can do for them. If any body can make anything decent, or tolerable, out of such material as those boys are, they can do more than I can, I'm sure."

Yes, my friend, you remind me of that good mother that gave her little sick darling, Johnny, three doses of calomel during the night and another larger dose in the morning: then sending for the doctor told him when he came: "Doctor, I'm afraid Johnny is going to die, I've done everything I could for him. I have given four doses of medicine, and he has got worse all the time." Johnny did die, the victim of his mother's overdosing.

Still again, I ask, what of the teacher, and the material intrusted to his skill and care? You will all agree with me, when I say that no amount of Parian or Pentelican marbles, nor brilliant and costly metals,—no rare and precious gems, whether rough or wrought, can ever compare in value or responsible results, with one human soul, endowed as it is with measureless capacity for intellectual progress and power, for good or evil. But the development of the intellect; the enlarging and intensifying of the capabilities of acquisition, retention, utilization are but the first and least part of your work, teacher. There is the training of that individual to a true, noble, and persistent purpose that shall control his fitful, impulsive, wayward, or indolent disposition. Does your very being stagger and shrink back, in view of such a work? Grant it. But here is the material susceptible of such results; a soul to be won or lost: not one, but many. Your skill and energy, your patience and fidelity, may be taxed to their utmost; and what artists are not, even on perishable material, when struggling only for human fame?

2. *Susceptibility of Transformation.*

But you work not for such an end. On your material your labor is for the weal or woe of the material, not for your own aggrandizement or reputation. Shall that pupil, under your influence, learn to love work, instead of play; under your inspiration, learn to study, because he loves to study, not because he is compelled to do so? If even so much is attained, he begins life a worker rather than an idler, a producer rather than a consumer, he leaves you advancing on an upward rather than a downward plane, and the difference is, in the one case, industry, energy, enterprise, thrift, success; in the other, labor is a burden, energy and enterprise, are all given to sensual indulgence, and life is a failure, death is a relief, and what after death? Such are the results, teacher, of your labor on the material on which you work. But, here, I want you to notice the increasing interest and ardor which day by day must characterize the work of the true teacher, as he sees these elements developed, cheerful industry, the love and power of investigation, energetic effort in the preparation of his class exercises, glowing enterprise awakened by his increasing success over himself and his difficulties Why, that boy is a new creature. He is born again. His school duties, before forced through on the rote system, a drag and a bore, are now his absorbing delight, and his increasing enthusiasm evinces a new nature and reveals to himself a new existence. But will not these same forces evoked by your skillful management go with him out of the school-room into his life-work? I tell you, teacher, such energies, thus aroused, are worth more to that pupil than all the knowledge, or all the culture, that school, seminary, or college ever conferred or can confer, without them.

But does then any teacher, under such responsibilities, and with the possibility of such results, yet say that he has no interest in teaching, and he merely teaches because he has to do something; and then is ready to apologize, at any time, for his being a teacher, saying that he is only teaching to help himself to some better business?

Why, the miserable creature! what sort of material is *he* made of? He ought to ask the children's pardon for what injury he has done them, and never disgrace a school-room again. A blackleg apologizing to his comrades for his being seen in so low a place as a prayer-meeting would present something like a parallel to his case.

3. *Power of Affection.*

Again, in this material on which we work, teachers, there are higher and purer powers and susceptibilities than any yet mentioned, among which is that of personal affection, and no master workman will overlook or fail to bring into requisition this power as an element in securing his highest success.

There is no man, woman, or child so bad, so perverse, so blinded, so hardened but that he can be reached, provided the proper and adequate means be used; and we ought to be exceedingly slow in giving over any particular case as beyond our power; feeling that in excluding any one from the pale of hope and kindly influence, we virtually confess our own incapacity; while it is surely possible that some other teacher might bring around that boy or that girl such influences as would convert him or her from a willingness to be considered the worst scholar in school, to a determination to become the best. Such radical changes in the character of pupils have blessed and encouraged many a faithful teacher, and are among the richest rewards that he ever experiences for his many anxious days and sleepless nights.

The power of affection, then, dwells in every heart, and the desire for consideration and esteem. Every pupil will love or hate you, and when your name is spoken, he will be inclined to take sides for or against you, to maintain your cause against whatever opposition, or to join with those who censure and revile you. That teacher who is sustained by all his pupils is safe, in any community, in whatever measures he may adopt. The best method I have ever discovered to win a bad boy is to find as much as possible in him to commend, and as little as possible to censure. Thus, as I take his part against accusers possibly against himself as an accuser, he begins to feel, that he has found a friend in his teacher; and it can not be long before his heart will respond, and his external bearing toward me will undergo an entire change. Now, in winning such cases, the "hard cases" of all former teachers and of the district, there must be a keen and pure delight. Here, then, in this power and susceptibility of affection dwelling in every bosom, the true teacher finds an element in his material which makes him love his work and glory in it.

4. *Power of Appeal.*

Again, there is the power of appeal possessed by every child; appeal from your decisions or actions, whether legislative, judicial, or executive, for in all these capacities you are compelled to act at almost any moment.

That child can and will appeal to his schoolmates, in case he feels himself wronged, and to his parents; or that young man will appeal to his associates in or out of school, possibly in the doggeries or on the street corners.

It is folly to ignore this power of appeal, teacher. It has its existence and influence, and, possibly, you lay yourself open so frequently to its effects that all your efforts for the good of your school are neutralized, and sooner or later you will be compelled to abandon your position. But beyond these courts of appeal already mentioned there is a higher tribunal to which you are brought by every pupil, however vicious or reckless. It is the court of conscience in which he will rightfully hold you amenable, though placing himself beyond its jurisdiction. He can pronounce judgment, in your case, with wonderful discrimination, under the eternal law of right. Such a decision, coming as it does from this self-con stituted judge, you can not afford to disregard or defy. You will do it at your peril.

Let us, then, love our work, teachers, because our pupils have consciences, a consciousness of right, ever active in our behalf, if not in their own. For who is not thankful for any incentives to right and restraints from wrong, coming from whatever source?

5. *Power of Combination.*

The next element in our material, fellow workman, and the last I shall notice, is the the power of combination. I have hitherto considered the character of pupils chiefly as *individuals* related to their teacher and friends beyond the school-room. But, bear in mind, it is not one individual, nor fifty individuals, that you are called on to raise up and develop like so many apple-trees in an orchard, each improving or deteriorating, as well or ill cultivated; but, altogether, they are so many currents in the gulf, flowing, interflowing, counterflowing; and what shall be the resultant current, a gulf stream to dispense warmth, life, and verdure on remote and otherwise icy and desolate shores; or a vortex carrying itself and all that shall be drawn within its reach to one common abyss of destruction?

Ladies, suppose as any one of you walks down the street to the post-office, a low fellow of the baser sort is standing in a saloon door; he will scan your countenance, person, and gait, but with caution, perhaps seeming respect. But if, on your return, he shall have been joined by a comrade, you will probably overhear a titter, or a low whistle, at your expense. But suppose to these there have been added three or four men, the next time you pass that way; you will very probably be openly insulted. It takes the combination of a half a dozen blackguards to insult one inoffensive, helpless girl; a dozen armed ruffians to attack one unarmed man; and then they are tremendously bold, brave, defiant. Such is the power of combination; it converts cowards into bullies.

Again, notice that group of boys sitting on yonder goods box, beyond the ears and eyes of their parents, as they suppose. In their chaffing, jesting, and ribaldry, which one dares intimate any dissent from the strain of impurity or profanity of the company? knowing well that he would be greeted, in such a case, by the leader of the "crowd" with—"You are getting mighty pious, arn't you? You'd better go home and say your prayers." How many boys in the thousands of such companies found everywhere, in city and country, dare attempt to resist the combined current of their respective "crowds?" How many are there, in any dozen, that will not the rather increase the general force in this vortex of folly and wickedness? Perhaps some boy who loves his mother has concluded, "it don't pay" to make his mother so sad and tearful; and he resolves to have better company, or none at all, and he tells his mother so. He probably finds none at all, save his sisters, his music, and his books.

Many a mother understands too well what I mean by the power of combination. It is ruining her noble boy, and blasting her dearest hopes, in spite of all her sighs and tears.

How can she break its spell?

Teacher, can you help her? Let us resolve to try.

I have cited some instances out of the school-room, in which this element is productive of evil. Let us notice one or two in which it has been equally efficient for good. The Washingtonian temperance movement, in its inception and wide extended progress, is one good example. The progress of Christianity and civilization, through the influence of revivals of religion, is another. And it seems to me that without these two applications of this principle we should only witness, in the world's history, progress in superstition, bigotry, and tyranny on the one side, sensuality, infidelity, and anarchy on the other; all conspiring to banish virtue, piety, and liberty from the earth.

But in no place is the power of combination more active than in the school-room, more to be dreaded, more to be prized. It remains for you, teacher, to convert this reciprocal influence, this power of combination from an agency of evil into an energy for good; and you *can* do it. Then you will find there is no element in your school-room so effective in working out splendid results as this. The popular feeling of a school, the *esprit de corps* of a class may be all wrong, or they may be all right. They may be all *for* the teacher or all *against* him and his measures. He can never justly claim any true success, till he has secured the control and co-operation of this all-potent spirit and power of combination.

The question then comes up to every one of us, how can I so gain the mastery over this element that it shall bring me, in my school management, and in my class exercises, a beautiful and glorious success, rather than a disastrous and lamentable defeat?

Forewarned, forearmed: all I proposed to show in this lecture was some of those elements in the material on which which we work that should incite love for our work. Some of you may say, "I see more reason why I should fear, dread the work of teaching from the exposition which you have given." Well, my reply is, "You may lack one important qualification of the teacher, or you may deny the truth of my statements." But I shall endeavor to show, in a future lecture, how these elements in human nature, so active in the school-room, so fearful in their results when ill-directed, may become, by the management of the true teacher, his surest means of success, and, of course, the strongest reasons why he should love his work and glory in it. Napoleon never underrated the forces of his antagonist, either before or after victory; well knowing that the more powerful the army defeated, and the empire subjugated to his sway, the more glorious was the victory obtained, and the more were his prestige and resources augmented for the achievement of further conquests.

LECTURE ON SCHOOL MANAGEMENT.

LECTURE V.

FIFTH QUALIFICATION. LOVE OF THE WORK.

LADIES AND GENTLEMEN:

In my last lecture, I tried to develop one reason why we should love our work. It was in the powers and susceptibilities of the human soul, as we find it in the school-room; also in its outlook for time and eternity.

In this lecture I propose to consider some other reasons why the teacher, more than any other man, should take satisfaction and pride in his daily labors, and why he should aspire to excellence and eminence in his vocation.

REASON II. VARIETY AND NOVELTY.

Conversation with Dr. and Mrs. W.

While enjoying the genial hospitality of Dr. W., then residing in an Ohio county town, I was addressed at the breakfast table by the Doctor, thus: "How is it, Mr. Holbrook, that a man of your energy and enterprise can content himself with going over the same round of the school-room, day after day? I should think it would be very monotonous. I don't see how you endure it."

Said I, "Doctor, I heard you leave your house at 5 o'clock, this morning; will you permit me to inquire where you went?"

"Certainly, I went to see a patient that I left last evening lying very low with typhoid fever."

"How did you find her, Doctor?"

"Her symptoms were slightly better."

"I suppose you examined her pulse attentively, noticed her tongue, prescribed according to your judgment of the case, and left."

"Yes, sir."

"If you please, Doctor, where are you going after breakfast?"

"To dress the broken leg of a patient, about two miles in the country."

"And what after that?"

"Why, I have several patients in town."

"And you will call on each of them, feel the pulse, examine the tongue, smell the feverish offensive breath, prescribe pills or powders, and leave for the next one, to go through the same order of operations."

Said Mrs. W., "I think he rather has you, Doctor."

"Yes," said the Doctor, "I see there are different ways of looking at things."

"But, I don't see," said I, "how a gentleman of your refinement and taste, Doctor, can endure such a monotonous round of repulsive duties, day after day, for so many years." "But," said I, addressing the lady, "Mrs. W., I was out in your garden before breakfast. You have a beautiful bed of flowers there; they must have cost you a large amount of time and labor."

"Yes, sir, I attend it entirely myself."

"The flowers speak well for your industry and skill in floriculture. But, did you not cultivate the same kinds of flowers and plants last spring?"

"O, yes, and I expect to do it next spring; in fact, husband says, he expects I'll soon turn into a plant, plantain, or something else more useful than beautiful, in the garden myself, I am so much engaged there, and sometimes to his inconvenience, I suppose."

"But, I don't see why you don't get tired of cultivating, over and over, the same flowers every season. I should think it would be very monotonous"

"Why, I never think of it as tiresome or monotonous; I

find something new every day, almost every hour for that matter, to excite my interest, and keep me in the garden. I suppose I am something of an enthusiast. Husband thinks I am about half crazy sometimes."

"Yes," he said, "every woman will have her pet or her crotchet. I suppose wife's is as harmless as any other."

"But you like the flowers as well as I do, Doctor, or I wouldn't spend so much time with them. Don't you like the flowers, Mr. Holbrook?"

"Oh yes, indeed I do, and I don't know that I ever enjoyed their fragrance and beauty more than this morning. But I think I find as great variety in the labors of my school-room, and find myself as much interested and excited in the development of those human plants, buds, flowers, that I find there, as I can suppose it possible for you to be, on your pet work; and I think much more so, inasmuch as it never escapes me, that I work not for the day, or the week, but for all time, and expect to see fruits, in the future lives of my pupils, answerable to the efforts and skill I put forth in their behalf."

"Well," said the Doctor, "you have your own views of things, I see; quite philosophical I admit. It is a very pleasant feature in human economy, that there is a place for every man, and a man for every place. But it is a pity that so few, comparatively, find their place, or are satisfied with it when they do find it."

Thus, Teachers, I claim that our business is an ever changing scene, of variety and novelty every new phase presenting some new call for effort, and exciting a new interest. Every pupil in the eye of a true teacher is a bud of promise, or a flower of hope and joy, responsive directly and immediately to his endeavors for higher improvement, and further development. But if there is an exception, in some rough boy, or pert girl, it's only an instance of novelty calling for new and varied expedients, for his or her redemption. Then, what satisfaction when the wished for results of our labor, patience and skill begin to appear. What vocation thus will compare with ours for novelty and variety, constantly improving, ever yielding more present satisfaction, and brighter promises of future reward?

If any teacher complains of monotony, and wearies in his daily round, each day more tedious than the preceding; the difficulty is in himself, not in his business. He or she is a lazy teacher, without energy enough to be interesting or interested in any business whatever, whose school is a chaos or a pandemonium; who watches the clock with more solicitude than the scholars, thinking the hands never will get around; and the term never will come to an end; or he or she is a force teacher, a rote teacher, attempting the impossibility of holding the restless spirits of children and youth down in the miserable grooves of his machine shop. Sooner let him attempt to bind the winds with a bed cord, and drive away the clouds with his scowling brow, or threatening fists. Immortal, responsible spirits forced by human power into anything truly noble or hopeful! What greater absurdity conceivable?

Reason III. A Field for Ingenuity and Enterprise.

You have all read of James Watt, the more than inventor of the steam-engine. When a boy, he was employed to open and shut the four valves of an immense cylinder, by working two rods, each attached to two valves. Now, you see the boy pulling with one hand, pushing with the other. You see that mighty piston ascend and descend, and obedient to those little hands and arms, throwing at each stroke a hundred barrels of water from the coal mine beneath. But *don't* his arms grow tired!

Now, thinks that weary boy, "Can't I connect the end of one rod somehow with one end of that great beam, and the other rod to the other end? They would never know the difference, and my tired arms would." So the boy, in his resting hours, planned, and arranged connecting rods, cords and pulleys, himself the meanwhile the butt of jest and ridicule, from all the other boys and workmen. At last he succeeded, and as he sat on a box and watched the successful working of his plans, the results of his ingenuity, wasn't he rich? Where were the jesters now? They had become warm admirers or silent foes. But what does he care? His plans worked. He had won success, and more renown than he knew of at that time. He soon succeeded in making one rod do the work, by passing one end around an eccentric on the main shaft; this arrangement virtually continues to the present time, though another nameless Watt has made one valve serve the purpose of four in giving ingress and egress to and from both ends of a steam cylinder.

When Charles Goodyear, by the ready use of an accident that nobody else would have noticed, succeeded in hardening or vulcanizing Indian rubber, and soon applied it to ten thousand purposes, from hair pins and combs to the construction of life boats, and pleasure carriages, was he not well repaid for his personal hardships, for the destitution of his family, for the jibes and jeers of his own and his wife's relations that he had endured for twenty years, in working to attain this very result?

I formerly knew a master mechanic, Thomas Keyes, who when a boy was employed in a cotton factory, attending a power loom. As often as a thread broke, he had to stop the loom, tie the broken thread, and again start the loom. If the loom was not stopped at the instant the thread broke, the loss from the resulting defect in the cloth came out of the boy's wages. The closest application was, therefore, necessarily given by all the boys and girls in charge of the looms, and it was a most exhausting kind of labor. Thomas, after working thus, for some months, and with little profit, at length conceived the idea of hanging a looped wire on each thread of the warp, over a grooved cylinder revolving slowly beneath. These wires were so arranged in a frame between the threads and the cylinder, that if a thread broke, the wire which it had sustained would fall, and lodge its lower end in a groove of the cylinder. This would check the revolution of the cylinder, and throwing the belt off the driving pulley upon the loose pulley, would stop the loom, at the instant any thread broke. By this contrivance, Thomas was enabled to attend three looms instead of one, saving himself the loss of wages from the defects of the cloth arising from missing threads.

Do you see our friend Tom seated on a stool, comparatively at ease, waiting for one of the three looms to stop, instead of watching most intently and incessantly every individual thread on a single loom. Tom is very much elated with the success of his contrivance, and the result of his ingenuity. And well he may be, for his invention is speedily adopted in all cotton factories everywhere. Why he never obtained a patent is a mystery; far less valuable inventions and improvements have given many a one an independent fortune.

But the fortune is the least of my consideration, here. It is the delight he must have experienced in seeing his plan work, and in the consciousness that it was saving thousands of industrious worthy girls from exhausting fatigue, and increasing their wages as well as the profits of their employers.

So far as this narrative of facts is applicable, you can apply it to your own case, teachers, in managing your schools. You can make the labor of school government as exhausting as the watching of a thousand threads in the warp of a piece of cloth; or, by the exercise of your ingenuity, good sense, and good feeling, in planning judicious arrangements, inventing happy expedients rather to forestall than to suppress evils, you can make your school government a matter of positive satisfaction and increasing pleasure, day by day; so much the more so, as your plans will ever be improving, and working more successfully. They will thus produce self-propelling and self-controlling industry, happy hearts and joyous countenances; where before there was repugnance for all your watchful anxiety, resistance to your most earnest efforts, continual conflict with your well-meant and energetic measures to maintain good order, and secure diligence in study.

In the times of '76 it was thought necessary by the British Parliament to hold secret sessions, to meet the emergences for the suppression of the rebellion in the American colonies, and it often required a heavy constabulary force to clear the galleries, from the fact that every person, on going out, stationed himself as near as possible to the door outside that he might be among those who would be able to crowd in after the secret session was concluded. But some M. P., the only man among them, perhaps, with wit and ingenuity enough to be a good teacher, suggested the plan of announcing to the people in the galleries, that they would be admitted by the doors at the other end of the galleries from those by which they went out. No sooner said than done, and the very cause which before had retarded, now accomplished the clearing of the galleries, with a rush, viz.: the desire to be among those who should first enter the galleries the moment the door of ingress was thrown open.

I have adduced these two or three examples, for the purpose of exhibiting the infinitely greater satisfaction we experience in removing difficulties by foresight, in flanking them by strategy, in turning the worst of them to our highest advantage, greater, I say, than we ever can by maintaining perpetual war to crush or restrain difficulties, which are only aggravated by our vain endeavors.

Teachers, there is no situation in life where ingenuity is so frequently called for, or can be so happily applied, as in the charge of a large school. In my last lecture, I tried to show some of the characteristics of the forces that must either harmonize or conflict with the teacher's purposes and plans, just as he has skill and ingenuity to manage them. He may expend all his time, energy and health in repressing and crushing those very activities which, with proper management, would become the sources of his highest satisfaction and success.

Now, I think you will agree with me that the chief satisfaction in prosecuting any successful business is that which the business man feels in the working out of his plans, in reaching his ends by his own skill in contrivance, in scheming. Read the life of Samuel Budgett, the model merchant, for an example. Should the biography of A. T. Stewart ever be correctly written, I have no doubt we would find the same fact splendidly set forth.

In order to illustrate the methods by which some of the common and the uncommon difficulties of the school-room may be forestalled, and either prevented, or converted into advantages, I shall devote one lecture in this course to School Strategy, in which I shall endeavor to show how much better contrivance is than force, *contrivance* to infuse better feelings and purposes into the active vicious spirits of a school, than *force* to crush them into obedience, and thus really intensify their energy for evil, or drive them from school, and, perhaps, beyond the last influence for good.

Reason IV. Love of Family.

Again, teachers have the same inducements to love their work that other men have. I suppose that Irish stone-breaker found not very much in his work to attract him, either because of the value of the material, or because there was exercise of skill in breaking it; but he labored diligently, because he loved his wife and children, and took satisfaction in making them comfortable. And you, teacher, can have the same relations and affections as other men and women, and you ought to be able to draw vastly more satisfaction from these than the majority of other men do. Why? Because you know how, or ought to know how, to give more satisfaction to your wife or your husband; and to train your children on the same principles that you find so effective in training other people's children.

Reason V. Love of Money.

If the love of money is the chief and all-absorbing motive of sordid men, it is none the less a good and forceful motive for noble men. It is true you may never become a millionaire, teacher, but by honest industry and skillful investment, multitudes of teachers have attained to competence, and not a few, to wealth. The ability to obtain a good salary, and to make money reputably, enhances your influence for good in school and out; and the business capacity to make good investments of your earnings, and to accumulate property, will enable the teacher to secure the confidence of business men, as a capable trainer of their children to habits of industry, economy, and thrift.

So, I say, the love of money is a worthy motive, and the possession of real estate, bank stocks, government securities, or mortgage notes, is no detriment, in any sense, and affords to some, in our profession at least, a powerful stimulus for higher endeavor in their legitimate work.

REASON VI. SOCIAL STANDING.

But some teachers complain, "We are not very much thought of." This is a mistake. The teacher will receive consideration and enjoy a social standing according to his merits, though his being a teacher will not compensate for every deficiency in his social or business character.

The lawyer, who is but a low driveling pettifogger, is none the more respected because he is a lawyer. But of all the professions, I really believe there is less *demanded* (perhaps I ought to say *expected*), of teachers to insure admission to the best circles in which they may desire to move than of any other. In other words, the teacher with a given amount of intelligence, social power, and cultivation, stands higher among the families for whom he labors than any other man, the minister not excepted; and, teachers, if you are not welcome to all family circles and social gatherings, it is your own fault; it is either from lack of social culture and moral stamina, or from excess of pedantry and egotism.

If there is any bore more cordially dreaded and more generally pronounced insufferable than any other, and the more so, perhaps, because he can not be snubbed, it is his little almightiness, the schoolmaster; not because he is a schoolmaster, but because he carries the stiff, didactic, dictatorial bearing of the school-room into his conversational intercourse; absurd enough in the school-room, but perfectly intolerable anywhere else.

Reason VII. A Field for Enterprise.

It is often remarked of us, teachers, that as a class, we are men of small calibre, of no particular force, and that few of us ever amount to much; while, if any of our profession do arrive at distinction, it is assumed that they are not teachers, but philosophers, presidents, doctors, or professors. For my part, I would rather be known as a "live teacher," than be dubbed with any or all those sonorous titles, so often the only reputable endowment of their possessors.

Unfortunately, there is too much ground for this slight opinion so generally entertained of the character and enterprise of teachers. While the ten-thousands know little of their business and care less for any real success in it, the tens, possibly the hundreds, just at this time, find here a splendid field of enterprise, not exactly in the sense that Vanderbilt or Fisk, A. T. Stewart or Solon Palmer, would count enterprise, but surely in a higher and a nobler. A determination for excellence in any reputable calling is surely praiseworthy; and none the less so, is a desire for eminence in a calling which, before all others, has blessed mankind, and will ever continue to do so. The world's roll of honor for teachers presents as many notable names, unstained with blood, as any other. Shall I mention Socrates, Plato, Aristotle, Pythagoras, Archimedes, before the time of the Great Teacher; of Leibnitz, Euler, Sir William Hamilton, Cousin, Dwight, Nott, and Wayland, since? If I mistake not, every individual in this list commenced business by teaching in a common school; that is, in a school made up from the common people. At all events the one nobler than all, is no exception, for his biographers all relate that "the common people heard him gladly;" and he never objected to being called by his pupils or "disciples" Διδάσκαλος (*Greek for teacher;* though the word is generally translated *master* in our common version, King James' Bible.)

A true ambition is a heaven-born inspiration, and being consecrated to God and humanity is the salvation of the world. A perverted ambition is the essence of diabolism, and being consecrated to self and Satan, is a rankling venom in the soul of the possessor, a withering simoon over the earth, blasting communities and nationalities with misery, sin and death.

A good teacher without a true ambition is a contradiction of facts, an impossibility. Teachers with no ambition abound everywhere; and teachers with a perverted ambition, are not rare in these days, and their baleful influence is one of the strongest barriers to the progress of our cause. I have neither time nor disposition now to characterize their action or influence, appropriately, whether as effecting states, counties, or single communities. But it is a notorious fact that many of the most active men in many of the state associations, even, are those whose unholy self-seeking is as obvious to every body as it is odious, repulsive and disgusting to all teachers not in their rings.

A man, woman or child that has no desire to shine is a poor thing indeed. The world has more respect for high success in wrong than for moderate doings in right. Thousands of men slaughtered give immunity from the penalty of murder; if not, hundreds of thousands will. The eminent villain who grasps at a nation's life, finds patriots enough to go on his bail-bond; but the timid, half-conscience-stricken wretch who murders stealthily only one, attains to the gallows and general execration. The man who steals a railroad and all its appurtenances, rides to opulence and renown on his prize; but another who steals a horse, finds himself transported to the penitentiary by the sheer insignificance of his crime.

Examples multiply, to show that the world respects eminence and enterprise, even in wrong. An atmosphere of admiration surrounds the atrocious scoundrel, when, in justice, storms of execration should sweep him into eternal infamy. What a perplexing problem is this in human affairs, that men are so fierce, audacious, persistent for Sin and Self; and yet so feeble, faint-hearted and hesitating for God and the Right. But my quarrel, this morning, is not with the world, the flesh or the devil, directly, but with teachers as a profession, for being so shiftless, for having so little professional zeal, so little personal pride. Take this one fact. There are few general gatherings of teachers, whether in the form of National Conventions, State Associations, or County Institutes, that do not invite some briefless lawyer, patientless doctor, or aspiring political candidate, to address them; and all quietly submit to the idea of receiving instruction in matters that numbers of them have made a life-work and a life study from an outsider, who, very likely, has made no headway even in his own vocation. To me this custom has always appeared as bald a profession of constitutional weakness and general debility in the body corporate of teachers, as it would be for a convention of physicians to call on a professional teacher, who was out of a place, to give his views on the best method of conducting a clinique, or to deliver a lecture on symptomatic diagnosis, or, perhaps, on the general bearing of the medical profession, or the means and methods of securing a paying practice.

I think I see the judges and attorneys of the Cincinnati bar, inviting Superintendent Hancock or Professor Venable, standing, as they do, in the front rank of our profession, to deliver an address on the uncertainties of the law, with suggestions of some methods of reform in conducting the courts so that clients may obtain more speedy and exact justice.

With this general state of affairs, ambition and enterprise pushing and crowding in every other calling, and so little motion of any kind in our profession save that of mutual jealousy and self-seeking, you are ready to inquire of me, teachers, "How can you make it appear that teaching presents a field at all worthy of a noble ambition, or in the least inviting to an enterprising spirit?"

If ambition, enterprise, and their success, are to be measured by the scale of political elevation, or by the amount of bullion and stocks accumulated in speculation and swindling, whether in an official or private capacity, the teacher is, of all men, the most unfortunate; and I rejoice in the fact.

But if ambition, enterprise, and success, are to be estimated by their results in training the incoming voters to put down swindling, and wrench the grasp of rings of speculators from the public treasury and national domain, I know of no business that affords a field in any way comparable to that of teaching.

Do you object, that this would be teaching politics; I reply, just such politics as justice in both parties demands.

But thorough-going enterprise can and will develop itself in a teacher, by his striving to make every school that he takes entirely superior to what it ever was before, and by his determination to win this reputation, for every school or system of schools that comes under his charge.

Indispensable to this spirit of enterprise in the teacher, as to a man successful in any other calling, are earnest effort, and self-sacrificing devotion, exhaustless ingenuity and good judgment in planning; promptitude and skill in executing every plan; constant aspiration for a still better condition of every school while remaining in it, and a persistent purpose to make it so, every successive day, and every successive term; and thus obtaining for himself continually a better preparation for a higher position, with a larger salary and more commanding influence.

But comprehended in this general view of the teacher's work as a field of enterprise, is the acquisition of the appropriate means of advancement; among which may be mentioned, a good library, a sufficient apparatus, and a practical knowledge of its use and repair; a determination to avail himself of the best facilities for improvement in the art of teaching and school management; especially of the advantages afforded by the most progressive institution, and thus of the most vigorous, thorough and masterly preparation for the highest positions the business can offer.

Again, in the fact that the existing colleges as a system are, to a large extent, effete in their aims and methods, handed down from the dark ages; feeble in the operations, and efforts of salaried professors; and any thing but progressive in their spirit and enterprise, lies a wide field open for private enterprise and competition, in fitting young people of both sexes for their life work, and giving them such a preparation as the present times demand. Already some have entered it, and are succeeding, for the most part, proportionally to the real advantages, which they are found, on sufficient trial, to hold out, as inducements to win popular favor, adequate patronage and support

The creation and management of a private institution of learning, entirely by one's own energy and skill, ambition to excel, and determination to succeed,desire to do good, and a humble reliance on the Master, without begging of any ecclesiastical or political body for endowments, or selling unavailable scholarships, and yet using the same legitimate means which give honorable success in any other private business open to fair competition, is a field of enterprise, perhaps, that comparatively few will desire to enter, but to those few it offers the highest style of attraction, and gives the richest kind of reward.

Reason VIII. A Field for the Exercise and Cultivation of Patriotism, Philanthropy and Spirituality.

There is still a higher class of motives to energize the teacher's activity, than any yet adduced, and enhance his love for his work; and while every Christian teacher will admit that in the scale of importance and dignity they stand the highest, he will confess with me his fears that in the scale of potency and appreciation they stand the lowest, with the great majority even of those teachers who are professors of religion. The love of one's country, or Patriotism; the love of one's kind, or Philanthropy; the love of Christ, or Spirituality, are each good and sufficient reasons why teachers should love their work more than should any other class of professional men; as much more as their opportunities are better for the exercise of these sentiments, and for witnessing the immediate fruits of their labors.

Let us, for a moment, compare the teacher's position with the minister's. Now, I hold myself second to no man in the amount and degree of respect, yes, reverence I would yield the devoted minister of Christ, and his calling. It is heaven-appointed; and if the world is as bad as it is, with the Church, its ordinances and ministrations, what would it be without them. But the minister, for the most part, labors with adults, whose habits and purposes are fixed, either for good or evil. His field, in the majority of instances, is restricted to his own parish, made up of the most moral and upright men and women in the community; those who least need the gospel preached to them.

The Christian teacher, on the other hand, deals with children and youth whose habits and purposes are yet in the forming state, and of consequence comparatively easy to influence and mold. Their affections and wills are yet in that incipient budding condition of activity, which renders them peculiarly responsive to kindly effort and example, whether it be in the direction of Patriotism or Christianity.

But, again, the teacher of a public school comes in contact with the children of all classes of families, those of every religious persuasion, and those who adhere to none; those of both political parties, and those who eschew politics; those who belong to every stratum of society, and those, may be, who are outcasts from all society; and if he can succeed, as I conceive every devoted Christian teacher may, he will win the majority of his pupils, over from bigoted sectarianism to true philanthropy; from bitter partisan prejudice, to a genuine love of liberty, and a just appreciation of the free institutions that make our country what it is, the Refuge for the oppressed of all nations.

Such being the facts, what responsibility devolves on us as patriotic Christian workers, that we do not permit that influence inseparable from us, to work injury to our country's liberties, or detriment to our Savior's cause. Shall we not rather the most earnestly consecrate our influence and our opportunities to the amelioration of society and the upbuilding of Christ's kingdom?

Shall we not, then, the more love our work, teachers, as we love our country, as we desire the general advancement of civilization and righteous governments in all nations, as we are grateful to our Divine Master for calling us to such a post of responsibility, to such a work of love, a work so pregnant with possible and glorious results in honor of his name?

Shall we not the more earnestly pray the Great Teacher, that he will endow us with a daily increase of the "spirit of a sound mind," of a fullness of purpose, and of a noble daring to do his will, that we may thus make some little return, meager though it may be, for his infinite goodness and forbearance toward us, in that we, so unworthy, are permitted to be co-workers with him in building up his Spiritual Kingdom.

LECTURE ON SCHOOL MANAGEMENT.

LECTURE VI.

DIFFICULTIES.

PRELIMINARY REMARKS.

IT is undeniable that many engage in teaching as the only course of avoiding "hard work." Such think there is little else to do in the school-room than to sit and hear the children read and spell, and *say* their lessons, and thus they are going to have a good easy time of it; certainly easier than chopping cord wood, or washing dishes and scrubbing floors; and, besides, they can get better wages.

There are too many boards of directors that are willing to employ just this class of teachers, because they can hire them for five or ten dollars a month cheaper than any others that offer. Such directors are willing to intrust the instruction and training, the formation of life-long habits and character of their children to a man or woman, to some boy or girl, that they would not think of hiring to take care of their horses or cows, fattening hogs or incubating poultry, even though in the latter case the work would come frequently under their eyes; but in the former scarcely ever, if at all. Such is the comparative value that too many respectable and intelligent fathers and mothers place on the moral growth of their boys and girls, and the money growth of their colts and calves, goslings and chickens. To this class of teachers I have nothing to say. They are not here. If they attend any institute it is an Examiner's Institute, as their only method of getting a *legal* certificate to teach. Let those examiners who hold institutes to fleece weaklings, and authorize them to abuse the children, deal with them as their advertisements intimate.

But to this large and zealous gathering of self-denying, devoted teachers, who here exhibit a willingness to spend some adequate amount of time, money and labor to fit yourselves honestly and honorably for doing a good work in the school-room, I have much to offer in the way of pointing out difficulties; not such as will stand in the way of your getting through a term and drawing your money; but such as will be likely to prevent your highest success as Christian artists, determined to do the best work ever done in that school where you shall engage, desirous of building up a reputation that shall bring you better opportunities to do a nobler work, and ambitious to occupy sooner or later an honorable position among the leaders in your profession.

Some of these difficulties I shall merely mention, here, deferring their discussion and methods of removal to the development of a plan of school management, which I shall bring out as a system in due time. Other difficulties of a more special character I shall now discuss, presenting some special methods for disposing of them in the discussion.

Difficulty I. Insubordination from Bad Predecessors.

The difficulty that will be likely to meet you in entering a new school will be the general spirit of insubordination, which prevails as the necessary result of bad previous management. From incompetent, inefficient teachers, who for want of moral or intellectual power were compelled to use physical force in government, the school has acquired a hard name, and you will hear it spoken of as the worst school in the county, perhaps. It has been growing worse for a long time. One teacher after another has been turned out by the directors, barred out by the boys, driven away by prosecution of some man whose boy he had knocked down in a fight; or he simply left in disgust. The boys by this kind of training, winter after winter, are, if you listen to their own account of themselves, a ruffianly set. In short, the school is about as bad as it can be.

Here is surely a difficulty, though in few cases has it reached the point here described. Still in the majority of schools in which you will engage, this difficulty will exist in a greater or less degree, generally in the greater.

Now, there are two ways of meeting it. One is to quell the insubordination and general spirit of misrule by your good right arm, as your predecessors tried to do; assuming that this is really the worst set of scholars you ever saw, and you are the man to bring them to terms, and that you will "take the kinks out of them." The result will be, probably, just as it has been with your predecessors, floggings, fights, and fusses without number, prosecutions from the parents, hatred from the children, till you will be glad to quit the field. But if you fight it through, and, with the help of the directors, expel some of the worst boys from school, and have comparatively quiet times afterward, you have achieved a barren victory, The results are terrible for a philanthropic mind to contemplate.

Another method of dealing with such a difficulty, and one in which a lady teacher will be quite as likely to succeed as a gentleman, I shall develop after a while. For the present, I leave the difficulty, with the remark, that I consider such a district, and such a school, rather a desirable field of labor; yes, a very hopeful one. The bad character will never deter a true teacher from engaging, but rather excite his spirit of enterprise and philanthropy.

Difficulty II. Insubordination from a Good Predecessor.

The next difficulty which demands our attention, is the insubordination arising from perfect confidence in the instruction and management of your predecessor. This is much more formidable than the difficulty just given, and requires special management.

First, let us see how the difficulty manifests itself:

Mr. Smith, you are compared in every act and plan with Mr. Smart, the last teacher. Whatever you do or propose to do, is brought to Mr. Smart's standard, and always to your disadvantage. If you wish a pupil to rise when he recites, "Mr. Smart, let us sit." If you desire the children to hang up their hats and over-clothes when they enter, "Mr. Smart, let us lay them on the wood-pile, or anywhere." If you desire them to come in from recess when the bell rings, "Mr. Smart always came out and called us in; he didn't treat us like plantation niggers." If you open the school with prayer and singing, "Mr. Smart closed the school with prayer, and didn't have any singing." And so on.

If you try to overcome this difficulty by showing the superiority of your plans and methods, and thus directly or indirectly speak to the disparagement of Mr. Smart, you will only increase the difficulty, and you will be charged with being jealous, and treating Mr. Smart "real mean."

A much better way is to grant every thing for Mr. Smart that the children claim, and even to exceed them in your praise, if you can conscientiously. Give the children credit for thinking so much of their old teacher. It really does spring from a noble feeling, and on this feeling you can base a good hope of like or superior success. After this difficulty has fully developed itself, and has become sufficiently annoying, I would take some fit opportunity and make a little speech something like this:

"Scholars, I am glad you think so much of Mr. Smart. I have no doubt he was a good teacher and a worthy man. The fact that you seem to esteem your former teacher so highly, speaks well for both him and you. I have no doubt his plans of management and methods of instruction were good, and I surely do not wish to blame you for thinking so. I think so myself.

"But while his plans and methods were good for him, and you like him for having plans of his own, you surely could not respect me for trying to imitate him. If I am to have your respect and enjoy your confidence, I must have plans of my own, and such as are adapted to my methods of instruction. His plans were good for him, mine are good for me. If you will help me carry them out, and try to feel that I am working for your advantage, and endeavoring to please and benefit you in every thing I ask of you, I think you will soon like my plans, and you will find that you are advancing rapidly in your studies, and enjoying yourselves well. On the other hand, by watching to find fault, and complying reluctantly with my requests and opposing my wishes for your good, you can defeat any thing I can do for you; and such a course would work in the same way with any other teacher, whoever he might be."

Now, by pursuing the course indicated in this hypothetical talk, modified to suit the circumstances, you can hardly fail to find reasonable pupils, and those who will soon take as much pride in the new teacher as in the old one.

Difficulty III. General Prejudice against Novelties.

You will probably take a school in some country district or rural village, where the "new teacher" receives the usual attention of a few days' gossip, and is the standing theme of remark in the shops and stores next in importance to the weather and the crops. If you follow the old well-worn track of rote or rant, you will presently fall out of the sphere of gossip, and be as thoroughly let alone as most of your predecessors were. But if you are determined to make a good school, and take measures accordingly, you will continue to be carped at and criticised in proportion to the novelty and efficiency of your operations.

Suppose, for instance, you require the grammar class to study their lessons by writing them out on paper. This method being new and requiring the extra expense as would be claimed of paper and pens, very likely would be stigmatized as a new-fangled notion, and would excite remarks and opposition in the district that would seriously interfere with its success, and with your success in carrying through other plans which you might well judge necessary to what you would consider a good school.

I only mention this one novelty as an example, and you could hardly proceed without offending the petulant wisdom of Squire Rote, and the critical asperity of Aunt Gossip more and more daily, till the restiveness and impudence of the

Rote children and the Gossip children would infect the whole school, and render your position very uncomfortable, if not entirely untenable.

The remedy for this evil, is not in riding over popular opinion, or in succumbing to it. Neither course will be likely to serve your purpose. I would rather recommend the plan of prevention, by first advising with the directors, and securing their assent and approbation; then I would carefully and clearly demonstrate to the pupils interested, the superiority of the new method over the old, showing a perfect familiarity with the old method by taking off its disadvantages, and presenting in contrast the excellence of the new. I would then propose that the class try the new method for a week or two, to see whether they would like the change, saying, that "If we don't like the new method, we can return to the old at any time."

Difficulty IV. Bad Habits in the School-room.

Their name is legion, but there is one which is the atmosphere for all the rest to live and breathe in. It is generally called whispering. I shall call it communication, as whispering is only one of the thousand ways in which communication can be carried on, in the school-room.

If this one bad habit can not be controlled little good can be accomplished. Do not suppose I wish you to subdue this habit by fear or force. It will be of little use for you to enforce a law against whispering by scolding or punishment. The evil will only be increased by such a course, and many worse ones introduced.

The description of some "better methods" of preventing whispering and other forms of communication will be given hereafter, also for removing other bad habits involved in this and sustained by it.

Difficulty V. The Interference of Parents.

This is a difficulty which it is hard to reach. I have often said, and you have often felt, "If I had only my scholars to manage I could get along finely." But a teacher has to manage a whole community. If he is a man of any force and dares to introduce new ideas and usages into his school, and when the parents and all the old crones and gossips set in to work against him, he finds a difficulty which can only be reached by the long arm of influence. It would better have been foreseen and removed before it had been met.

It is exceedingly important that the teacher carry the popular voice with him, both of school and community; but he will almost always find that the very cases, which cost him the most labor and self-sacrifice, are those which bring upon him the most censure; that those parents, whose children have taxed his ingenuity, toil and patience the most, are the first and only ones to complain.

Such interference will, of course, have a tendency to chill a teacher's ardor and repress his energy; but to the true teacher it will act as the highest kind of stimulus, and arouse a degree of spirit and determination that will compass the difficulty and turn it to his ultimate advantage. In the lecture on strategy, I shall show how this was done in one case, at least.

Difficulty VI. Amount of Labor to be Performed.

1. *Recitations.* As your success in managing a school will depend mainly on your power in conducting recitations, and in exciting your pupils, not only to activity in close attention and real work during the recitation, but in arousing such an earnestness in the subject matter as will secure energetic study during the study hours, it is essential that you have sufficient time to accomplish this. It takes time to wake up mind and bring it into vigorous, working condition.

In this school our recitations are fifty or sixty minutes long, and we always think them too short to do what we desire to. But let us see how long they will be in an ordinary district school, where a tolerably good classification can be effected. There will be three classes in Arithmetic, two classes in Geography, two in Grammar, five in Reading, five in Spelling, one in Writing. But the Reading and Spelling classes must be attended to twice daily. So much for the common branches. There are then about twenty different recitations or drills in the common branches, saying nothing of two or three classes in higher branches, which you are expected to have in almost any district that would offer paying wages. But how many hours do you teach? Not less than six, nor more than seven. What then must be the average length of a recitation, after taking out a half-hour for recesses and changes of classes? Hardly fifteen minutes. An hour is too short for us where all our pupils are anxious to do their best, and the teachers have no interruptions in keeping order or otherwise. What then can you do in fifteen minutes where you find anything else than willingness to work, and when you are subject to frequent interruptions? Under such difficulties more time is required to bring your classes into good working order, instead of less, one quarter or one-third as much, as you see you really have. Then we find the labor required of a teacher in conducting his recitation is enough for two persons at least; in other words, he ought to have an assistant, and his school ought to be a graded school, with at least two departments.

In fact, the labor of *properly* teaching and managing a district school, or an academy of sixty or eighty pupils, is just about equal to teaching and managing the three hundred, and more, that we have here. Now we employ from six to ten teachers, in regular branches, besides others in extra branches, and none of you have reason to complain that your teachers do too much for you, I suppose, or that we perform work which properly belongs to you.

If hearing recitations were the only labor, even though twice as much as you can do well, you might consider yourself fortunate.

2. *Attending to necessary wants.* Though your pupils may be comparatively orderly and well disposed, the wants which they think necessary will be numerous and must receive your attention, or disorder and confusion are the result. One wants to borrow a slate pencil, another a pen, a third a dictionary, a fourth a piece of paper, a fifth some ink, a sixth a knife. One asks, "May I go out?" another "May I get a drink?" a third, "Mayn't I fix the fire?" a fourth, "May I raise the window?" a fifth, "May I speak?" a sixth, "I don't

know where the grammar lesson is;" and thus your time may be given entirely to satisfying the pupils in what seems to them reasonable wants, to say nothing of unreasonable ones. But how is your recitation progressing the meanwhile?

3. *Watching idle and mischievous pupils.* If you are endowed with a good degree of patience the two difficulties previously mentioned may be endured, and the day pass without being entirely wasted, but the idle and mischievous must have your constant attention; or, from lack of interest in any good direction, they will furnish you with enough business to occupy your time, in quieting the disorder which they in wanton sport or designed annoyance, create. Now these mischief-makers must be managed; a school without them would indeed be a dull, monotonous place; but it takes time and labor to convert the spirit of mischief and love of fun, into the spirit of enterprise and the love of study. It can be done, however.

4. *Discipline.* The general arrangements and ordinary management of the school take some considerable time, which of course must abridge the time for recitations. But the special cases of delinquency; as whispering, idleness, mischief; tardiness, absenteeism, quarreling; etc., etc., etc., must be corrected, each separately, and thus, were there no other interruptions, these would necessarily very much impair the interest of recitations.

It may be said, that most cases of discipline may be deferred till after school hours. In other words, scholars should be "kept after school" when they misbehave and neglect their studies.

I have three serious objections to this very prevalent method of discipline.

Objection 1, "*to keeping pupils in.*" It requires my own confinement with the pupil, when I need the time, for rest, recreation or study.

Objection 2. It makes the school room a prison to the pupil. Those teachers who use this kind of punishment, need not be surprised to hear pupils long for the close of the term and freedom from such a prison, rather than the expression of regret that the school is so soon to close.

Objection 3. Compulsory study can never be otherwise than oppressive and odious; whereas the true teacher's constant aim is to make all school duties pleasant and attractive. And then the only punishment that such a teacher need inflict, is the deprivation of the privilege of engaging in some school duty, instead of compelling the pupil to work in extra hours.

5. *Writing copies.* When will you set copies for writing-lessons?

6. *Working difficult Problems.* How are you to work out the "hard sums" for those who say "I *have* tried and can't do it.'

7. *General Business.* When is the time for general exhortation, encouragement, reproof, restraint, and the transaction of other general business?

Thus, we see that the one who sets up for a Lazy Man has missed his location, wonderfully, when he takes a country school. He'd better take a contract for cutting and piling cord-wood, at the rate of three cords a day; or undertake to 'tend sixty acres of corn in a season, than attempt to pursue his vocation in a school-room.

It was not my design to show, here, how this seven-fold amount of labor can be reduced to manageable limits, and how the teacher can do much good, under such adverse circumstances, and even acquire a good reputation for efficiency and success; I shall defer this to *a general scheme of school management* which I hope to offer for your consideration in due time.

Difficulty VII. Irregularity in Attendance.

This evil is most likely to occur in the case of those pupils who are least interested in their studies, and who from want of natural quickness or from meagerness of opportunity, have never been aroused to feel any relish for reading, study, or any other intellectual effort. Such being the dullest and most backward, need every day and hour of school to keep up with their classes. A pupil of the more energetic and interested class can be spared a day, now and then, without special injury to himself, or disturbance to his classes. Such a pupil is seldom or never absent.

But there is James Carrington, a boy hereditarily sluggish, and for want of interest on the part of his parents, has been permitted or required to attend school but little. He is the most backward in every class, and little inclined to hold any other position. In his classes, James excites your sympathy, and you give him your most special and earnest efforts, in all kindness, and patience, and you bestow them day after day, till you begin to feel somewhat encouraged in his behalf. Here, let me say, parenthetically, if you feel any prejudice or repugnance toward such a pupil as James, begin to work for him, and try to do him good, and your antipathy will soon be superseded by a real interest in his case. Still the difficulty is that just as you are able to notice that James is becoming somewhat diligent, and his ambition is at last reached and for the first time in his life he is taking some pleasure in mental effort, he is absent from school.

What is the matter now? Why is James out of school a day? "Why, father was going to the city, and said I might go along if I wanted to."

Thus your labor all has to be done over again, and it is often more difficult to interest James the second time than the first. But, you try again and partially succeed again, and about this time James is missing again; and so on, till he must fall back into lower classes, and then begs his father to let him go to work. The father is not unwilling, thinks James has more *larnin* now than ever he had, and he can't afford to lose James's work any longer.

This kind of school labor is the most trying to a conscientious teacher, taxing his energy and ingenuity, his patience and charity to their utmost limit. How many, even of conscientious teachers, are willing to work continuously for such a boy against his own desire and the interference of his parents, and try to make something of him in spite of such difficulties? I have known a few who have done it, and with success.

Some superintendents and teachers require pupils to "bring up" their lessons lost by absence, and detain them "after school" for the purpose. In my mind this is all wrong. For, admit that the missed lessons are learned by this imprisonment, it is very oppressive to the teacher to be compelled to remain in the school-room extra hours, forcing children to study, being made both a jailor and constable in the operation. But the worst feature is that the remedy only increases the disease. This imprisonment and compulsory study only make the school-room more repulsive, study more irksome, and the teacher more hateful, to the pupils whom she wishes to win.

Now, the knowledge any pupil may acquire of geography, or grammar, or arithmetic, is not the only object to be aimed at, and worked for, by the true teacher; but rather a thousand fold let the teacher work to excite a thirst for knowledge, a love for school duties, and an earnest desire to prepare himself in his school work, for his life work; all of which objects are most surely defeated by this prison-labor, force-work operation.

But, some one present inquires, how are my pupils to get good per cents at their examinations, if I let them have their own way? I reply that this course you are pursuing is forcing them by antagonism to hate the very things that you want them to love, and brings all the burden of good per cents for your pupils on yourself, the pupils working as far as they dare against you. I would prefer such a course, even in a per cent system, as would secure the co-operation of the pupils rather than their opposition.

Do you wish to know how I would do it? Before I close this course of lectures I shall try to point out some of the various methods by which a higher and more energetic course of school ambition can be excited and maintained.

I have, now, given seven difficulties, in this lecture. In my next, I shall consider seven more, equally potent for your annoyance or defeat, in your good work.

LECTURE ON SCHOOL MANAGEMENT

LECTURE VII.

DIFFICULTIES IN SCHOOL MANAGEMENT.

DIFFICULTY VIII. TARDINESS.

No school difficulty has received so much attention in our educational periodicals, and none is so often called up for discussion in teachers' gatherings as this. It is, indeed, one of the most trying and vexatious. The causes are numerous in the pupil, but more numerous in the parents, and vastly more unmanageable.

One of these is the *overwork of mothers*. The mother may have five or six children to take care of, she must try to please her husband, and see that the coffee and steak are not spoiled for his breakfast. She has to oversee a servant or two, when it would always be easier to do the work herself, if she had the strength. She has several hired men to board, and not unfrequently company to entertain. How can she always get her children off to school in time?

The first bell strikes for school, and the good mother, full of all sorts of work and care, hears it. She calls Mary; tells her to find Julia, and comb her hair, and put on her clean apron; tells James to wash his face and hands and start quick, or he'll be too late again; and the rest, the little ones she tries to get ready for school, in less than no time. She knows all this ought to have been done before the first bell struck, but she had more of other things on hand than she could possibly manage. How can she, I say, always see that her children are away in time for school?

But mothers and their cares are not the only obstacles. The father says to James, just as he is starting for school, "There, James, I forgot to have you take Charley to the blacksmith's before breakfast; you must do it now." "I shall be late to school, pa, and the teacher won't like it." "I'm sorry I didn't think of it before, James; but you will have to be too late this time, or I shall have to send a hand and he'll lose a half-hour's work."

From the unmanageable character of these affairs at home, and the desire to be reasonable with pupils, many teachers adopt the plan of receiving written excuses from parents. Though I do not condemn this practice as bad in all cases, it generally tends to increase the evil; and worse than that, it offers a strong temptation to deceit in getting forged excuses, and in loitering by the way longer than if the excuse were not in hand for protection. Thus, it seems to me that it requires more care and time to watch these written excuses, and see that they are not the means of deception, than to watch the pupils without them. But I would try to arrange matters so as not to be compelled to do either.

So far as I am concerned, I never would receive any excuses, either oral or written, for tardiness, nor absenteeism; but always try to hold the school and school privileges in such estimation, that the pupil would consider it punishment enough to be kept away from school, and thus instead of complaining of the pupil for tardiness or absence, and punishing him, I have to express my sympathy with him, for his loss in being kept away from opening exercises, or in being deprived of the pleasure of his class recitations.

But, perhaps, some one of you will say, "That will do very well for you, Mr. Holbrook, and it sounds very well in theory, but in practice, I expect to find in skating time or marble playing time, that several of my boys, and those I am the most anxious for, will frequently be tardy, and even play hookey now and then. It is such cases as these, that I would like to have you tell us how to manage."

Well, I'll try, though I never had any such cases, and

you ought not, and will not, if your school is sufficiently attractive. It will require some power and skill on your part, to make your general exercises and your recitations more interesting and attractive than skating and marble playing. But you can do it. I have known many teachers to control the evil so far as to make it a real advantage in stimulating themselves to extra and continuous effort to make themselves interesting—even using the comparative amount of promptitude or tardiness, as a scale by which to judge of their own power and skill in working for the good of the school.

I shall now proceed to give some of the methods or artifices by which tardiness has been in many instances reduced to an inappreciable quantity, if not entirely removed.

Artifice 1.

For securing promptitude in attendance. I would place some attractive exercise, in which all the pupils can engage, at the opening of school in the morning, also some interesting recitation or general drill at the commencement of the afternoon session.

Some of these exercises which I have made sufficiently attractive *to draw*, for a while, I will enumerate:

1. *Object Lessons.* It is my purpose to give one lecture in this course on object lessons, in order to show how they can be used for this purpose without waste of time; for it can be done, as badly as they are generally abused.

2. *Scientific Experiments and Instruction.* In our Natural-science classes here, Botany, Physiology, Natural Philosophy and Chemistry, the teachers give especial attention to this feature, in the management of these classes; and any pupil teacher who desires it, will qualify himself or herself in these classes to give an interesting and attractive course of experiments and illustrations, with little outlay for apparatus or materials, and with great advantage to his own practical scientific knowledge.

Botany, especially, affords a theme for a very exciting and profitable course of morning exercises during the flowering months; only one book is necessary, (a Gray's or Wood's

Manual), but the scholars should supply themselves every morning with fresh flowers, of such a kind as the teacher shall direct the previous morning.

So, Physiology may be used as a subject in flowerless months; the teacher and pupils furnishing specimens of bones, muscles, eyes, etc., from domestic animals, and to some extent using their own persons for illustration.

3. *Daily School Paper.* This may be prepared and read alternately by a girl and boy, on successive mornings. The respective editors can be designated by the teacher three or four days in advance, so that the labor of preparing a paper may not interfere with regular school duties. I have known school papers thus conducted to prove of great advantage, otherwise than in inciting to promptitude.

4. *Mental Arithmetic.* A drill in this branch may be so managed as to interest *all* grades of pupils, for a time, and prove very profitable as an aid to the study of written arithmetic.

5. *Orthography and Orthoepy.* A drill for the whole school in the elementary sounds, and orthographic parsing, has been made very attractive for a few weeks, winning prompt and eager attendance of all pupils. You will find a description of a course of drills in orthography, orthoepy and orthographic parsing in my Normal Methods of Teaching—pages 92–96.

6. *Penmanship.* This exercise ought always to be general and the teacher ought always to give it his entire attention, while it is in progress. It is the only class exercise in school in which prizes can be given without decided injury to some pupils. In this, however, prizes can be offered in such a manner as to stimulate the most backward, instead of the most advanced pupils; and the prize system may continue from term to term in writing, with increased advantage, if properly managed. The objection to placing this exercise at the beginning of school in the afternoon, that it is imme diately after severe exertion in play, and the muscles of the arm and hand are unsteady, is more than counterbalanced by the advantages of placing it there.

7. *Vocal Music.* We give opportunity here to all our

pupil teachers, not naturally disqualified, to prepare themselves to teach vocal music by such a method that the youngest pupils as well as the oldest in almost any public school, can learn to read simple music, from notes, at sight, in the course of a school term, by daily lessons of ten minutes each. There is every reason why vocal music should be considered one of the common branches, and taught as such.

General Remarks on the First Artifice.

These are some of the exercises, which being sustained with energy and skill by the teacher, will draw each *for a time.* Some teachers will succeed better with some of these, and some with others. No teacher would find it profitable to continue any one of these exercises indefinitely, to the exclusion of all the others. But there will be necessity and advantage in changing the programme for commencing exercises, both forenoon and afternoon, whenever the exercise is found to have lost its effect in securing prompt and cheerful attendance. Perhaps no general exercise except penmanship ought to continue more than ten minutes at a time; and in the morning the teacher would do well to place it *in his own time,* before roll-calling, rather than in the time that he is paid for, by contract with directors.

Artifice 2.

I have sometimes requested pupils to answer at roll-calling, by giving the number of minutes tardy, both for morning and afternoon, the roll being called in the evening for this purpose, also for taking grades in decorum, during the day as I shall explain hereafter. The number of minutes is determined by the pupils from the school clock, or from a watch hung near the door, for this purpose.

Artifice 3.

In a graded school of several rooms I have known a picture to be hung for a week in that room, which had reported the fewest cases of tardiness for the previous week. There is danger that this plan may increase the evil in some of the departments, which, from having a few careless pupils in them, find it impossible to win the prize.

6

Artifice 4.

I have known some very successful teachers to require tardy pupils to write their names on a slate hanging near the door, with the number of minutes tardy annexed, or in case that the pupil was unable or unwilling to write, a monitor appointed for the purpose, and always one who had not been tardy for a given length of time, made the requisite entry on the slate.

Artifice 5.

The daily reports of tardiness and half-days' absence are read every Friday night before the school.

Artifice 6.

Weekly reports of tardiness, and half days' absence, with grades of studies and decorum may be sent to parents on printed cards every Monday.

Artifice 7.

The unvarying and earnest desire to please and benefit every pupil, and a determined effort to accomplish this, at whatever expense of labor or self-sacrifice, will be worth more without any of the other artifices, than all together without this essential one.

DIFFICULTY IX. INDIFFERENCE OF PARENTS.

The utter indifference of parents as to the educational interests of their children would be astonishing if it were not so universal. It is true, some noble exceptions are found, but the great majority even of intelligent, respectable parents seem to be so profoundly absorbed in making money, or in other necessary family cares, that the true ends of life are entirely lost sight of in raising their children.

See that mother. She can go out to the nest two or three times a day for several days to see whether any of the goslings have made their appearance; and when they are hatched she can find time to feed them frequently, watch them carefully, and nurse them tenderly. Why? Because there is money in them.

But what does the same mother know about her children's operations in school?

They go to school, term after term, and she does not know whether they are learning to love knowledge and virtue, or hate them; whether by school influence their personal habits are improving or deteriorating; whether their teacher is inspiring them with a love of industry and probity, or training them by bad management to a hatred of labor and honest exertion. How can she know? She never visits the school, nor invites the teacher to her house, nor converses with her children about school matters, unless it is to listen to their complaints of the teacher, and their accounts of their own mischief and wickedness at the teacher's expense.

The father is greatly interested in his new breed of pigs, and never wearies in descanting on their superiority in making the most pork from the least corn. He can spend any amount of time in leaning over the sty; and seems to enjoy the crunching of the corn almost as much as the pigs do. If any pig loses his appetite, he knows it, or if any pig is missing at feeding time, he knows it, and hunts him up. He doesn't trust the care of his pigs to any hired man.

But his children may go to school or not go; they may be improving their time or wasting it. It seldom enters his head, that it is any concern of his to know whether the teacher is a faithful workman or a shirk; he is too much absorbed in his pigs and colts, corn fields and wheat crops, high prices and low taxes.

But worse than this, you have not only seen this kind of parents, if there were any in the district where you taught, and not improbably the majority were of this kind, take no interest in you or your work as a teacher, giving no encouragement to your protracted efforts to help their children to overcome their lazy, vicious habits, to stimulate them to earnest activity in their school work; but they are the first to make a fuss if in your anxiety to save and bless their children you have incurred their displeasure. They will then take an active part against you, and try to injure you, always assuming that their children were right, ready to believe every story they tell about you, however ridiculous or absurd;

when they know that these same children are caught in lies at home almost every day.

School directors, too, are frequently very little inclined to give you any aid or encouragement in such cases. They are more likely to be the men who make a fuss on behalf of their children, laying all the blame on you, rather than giving you their sympathy and co-operation in trying to correct the bad habits of their children.

In view of these facts, far too prevalent, teaching is not unfrequently, a thankless business; and it is no wonder that so many are willing to leave it for almost any other pursuit.

But let me here tell you again, as I have several times before, that this difficulty with all the rest in our profession should not dishearten the true Christian teacher, nor turn him from his work; but rather excite him to greater patience, keener ingenuity, higher efforts, nobler self-control, loftier daring, firmer trust, and a purer consecration to his work.

DIFFICULTY X. WANT OF UNIFORMITY AND SUFFICIENCY OF BOOKS.

It is indispensable to a well-managed school, that every pupil have his own books, as it is impossible to carry out any regular programme for study hours, if brothers and sisters, or others, are compelled to use each other's books. And it is impossible to avoid communication, if two pupils study together from the same book. Still many parents are very reluctant to furnish the requisite books, thinking that one geography and atlas, sadly dilapidated, as they are, will answer for two or three children; as they can either study together or use the same books at different hours.

Then, in order to secure any economical disposition of time for recitations, and so reduce their number that there will be time enough in each to excite any wholesome interest, it is necessary that all pupils who can possibly be classed together have the same kind of text-books. But parents can't understand this. Too many think if John has an arithmetic of any kind, he can study arithmetic, and the teacher can attend to him separately; and so of an old Murray's or

Kirkham's grammar. And very likely a director's daughter brings a new grammar or arithmetic, which some agent has left with him for examination. So uniformity is disturbed, and desirable classification rendered difficult if not impossible.

What is the teacher to do under such circumstances? I can tell you what has been done by many a teacher. He has bought the necessary books with his own money, and lent them to the pupils, and thus removed this obstacle to good order, diligence, and the necessary condensation of classes. He can thus by a comparatively small outlay secure double or triple the time for the more important recitations, and a higher interest from having larger classes. He also makes it practicable to arrange his programme for study hours, for each class in each branch as well as for recitations. It may be true that the directors have the power by law to prescribe the kind of text-books, and to require that the pupils are supplied with them, but very few use this legal power. More are backward in supplying their own children.

In lending books to pupils, I have almost always been paid for them. The only fathers who stand out, and refuse to pay, are those who spend dimes enough daily for whisky or cigars to buy one or more books, growling when a book is called for, "There it is again, every new teacher must have a lot of new books bought. The old ones are good enough. I'm not a going to submit to it any longer. They can't speculate any more out of me, not easy!" Whether the books are paid for or not, I am compensated in having a more interesting and successful school, and in the feeling of the pupils, that I am willing to do a little more for them, than to keep them in the school-house hours enough in a day, and days enough in the term to get my wages.

Such outlays, judiciously made by the faithful, earnest teacher, often pay a hundred fold.

Difficulty XI. Want of Sufficient Desks and Seats, Recitation Benches and Blackboards.

Since you are a good teacher and are receiving extra wages, the school will be fuller than ever before, and the crowded seats will militate against good order. This difficulty can be removed by the directors, who have the power to levy a tax for necessary repairs and supplies, without a vote of the district. Provision should be made with the directors for this difficulty before engaging with them.

In contracting, they will tell you, "We have a small school, only about twenty or thirty scholars." But you will inquire for the number enumerated; and if you find it eighty or a hundred, you will make your calculation for fifty or sixty. And if they don't attend afterward, conclude it is your own fault, and the difficulty is in your want of energy or power to draw. Thus you will find stimulus for your highest exertions.

Difficulty XII. Want of Properly Prepared Fuel.

Every teacher, almost, has felt this difficulty as a sore annoyance. Sometimes it is the want of fuel of any kind. Sometimes the wood is not chopped, and it is expected that the larger boys will chop it, or that the teacher will do it himself. Sometimes the wood is sap-rotten and water-soaked, a load that the director could neither use nor sell, so he charged the district full price for it, and hauled it to the school-house.

Having shivered with my pupils for a day and more, expecting a load of wood every hour, I dismissed the school at evening, and went the third time to see the director about the wood previously promised. He charged the delay upon another director, who had promised he would send a load to the school-house three days before; but said he would send a load himself, the next morning before school time. Sure enough, I found the wood, a jag of swamp-ash saplings. I tried an hour to get a fire started, but in vain. Still shivering with the children, I sent a note to the director, requesting him to send me a basket of icicles off his wood shed, for kindlings, as I could not get the swamp-ash to burn. He came over, somewhat angry, and somewhat amused, with some fragments of old rails, with the help of which we managed to shiveron until the other director fulfilled his promises. After threatening to leave the school, I secured fuel enough ready chopped and split to last through the term.

The remedy for this evil, want of properly prepared fuel, is in your contract. Make the written agreement that, if the school stops for want of fuel or any other cause for which you are not responsible, that your wages shall be fully paid; but if the school is suspended from any failure or disability on your part, you will not expect pay for lost time.

Difficulty XIII. Hard Cases.

It is sometimes said, "There is a plenty of fine-spun theories about governing schools, but none of them tell us how to manage the hard cases; these theories do well enough for plain sailing, but they fail us just when we need help, in rough weather, or when driving toward the breakers." So, "theory and practice" are scouted as of "no account, any how."

With regard to this difficulty, "Hard Cases," my first remark is that he or she whose theory and practice are *normal*, and right, seldom has any hard cases to deal with, and even then they are so speedily softened, that the fact of hardness is hardly recognized or remembered. Such a pupil as had borne the reputation of being the "worst boy in school," is rather known as among the most diligent and loyal. Why? and how? I answer, (1,) because his antagonism is not excited by suspicious measures of unusual rigor toward him, particularly; (2,) because the teacher perceiving or discovering the particular bent or idiosyncrasy of the boy, or young man, furnishes him something to do that will occupy his time and engage his attention, in some useful direction, and the pupil begins to feel, as he never felt before, that the school is going to be of some real advantage; and having his interest aroused, and his mind fully occupied, he forgets his old school tricks and former bad habits, and becomes one of the most diligent students.

I have found book-keeping an excellent study to win over such hard cases. The idea of making some definite and valuable use of school acquisition is a new one, to this pupil, and is generally adequate to dispel the old one, of considering the school only a place for resisting law, and the practice of mischief and rowdyism. So, I repeat it, the teacher who adopts this plain *normal* principle, of school management viz, *I must furnish every pupil something to do that will be useful and interesting, or he will furnish me something to do that will be vexatious and exhausting;* and carries it out with any degree of faithfulness and tact, will have no hard cases, or, if he has, the popular current of the school will be too strong for them to resist, and as they perhaps took the lead in fun and misrule before, they will strive as hard to shine in leading the classes and promoting the general interests of the school.

☞ But you say, "Suppose a boy or young man still holds out and I am unable to reach him; he still continues troublesome and rebellious, in spite of every thing I can do, then what?"

My answer is, You must acknowledge to yourself that some teacher can be found who can manage even this hard case, that proves so refractory with you. In other words, if you had more skill and patience, you could manage him yourself. Then I say study the case once more, before you own up beaten. Tax your own resources of ingenuity in expedients and artifices, once again, before you are willing to acknowledge yourself utterly vanquished in this contest: you, fighting for the boy and his best interests; he, fighting against himself and for his own destruction. Can't you make him see it?

Try again, find some other expedient, convince him, if possible, that you only design to do him good, and he alone prevents it.

But at last, one or the other must triumph, you for his salvation and your own higher success in all your plans for the good of the school; or he for his own ruin, your discomfiture and the demoralization of the school. Unless you voluntarily resign, as incompetent for the position, and leave the field free for another to win where you lost the battle, it becomes a matter for the directors to decide, whether you or he ought to leave the school. It may even be necessary to suspend the pupil till a meeting of the directors can be called.

Now, in resorting to the directors for "aid and comfort," the teacher must be on his guard against two extremes.

1. He or she must not *threaten* in every slight difficulty 'I'll call in the directors if you don't behave better."

2. He or she, the teacher, should not defer the matter too long, or until he or she has lost all respect of the pupils, and the work of disorganization has proceeded too far to admit of recovery after the principal cause has been removed.

The directors should never be called *into a school*. If they are called once, it will soon be necessary to call them again, and it will not be long before they will be needed all the time. A special meeting should be called for the hearing of such a case, both parties being present to make their statements. If the contumaciously incorrigible, or his parent fails to appear, you will state the case with such witnesses as you think best to call.

If the directors then decide to retain the unmanageable pupil in school, by all means you ought to resign. You can not do a worse thing than to continue a fight after being so thoroughly worsted, routed, and all your subsidies gone over to the enemy.

You may profit by your experience, in another field, but your usefulness here is at an end.

Difficulty XIV. Low Wages.

I look upon this difficulty somewhat differently from most of you, perhaps. You think it a necessity that you would avoid if you could. I think it a misfortune that comes from want of sufficient energy, foresight and tact. "Perhaps so," you say, "but how can I relieve myself of it?"

I will first try to show you how the difficulty works.

You have attended a normal school, and spent all your means in qualifying yourself well for your work. You are anxious now to get a situation, and you hardly dare ask living wages, fearing that you'll not succeed immediately in getting one.

The directors discover your necessities, and jew you down till you engage to teach for half wages, less than any ordinary mechanic is receiving, say thirty dollars per month. Now, what is the consequence? Why, those very directors, who by taking advantage of your necessities, jewed you out of half your wages, are boasting around the district that they have hired a cheap teacher, and you will have to enter that school under the disability of poverty and dependence—two unpardonable sins in these times. Yes, you are a poor, cheap teacher, and all the children have heard of it, especially the directors' children.

The best scholars in the district will not patronize such a teacher; they prefer to go away to school. The worst are sure to be on hand; they expect to have a good time at your expense. How are you going to rise above all this; make a good school out of the worst of materials? How can you convince the children that you are worthy of obedience, and their parents that you have any just claims on their sympathy and co-operation? you poor, cheap teacher! You will find it somewhat difficult, I imagine, whatever may be your qualifications. Yes, low wages is indeed a sad difficulty, and hard to overcome.

Let us now consider the advantages of good wages for a moment.

You meet an honorable board of directors anxious to have a good school, whatever may be the cost. You present your views of teaching and school management, and succeed in enlisting their attention and interest, in the plans and methods you propose to pursue. They feel that money will be well expended in hiring you at an extra price; in fact, they can not afford to let you go. They agree to pay you much higher wages than the district has ever paid before. Now what is the consequence? These directors, in order to sustain themselves with their constituents for paying such an extraordinary price, three or four dollars a day, when the district had never paid more than two dollars before; instead of bragging of their own sharpness, at your expense, avail themselves of every opportunity to speak well of your qualifications, and to set forth your *normal* views and methods in their true light, before the people of the district.

Being thus committed, they are prepared to stand by you, and assist you in carrying out your plans, as well to justify their course, as because they are really interested in the development of your plans, and in the increasing success which attends them.

You are thus introduced under the most favorable auspices, and sustained and encouraged by the hearty co-operation of your patrons. The more advanced pupils of the district and surrounding districts will attend your school, instead of going abroad to boarding-schools. The good students are now all on hand, and are in ascendency; the bad boys and frivolous girls say with the rest, "We are going to have a good school, and I am going to learn something this time."

I say then, teachers, "covet the best gifts," claim the highest wages—only first thoroughly qualify yourselves that your claim shall prove to be a just one—and then, secondly, and always, don't work for high wages—but for infinitely higher ends. But working for such ends is the remedy for low wages.

LECTURE ON SCHOOL MANAGEMENT

LECTURE VIII.

SELF-DIFFICULTIES.

In the two previous lectures, I treated of some of the leading difficulties in the school-room, numerous and formidable enough, it would seem, to intimidate any one who should fully realize their extent and power; but in this lecture I design to bring to view another class of difficulties in many cases still more subtile and unmanageable, than any that can exist in the school-room; they are such, teachers, as are a part of one's self, one's own bad habits, weaknesses, and disabilities. The former difficulties may be overcome or provided for by sufficient energy, foresight and ingenuity; but who is fully his own master? "He that ruleth his own spirit is mightier than he that taketh a city," or governs a school by positive enactment, and rigid enforcement. The teacher who is thoroughly master of himself and possesses the requisite qualifications otherwise, has a school that will call for very little positive government, at least such as manifests itself.

Self-Difficulty I. Bad Grammar.

Let me first notice, my young friends, your use of the English language. You will frequently find yourself making mistakes in the use of your vernacular. These erroneous forms of expression were taken in with your infantile breath, as it were; at the fireside, or on the play-ground, and possibly some of these uncouth localisms, or barbarisms, cling so closely that you are entirely unconscious of them, and probably no friend has had the kindness, or the hardihood to advise you of them.

I know a young man, here, who will persist in his home habit of introducing the preposition, for, before every infinitive, as "I wish *for* you all to come early." "He said *for* us not to mind it." As offensive as this is, to most of you, he is frequently inclined to boast of his knowledge of grammar, and is obviously unconscious of this and other similar deviations from correct language. Probably if you were to tell him of the error, he would reply, "Certainly, I would like *for* you to correct me, when I'm wrong; but you must make *for* me to see that I'm wrong, first."

But, suppose you try to correct your own home-bred errors, and you frequently catch yourself uttering impure colloquialisms—not to say, vulgarisms or slang phrases—the difficulty is then not so much in the fault itself, as in the attention you attract in endeavoring to overcome it; especially, as you will almost surely make the matter worse by overdoing it.

For example, I have heard some pupil teachers here in this effort at self-correction use the forms "I do not," "He is not," instead of the proper colloquial forms, "I don't," "He isn't;" also "I arn't" for "I'm not."

Now I beg, that you don't do such foolish things; rather let your expressions be easy, and free, even though the home-bred uncouthness does show itself now and then. It will not be as likely to excite ridicule as your over-much nicety in grammar. It is generally and correctly assumed that a man who is ostentatious of his grammar, has little else to boast of. Pedantry and ignorance are never far apart.

When you go into society, don't make every one you come in contact with uncomfortable from your extreme effort to be remarkably accurate in your syntax and etymology: more than likely some fast boy or girl will be ready to take you off the moment you are out of hearing.

I once visited a family where a teacher of this stamp had formerly boarded. The good hostess evidently entertained the idea that all teachers were exacting in their grammar. She was painfully precise in her language. For instance, "Mary, *sit* the chairs up to the table, and we will *set* down to tea." If the teacher had not been there she would probably have spoken correctly.

Now, teachers, don't make yourselves and your profession so oppressive. Let those around you feel that you recognize them as fellow-beings, even though you do think you understand grammar so much better than they.

It may work well in your school, however, to call for reports from the members of your grammar class of any instances of supposed bad grammar coming under their notice. These reports should be called for at the commencement of the grammar recitation, and the criticisms should extend to the teacher as well as to fellow pupils. A mutual interest excited in this way, and sustained in the spirit of kindness and humor, will do more in one school term to help teachers and pupils in practical grammar, and in appropriate use of language than memorizing all the definitions, rules, notes, remarks, observations and exceptions in the bulkiest of grammars, or in Brown's Grammar of Grammars.

When judiciously managed such an exercise will soon create in those engaged in it a kind of grammatical conscience, which will hold its sway with increasing integrity, and yet with more ease and grace all through life.

SELF-DIFFICULTY II. USE OF TOBACCO.

This difficulty, I hope very few of you have to contend with. Still for the sake of these unfortunates, although I confess I have very little hope of benefiting them, I will dwell for a moment. I hardly know where to begin, so I'll give you little of my own experience. When about fourteen years old, I noticed that many of the most taking young fellows smoked. It looked smart, and so I thought I must smoke. The first time I tried it, a few drafts were enough to make me "awful" sick; but I was determined to be a man if it did make me sick, and I worked at it till I conceived I could handle a cigar with as much grace as the smartest of them. Not yet having acquired any particular love for the weed, I chanced one day to enter a grocery where three of the most brutal, vulgar bullies of the town were smoking with particular gusto, each with his emptied beer glass standing near him. I pulled my cigar from my mouth, and whirled it out the door, mentally resolving that I would never smoke again or do anything else in which such wretches as they could beat me; and I have lived up to my resolution, at least, so far as smoking is concerned.

But some of you say, "I was advised by a physician to smoke to cure the toothache." Yes, and I suppose you are curing the toothache yet. I would prefer some more effecttive remedy. You remind me of the Irish doctor's bill for services rendered, "To curing your wife till she died, $50."

A young man here last summer said his physician had prescribed smoking a pipe to help his dyspepsia, so he is still smoking for the dyspepsia, when he is able to eat any thing. Why, I would as soon think of polishing my eye-balls with shoe blacking to improve my impaired vision, as to use the poison of tobacco to strengthen impaired digestion. "But a poor excuse is better than none," you know.

If any one of these unfortunates, present, can adduce one positive advantage from smoking or chewing, I would advise him to write it down and give it a whole column. But against that column let him fill another with the evils connected with the use of tobacco, and with the sin and moral degradation resulting from his slavery to so vile a habit.

The list, honestly made, will be appalling. The idea of being a slave to any habit, it seems to me, is demoralizing to all integrity, and a teacher, of all men, ought to be his own master, and in the highest sense a noble, pure and Christian freeman.

Some twenty years since I was conducting an Institute. Two leading teachers of the State were assisting. One the noble and lamented Andrews, the other a Mr. Nameless, though not to know him is to be yourself unknown. The wife of a physician, from the city in which Mr. Nameless was Superintendent of Schools, was dining with us. As soon as our meal was dispatched, Mr. Nameless drawing back from the table, Mr. Andrews says, "Well, Sam, I suppose that cigar has to be attended to now." "Oh yes, every dog must have its day you know," replied Nameless.

Said the lady visitor, "Mr. Nameless, do you know what Henry told me yesterday?" "Of course not." "Do you know that we have been trying for a year and over to break our Henry of smoking; and with his frail constitution and highly nervous temperament, we feel that smoking is ruining him?" Said Mr. Nameless, "Oh smoking doesn't hurt any body; and if it does, they ought not to smoke." "But," said she, "how could it escape your notice, that Henry is making himself almost an imbecile by the practice? His father and I had entreated him to give it up, and he promised us he would; but yesterday I discovered from the odor of his clothes, that he had been smoking again. We charged him with it. He did not deny it. But what do you suppose was his argument this time? 'Why, Mr. Nameless smokes all the time, and it doesn't hurt him.'" Now, teachers, who could bear such a remonstrance from a mother? Surely no man whose every moral sensibility had not been paralyzed by the use of the fell narcotic. Mr. Nameless smokes yet. But what has become of Henry?

SELF-DIFFICULTY III. WANT OF SELF-CONTROL.

I remarked, to be one's own master is more necessary for a true Christian teacher, than for any other man. I shall proceed to specify a few points where the teacher especially needs this self-mastery, and where, if wanting it, he finds a difficulty to which he will sooner or later be compelled to succumb, and thus abandon teaching, or be recognized only as a failure and a disgrace, cast off from one place after another, till life itself shall become as great a burden as he is a nuisance in the school-room. But the teacher who shall exercise due self-control in these particulars can not fail to be a growing teacher, growing in reputation, position, and in usefulness.

Specifications in Self-control.

1st. *Early Rising.* There is no deservedly eminent teacher in these days anywhere to be found, but finds it necessary to study. Such are the advancing claims of Science, Literature and Art, in all directions with which every live teacher must keep pace, aside from the spirit of progress in his profession, and being posted and especially prepared in the matter and method of the branches he is teaching, that the utmost economy of time is demanded, to hold or win any advanced position. Though some successful teachers of uncommon physical development may differ with me in practice, I am prepared to say without fear of successful contradiction from those who have tried both plans, that *early rising* and study before breakfast is immensely more economical than study at night into late hours.

Morning study is better than night study for several reasons.

1. Night study is performed when the physical energies are more or less exhausted, and the mind can never do its best, without a full supply of nervous power. Hence, such study is often abortive, always less effective, even though it may be very laborious.

2. Morning study is performed when the physical energies are the highest, and of consequence the mind is the keenest. The difficult problems which baffled the student's best efforts the night before, he has found comparatively easy after a good night's sleep.

3. Any study to be effective must be exciting. Excitement and fatigue combined in night study, render sleep dreamy, fidgety, and unrefreshing, as every night student knows.

4. For want of sufficient and invigorating sleep, the teacher is unfitted for the duties of the next day, for, however much

he may have gained in preparation for his recitations, he has lost much more in good humor and cheerfulness and vivacity.

It is safe to say, then, that an hour for study before breakfast is worth two hours after supper to the hard-working teacher.

Study before breakfast is healthy excitement. Study after supper is often exhausting and feverish fatigue.

Study before breakfast is both mental and moral power that flows over copiously and bountifully into the schoolroom. Study after supper is the result of moral weakness, and ends, sooner or later, in mental incapacity.

Study before breakfast enhances every excellence, enriches every pleasure, and dissipates almost every difficulty of a teacher's life. But it requires self-control to rise early. Such as I am afraid but few teachers can persistently practice.

But if it requires self-control to rise early, it requires true heroism to retire early enough and continuously enough to make early rising habitually practicable.

LECTURE VIII—Self-Difficulty

Heroism, did I say? Yes, heroism, to break off from an interesting book, to withdraw from a lively circle, to excuse one's self from a charming chat with some fascinating friend. Gentlemen, Ladies—"One man among a thousand have I found," says Solomon, "but a woman among all these have I not found." By which, I suppose, Solomon intends to say, that it is more difficult for a lady teacher to exercise self-control, under such trying circumstances, than for a gentleman. But, I confess, I have my doubts.

2*d*. *Compliance with our own requirements.* For example, promptitude. How many teachers have self-control enough to be at their post, without one failure for a term, not generally, but always, without a single failure? But how can a teacher expect to remove, or even abate, the nuisance of tardiness, while he himself is chargeable with the same crime?

This unvarying promptitude requires that energy in character, and foresight in the arrangement of minor matters, that control of self, and mastery over circumstances, which make the successful man in any other business or profession.

Take another example: I once felt it necessary to request my pupils not to whistle in the school building, the school rooms or halls. The request was very generally complied with. But while solving an algebraic problem during recess, I was heard whistling continuously by all the pupils in the room. The unusual silence among the pupils attracted my attention, and brought me to a consciousness of my whistling. Under the circumstances I found it necessary to make a full confession of my delinquency—and tried to turn the accident to good account, by thus showing my own respect for law and order. But such accidents should not happen too often.

3*d. Controlling one's temper.* The true teacher is full of excitement and enthusiasm; and if he is not exceedingly watchful, especially when tired or ill, his excitability becomes irascibility. Thus his highest element of success, for want of adequate self-control, defeats itself. I know of no better means of controlling one's self under such circumstances, than a persistent determination to return good for evil. Simple will-power may do much, but acting under the guidance of the higher law, it can seldom fail.

A tired, overworked, harassed teacher too often claims the ass's ears. I will explain: *One cold morning last winter, a teacher, hurrying to his school room a half an hour earlier than usual, with his ears protected by fur lapels projecting upward, heard a group of boys he had just passed, vociferating, "What ears! what ears!" Turning around to resent the insult, by "pitching into" the boys, his anger was converted into laughter, by noticing the flopping of a remarkable pair of donkey's ears, not far off in the street. The teacher passed on, resolving, thereafter, to let the donkey always have the advantage of his own ears.

4*th. Controlling one's affections and preferences.* Self-control is again needed in managing one's affections and pre-

*Narrated by Captain Williams.

ferences. We naturally love those who esteem us, and try to please us. It is well that we are so constituted. We teachers have hearts, as well as other people. If a pupil, especially one of the opposite sex, is more attractive than others, the teacher would be more or less than human not to be influenced accordingly. But so to control affection and preference under such temptation, as to escape the charge of partiality, or greater weakness, requires that quantity and quality of self-control that very few even good teachers are found to possess.

Self Difficulty IV. Want of Social Power.

Teachers, as a class, have less social power and social influence than any other profession. We are, if at all successful in our calling, fully absorbed in its duties; rather, entirely overwhelmed with its cares, toils, and anxieties. Why, then, should we try to cultivate the power of making ourselves agreeable and popular with all classes of men and women? Why? Because, being recognized by our patrons as worthy, intelligent, and affable, being sought after and courted in general society, so much the more respect is accorded by our pupils, and thus this social power becomes a potent element in aiding the teacher to attain that ideal school government described in Lecture III, as the Personal Influence Plan.

Besides, the teacher whose studious habits seclude him from society, almost necessarily falls into odd ways and noticeable peculiarities, which much impair, if they do not entirely neutralize, his personal influence in the school room; making a resort to the Force Method necessary to sustain order.

I say, then, that the teacher should avail himself of every practicable opportunity, with his pupils and with his patrons, to cultivate his social power. Now, as it generally devolves on a teacher to lead in conversation, with whomsoever he may meet, he must learn to interest every individual, by *drawing him or her out* on topics concerning which that individual ought to know more than the teacher. Social power is thus evolved and rendered more available in directing conversation and in being an inquirer, than in being a voluble talker, especially about one's own superior abilities, remarkable adventures, and astonishing successes. EGOTISM is a too common fault with talking teachers.

I will add a word or two on *Dogmatism* and *Pedantry*, banes of the teacher's social influence. The control of children and youth, and their necessary subordination to school authority vested in the teacher, will sooner or later give the teacher who does not mingle in society the air, at least, of overweening confidence in his own opinions, and disagreeable restiveness and petulance, whenever his views or statements are questioned or contradicted. This tendency to dogmatism should be most carefully guarded against. The practice of free discussion between pupils and teacher in recitations, within the proper bounds of mutual respect, inciting as it does to breadth and liberality of opinion, will best counteract this tendency. As common as PEDANTRY is with the most assuming and pretentious of our profession, I have not yet learned to treat it, or its possessor, with much patience or respect. The pedant knows a little grammar, that is, he thinks he knows some one grammar by heart; he knows a little arithmetic, that is, he thinks he can do all the sums in some one arithmetic, and explain them, etc.; and you will see these *littles* projecting themselves in all directions, on all occasions; and the man or woman that does not understand grammar as he understands it, and give a definition or a rule as he has memorized it, he denounces as ignorant and low-bred. And so of other branches. Pedantry is the pride of littleness.

A little knowledge is an odious thing. A full and systematic knowledge of any one branch, as treated by various conflicting authors, will free any man, not a born fool or a hopeless knave, from this stench of pedantry. Teachers, beware, then, that you acknowledge no one text-book as your master; but rather use all text-books as your servants, all reference books as your counselors; nature and revelation, under the guidance of a humble spirit of inquiry, as your only adequate authority, your ultimate court of appeal.

But I am not quite done with Pedantry yet. If you will notice from the beginning in the mechanical arts, say, penmanship, up to the highest science we can grasp in this mortal state, the science of holy living; you will find this assertion sustained by facts. The more one knows, the more eager he is to learn. The most beautiful penman I ever knew, Mr. Lusk, was the most assiduous in his efforts still for higher improvement; and the most earnest and lovely Christian I ever knew, I will not mention her name, is the most prayerfully eager for higher attainments in the divine life.

Pedantry, then, makes itself odious by the satisfaction it enjoys in knowing all that needs to be known on any subject, and by rejecting all further investigation as useless, and its results as "positive error."

Self-Difficuty V.—Want of Confidence in One's Self.

It is no wonder, teacher, that whenever you take a comprehensive view of the innumerable duties, the immense responsibilities, the exhausting labors, the perplexing anxieties of the teacher's life, that you often cry out, "Who is sufficient for these things?" and feeling your own inadequacy, you, for the moment, stagger, as powerless for the conflict.

I suppose every truly successful teacher has such experiences. It is only shams and quacks that do not.

But if this spirit of self-distrust is in the ascendant, you are already a failure. No; true manhood, true womanhood is only incited, thus, to more earnest effort and cheerful daring, and declares, "I'll win, or die in the attempt."

Nor is this all; every such noble spirit resolves that every day's labor shall be more effective than any past one; that every term's experience shall make the next a higher success; that every successive class taught in any given branch, shall be better managed, more effectively drilled, more deeply and thoroughly roused to an earnest and cheerful activity, than any preceding one.

But there are multitudes of quacks in our profession—hodge-podge teachers, humdrum teachers, force teachers, talking teachers, everlasting *I* teachers, and yet other like classes, who know no more of these responsibilities and difficulties "in the school-room," and in one's self, which I have been describing, than the latest and veriest humbug advertiser of buchu or bitters, that cures all the complaints and catastrophes of this earthly existence, can be supposed to know of the laws of life or the righteous retributions of Divine Providence to guilty men like himself.

To such teachers, more than life destroyers, I have nothing to say. They are not here. They will continue to bluster and bruise, to imprison and dishearten, to turn a labor of love into the impositions of tyranny, to make the school-room and all remunerative labor hateful and oppressive, to render their pupils as unfit to enter on any rational and honest course of life, as they themselves are to perform the duties of the school-room, in spite of anything I can do for them.

But I address myself most hopefully to you, my friends, feeling that we have considered all these difficulties thus far with a common appreciation of their magnitude and force; and yet feeling that this consideration has the more fully prepared us to grapple with and turn them to good account, instead of being disheartened or crushed by them.

SELF-DIFFICULTY VI. WANT OF CONFIDENCE IN HUMAN NATURE.

By this confidence in human nature, I do not mean that easy, slip-shod goodness which will make you the constant dupe of every ready-mouthed pretender, whining hypocrite, or self-excusing shirk, in your school; nor yet, that confidence which trusts no pupil any further than you can watch him. Of these two extremes, I believe the former the least pernicious, however, in its school results. I will try to show you what kind and extent of confidence, I think, we teachers ought to exercise toward our pupils.

While I am a believer in general depravity, I do not believe that any person is so bad that he can be no worse; but rather that there is no person so entirely corrupt, but that yet there remains in him, deep down, perhaps, some lingering, not quite extinguished susceptibility for kindness, some generous feeling not quite smothered, that you can reach, teacher, if you have the power, the tact to seize upon and apply the proper means, at the proper juncture. If you can possibly discover any good quality or capability in such a pupil, or can learn of any good act that he ever performed, it may become a basis for a sincere recognition of some real worth, which may be succeeded by such a course of kindly appreciation and healthy encouragement, as he has never before experienced; and which, if pursued with some adroitness and much patience and charity, will win his friendship and cordial esteem. Thus, not unlikely, you may have his life-long gratitude, for his redemption from ignorance and crime.

Do not drive any bad boy out of school on too slight grounds. Exercise faith and patience a little longer. When you are compelled to suspend or expel a pupil, you really acknowledge your own incapacity to manage his case; besides, not unlikely, you thus take from him the last opportunity for reformation and the last prospect for a useful life.

SELF-DIFFICULTY VII. WANT OF CONFIDENCE IN GOD.

I claim, that the teacher, above all other men, needs a living Christian faith, a childlike, loving obedience to divine behest, and a perfect and filial submission to the Master's will.

Such are the trials, vexations, and difficulties, such the claims on his charity, patience, and fortitude, such the demands on him for ingenuity, foresight, and strategy, that no human ability would seem adequate to the case. If then there is any man that needs to live by prayer and close communion with God, and thus be permeated and energized by the might of the power of the Spirit of all wisdom and goodness, it is the teacher.

I doubt whether there is a Christian teacher, in this hall, but has come to a point sometime, many times, when he felt that he did not know what to do, or how to manage the particular case. He is unable, perhaps, to decide whether this new difficulty, or complication of difficulties, that presses upon him, demands definite and summary action, or yet forbearance and prudent delay. Now there are times like this, in the experience of every working, hopeful, teacher. "Every heart knows its own bitterness."

In such emergencies, the devoted, Christian teacher brings his grief, his perplexity to the Master. In the spirit of humble confidence he rolls the burden off upon Him who is waiting to receive it. He finds relief, deliverance. A light break up in his path. That which was about to crush or undo him, is seen necessary to his highest success. Thus he is led in a way that he knew not, and the eternal promise again made sure.

Shall we not glory in our profession then, my Christian friends, as that which more effectually, than all others, trains us to a humble and constant trust in the Redeemer's love?

The devoted teacher, sensible of the high trust committed; inspired with the honor conferred by the Master, in calling him to this work; aspiring always for improvement on his own plans, methods, and previous successes; filled with a firm trust that his lack will be more than made up by the presence and guidance of the Master; encouraged by the daily increasing energy, docility, and enthusiasm of his pupils; sustained by the consciousness that he is energizing these pupils for a beautiful and true life, and by the feeling that he may be instrumental in saving some soul from death, even in this his legitimate school-room work; and yet more and more uplifted by the smiles of the Master on his efforts; the days glide swiftly by, every day too short to complete its labor of love; but each succeeding day more and more characterized by the abounding goodness of God, in his successes, his victories, his triumphs over every obstacle, over himself, and this last difficulty, want of confidence in God. How can the teacher be otherwise than blessed in his work? How can his career be anything less than that of "the shining light that shineth more and more unto the perfect day."

LECTURE ON SCHOOL MANAGEMENT.

(COPYRIGHT SECURED.)

LECTURE IX.

HUMAN CONSTITUTION.

With Some Views of its Proper School Training.

PRELIMINARY.

I HAVE, thus far, ladies and gentlemen, been considering with you, the teacher's QUALIFICATIONS, DIFFICULTIES, and RELATIONS, making the teacher himself the central objective point of investigation.

With the QUALIFICATIONS, I have endeavored to give some principles, directions, and incentives, designed to elevate our views of our work, and to arouse us to a higher appreciation of our duties, responsibilities, and rewards, in order to stimulate us to a higher order of qualifications. With the DIFFICULTIES, I have endeavored, incidentally, to point out a few specific remedies for some of them, but more particularly to impress on our minds that there are few, if any, difficulties that, with sufficient skill and patience, may not be converted into real advantages. The general system of Normal School Management, by which all these difficulties and all others are to be met and converted, is of course yet to come. In discoursing both of QUALIFICATIONS and DIFFICULTIES, I have constantly desired to impress on our minds the true RELATIONS of the teacher to the present status of the pupil, to his future temporal life and to his eternal well being.

I shall, in the remaining lectures of the course, take the INDIVIDUAL PUPIL, and the SCHOOL, as objective points for consideration, and try to show the elements and workings of human nature in its complex mechanism in the individual, and still more complex bearings in the school, keeping in view always its relation to the external world, *i. e.*, to the life-work in business, in family, in church, and in state. I shall endeavor to keep in view also, the subordinate, final, and supreme ends of human existence, as revealed in experience, observation, and the Word of God; and with these lights to present a system of school management which will be worthy of your careful consideration, and, I trust, of your hearty approval and ready adoption.

Few, if any,of all the multitudinous and elaborate works on education, with which I am familiar, give any exposition whatever of the human constitution, and no professedly educational work, so far as I know, gives any adequate outline even, of this complicated machine, human nature. Availing myself of the best aids within my reach, I have made out such an outline, which I present here. It is not my purpose to give an exposition of this outline. I present it in order to give some idea of the immense complexity of the mechanism on which we work—with the hope, also, that you may be incited to study the appropriate works for the elucidation of this outline; I take great pleasure in commending for this purpose Hickok's Science of the Mind, and Hopkins' Moral Philosophy—as among the best books you can obtain for this purpose.

I shall have occasion in my subsequent lectures to speak of the various capabilities of human nature as given in this chart. For this reason I wish you would copy it carefully from the blackboard and preserve it for frequent reference.

OUTLINE

OF THE

HUMAN CONSTITUTION.

I. Powers. II. Susceptibilities. III. Ends.

I. Powers, body or matter, soul or vitality, spirit.

A. BODY, material element, indestructible, wasting and renewing.
a. Intrinsic Forces, gravitation, repulsion, polarity.
b. Extrinsic Forces, light, heat, electricity.
c. Susceptibilities, crystalization, chemical change, vitality.

B. SOUL, vital element, perishable, waxing and waning.
a. Vegetable Life, reproduction, growth, repair.
b. Animal Life, locomotion, sensation, instinct.
c. Rational Life, thought, volition, enjoyment.

C. SPIRIT, divine element, immortal, ever progressive.
a. Intellect, perception or senses, conception or understanding, acception or reason

1. *Perception,* {external, senses; / internal, consciousness,} attention, observation, penetration.
2. *Conception,* m, presentative: imaging, creating, combining.
n, representative: memory, association, imagining.
p, reasoning or judgment.
x, abstraction, classification, generalization.
y, comparison, inference, application.
z, construction, systematizing, utilizing. {for profit. / for pleasure. / BY COMMUNICATION.

3. *Acception.*
m, accepts or realizes truths: x, original; y, necessary; z, universal.
n, in primary x, cognitions; y, beliefs; z, judgments.
p, for intuitive ends: x, beauty, y, goodness, z, holiness.

b. Sensibility: 1, appetites; 2, desires; {of property. / of knowledge. / of power.} 3, affections.

c. WILL: divisions, {choice or election, {purpose or determination, {energy or enthusiasm.

1. TENDENCIES, hereditary, social, habitual.

2. MOTIVE POWERS: bad {world, flesh, devil. good {heaven, conscience, Holy Spirit.

3. MEANS OF TRAINING OR FORMING HABITS. {home, school, business.

II. Susceptibilities.

A. HABIT, trained by repetition, effort, rewards.

B. EXCITABILITY, aroused by {pleasure, pain; {love, hate; {pride, anger; {sympathy, antagonism.

C. MORAL STATE, determined by faith, works, supreme end.

III. Ends.

A. CLASSES, subordinate, final, supreme.

B. FIELDS, school, life, eternity.

C. OBJECTS, self, neighbor, God.

D. AIMS, happiness, usefulness, blessedness.

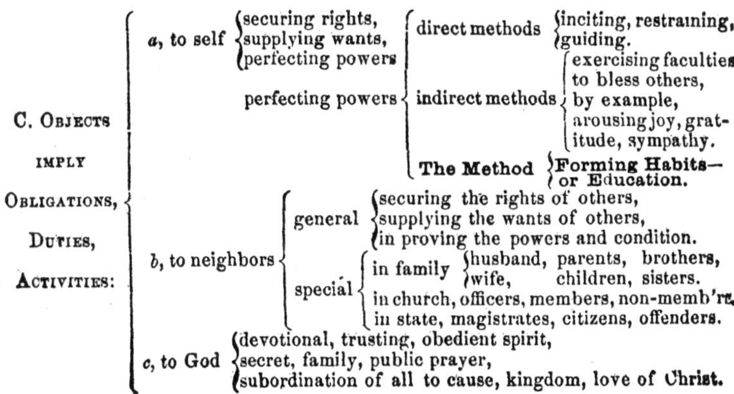

C. OBJECTS IMPLY OBLIGATIONS, DUTIES, ACTIVITIES:

- *a*, to self {securing rights, supplying wants, perfecting powers
  - perfecting powers
    - direct methods {inciting, restraining, guiding.
    - indirect methods {exercising faculties to bless others, by example, arousing joy, gratitude, sympathy.
    - **The Method** {**Forming Habits—or Education.**
- *b*, to neighbors
  - general {securing the rights of others, supplying the wants of others, in proving the powers and condition.
  - special
    - in family {husband, wife, parents, children, brothers, sisters.
    - in church, officers, members, non-memb'rs.
    - in state, magistrates, citizens, offenders.
- *c*, to God {devotional, trusting, obedient spirit, secret, family, public prayer, subordination of all to cause, kingdom, love of Christ.

SCHOOL TRAINING DEFINED AND EXEMPLIFIED.

False and True Conceptions.

With this chart of human nature before us, I shall proceed to evolve some aspects of what I conceive to be the true conception of our school work as teachers, remembering that the objective field of consideration in this lecture is the school and every pupil in it.

Bacon's apothem, "*Knowledge is power*," is the claimed base of the false conception of school work: "*Well trained and well directed activity is both power and happiness*," is the real base of the true conception. This truth is found not in the works of Bacon nor Aristotle; but in all the animate works of God.

The false idea accepts acquisition of knowledge as its aim, culture and scholarship as its ends, and the life of a refined and polished gentleman as its legitimate result.

The true idea claims the training of every human power and susceptibility as its aim; an energetic, varied, and joyous activity as its end; and the life of a successful business man, of an influential citizen, of a *working* Christian, as its result.

The false idea makes cramming the memory with facts definitions, rules, observations and remarks, its chief concern; it has also some sordid, meager views of preparing for business in working at arithmetic and penmanship; and more recently reaches its climax of absurdity, in going to a Commercial College to *complete* a business education.

The true idea makes cheerful, interested study, continued and earnest application, close and patient thought, its immediate and constant aims, ever feeling that these habits give sure promise of abundant *success* in business life.

The false idea *compels* the pupil to study, ever regarding study as an irksome toil, and exemption from it as the highest reward in school life.

The true idea incites, *permits* pupils to study, ever regarding study as an exciting activity, and imposes privation of it as a sufficient penalty for any derelictions in school life.

The false idea conceives that study and education are finished in Seminary or College course, and that study is too dreadful a thing ever to think of after graduating.

The true idea claims that the pupil has only acquired correct habits and effective methods of study, and its profitable application; so that the real life work in study and business is reached only when the pupil has become independent of his teachers and professors, and he studies and works because he can't help it.

The false idea studies to make good recitations, in order to pass reputable examinations, and to secure promotion, or exemption from penalty and disgrace.

The true idea studies *to learn how to study*, to train and energize the mind to higher effort, and more beautiful results in the study and class-room, but immeasurably more for preparation for the responsibilities of life.

The false idea prepares for recitation with the expectation of answering such questions as are proposed by the teacher, either in the words of the book, or, at most, by giving the ideas of the text-books.

The true idea prepares for recitations with the expectation of being called on to engage in a definite and accurate report on some principal or subordinate topic involved in the subject-matter of the lesson assigned.

The false idea conceives composition writing a regular humbug, to be squelched; an intolerable bore, to be shirked or shammed; or an insufferable nuisance to be abated by any possible means, either fair or foul.

The true idea is eager for frequent opportunities to give written reports on any included or concomitant topic of a lesson; enjoys it as a real privilege to engage with others in writing essays on topics assigned for such purpose, realizing that every such effort gives new power of investigation, new energy and grace in an expression of thought.

The false idea memorizes *one* text-book and groans over the task of memorizing the words, or mastering the ideas of this one text-book.

The true idea is never satisfied with the views of one au

thor, however reputable, but seeks spontaneously to collate the views of other authors, that thus, by studying the subject in various aspects, it may be understood in all its bearings.

The false idea is quite satisfied with the statements and reasoning of one book, and thus meeting the demands of recitations and examinations, never dreams that books and book lessons have any further connection with life, or that they can be made of any further practical value, in performing the duties of life.

The true idea thus works with an object beyond recitations and examinations, and thus its "object" lessons are as much above those of the false idea, as the true object illustrations are above the so-called "object lessons," imported a few years since from Europe.

The true idea is never satisfied without *making connection* between the ideas of books, and the facts gathered from experience and observation, in the common or uncommon affairs of life; reducing the ideas of books into living and working harmony with the actualities of life, and feeling an eager and determined purpose to make the school work a noble and beautiful beginning of the life work.

REMARKS ON LECTURE IX.

This lecture is brief, for the reason, that time was given during the hour of delivery, for the pupil teachers to transfer the Outline given, here, on pages 360–61, from the blackboard to their note-books. The next lecture hour was taken up in discussing the Outline in a general way.

1st. By calling for inquiries in case of any difficulty on the part of any pupil teacher in understanding the significancy of any terms used, or the relations of any of the divisions or subdivisions, and of course in giving the necessary explanations.

2d. By calling for any objections to any feature in the arrangement, and answering such objections.

3d. In challenging the class to mention any omissions in the wide range of human nature or experience, and showing how the apparent omissions were provided for in the Outline.

4th. In showing some of the uses and applications of

this Outline in arranging and prosecuting a course of Education.

5th. In assigning special topics to individuals for investigation; stating that reports not exceeding ten minutes in length would be called for on the next and succeeding days. These reports and full discussion of each by the members of the class gave, perhaps, a more practical knowledge of Psychology and Ethics, than is ordinarily obtained by the study of each of these sciences for a full term.

LECTURE ON SCHOOL MANAGEMENT.

LECTURE X.

SCHOOL MANAGEMENT, IN CLASS MANAGEMENT.

WITH this chart of human nature, as given in this outline (page 360) before us, and with these aspects of the true idea of school work designed to be made more palpable by contrasting them with the prevailing false views and practices as given in my last lecture, I shall proceed to more direct statement, or the evolution of the Normal Method of school management. As this method claims that all *right* mental and moral action is free action, and as this school management operates by inciting and guiding the WILL to free and cheerful action, it will be seen that the teacher's WORK is chiefly done while in mental and moral contact with the pupil, viz: during recitation, though his influence must pervade, and in no small measure control, the entire being of the pupil.

The management of a class, then, during recitation, must have for its concern the entire training of the man or woman; not that this training is then and there accomplished, but that it must be aimed at, provided for, worked for, most strenuously. Nor is it to be inferred that the teacher is to have no other interest, than what he can exercise in his class drill, but rather that he is to observe out of the class with increasing satisfaction, daily, the results of his labors in the class, and thus to obtain the data by which to guide his own further efforts and inspirations. He is also to notice those errors and weaknesses in the habits of the pupil which need special attention and special arrangements for their correction.

It is still claimed, however, that the class drill is the time and place where activities are to be roused and directed, corrected and stimulated, from day to day, and thus good HABITS of study and labor formed and established; and thus the Normal method places class exercise and class management as the necessary BASIS of all *correct*, or *normal* school management.

Education, the Formation of Habits.

A good education is the accomplished fact of good habits, established in the man or woman; habits in that direction which shall produce the best results the individual is capable of, for the good of society, and for his own individual happiness both here and hereafter.

The most that the teacher can do, or need do, for his pupil, is to aid him in forming and establishing good habits thus preventing him from forming bad habits, by forestalling rather than by repressing them. If the heart and will are habitually and earnestly engaged in the practice of good for good ends, there is no opportunity for temptation to evil, no possibility of it.

Hence, I repeat: that class management, which by so continuously directing and stimulating the mental and moral action of the pupil as to form correct and established habits, is most essentially the correct, or normal management, not only of the class but of the school; and that class management which forms bad habits, or does not positively and effectively form good habits of mental and moral action, is incorrect, vicious, abnormal.

HABITS TO BE AIMED AT IN CLASS MANAGEMENT.

1. The Habit of Cheerful, Earnest Industry.

This industry must be incited by legitimate ends and sustained by appropriate means. All labor or study performed from the fear of punishment, is eye-service, slavery, and fixes more deeply the hatred of work, and the habit of laziness. It is strange that parents and teachers can not see it. Slavery has ever been a failure, and the misfortune or ruin of all who were engaged in it. Why should we practice it on those we love and desire to bless?

All labor or study,performed from the desire or hope of some extra sensual gratification, is mere animalism or diabolism; and no such motive should be resorted to by teachers or parents who desire to promote the permanent well-being of the pupil or child. Hence, rewarding children for some good act, or some right course of conduct, as staying in at night, or milking a cow regularly and thoroughly, by giving some extra indulgence, as money to go to a circus, is training the child to both laziness and lust.

And that teacher who rewards his pupils for good recitations and good order, by giving a half-holiday or by letting out school a half-hour earlier than usual, while he punishes pupils for remissness or failures in study and order, by keeping them after school, and compelling them to take an extra half-hour of prison work or confinement, is training those pupils to hate study and the school; and he unwittingly, but most effectually, fixes the habits of laziness and shirking on the life and heart of those pupils.

The only industry in school life that is of any permanent value, is that which arises from voluntary action in a state of freedom, the industry of choice; eager, earnest occupation of the whole mind, from the irresistible impulses of a cheerful, willing heart.

Such a HABIT *of earnest industry once fixed, is worth more, as an education, than all else that can be acquired in school or college life without it.* And that habit of laziness, so often the direct result of school and college training, which shirks or shams all real work whenever it is possible without immediate disgrace, is a rottenness in the bones that no acquisitions in knowledge, no attainments in culture, no graces of manner, can ever compensate or atone for.

What a pitiable object such a lazy wretch is! a failure in

himself, a burden to his friends, a curse to society. How long will it be before he is a hopeless inebriate, or an abandoned debauchee—this highly educated gentleman?

It is true that some escape the blighting effects of this kind of school and college training, and in spite of it become useful men. If they do surmount such influences and leave college with any determining moral principle, any inspiring love of work, they surely may be expected to overcome all other difficulties in their way to eminence and distinction.

2. The Habit of Careful, Thorough Investigation.

No one cause will incite children and youth to cheerful and eager labor, more than the desire of knowledge. (See outline, page 360.) It can be made constant use of by the judicious teacher, in inciting to diligent study. But it requires skill, patience, and foresight, on the part of the teacher, to make this natural stimulus, healthy and powerful as it is, ever available, ever increasingly available. Hence the necessity of considerable breadth of practice and variety of exercise, to promote careful and thorough investigation. The memorizing of one text-book, however good, is in most cases the bane of industry, and the impassable barrier to investigation; and the teacher must contrive other methods than "learning a book through by heart" to secure any good habits whatever.

To secure persistent industry *as a habit*, by means of the habit of investigation, I would make use of two artifices:

Artifice 1.—To secure thorough investigation, I would have pupils *write their lessons*. This artifice requires management, of course, to obviate all the objections which any old fogy teacher will necessarily raise against it. In each branch some peculiar plan must be adopted to secure the ends, viz: thorough investigation and cheerful industry.

Advantages of the Writing Method of Study.

1. The pupil is constantly practicing and improving in his penmanship, capitalizing, spelling, syntax, and punctuation,

which exercises are all avoided in the common book method of study, or the *whizza-whizza* plan.

2. The mind of the pupil is very much aided and encouraged by the employment of the fingers, and by seeing on paper or on slate the results of its labor.

Remark.—This is a kind of object lesson drill that amounts to something in developing attention, observation, penetration, clear conception, correct, free, and happy use of language in the expression of thought.

3. Whereas, by the common method of study, the slow, honest student is constantly discouraged by his mistakes and inefficiency, as they are brought out and censured in recitation; while the quick and mischievous pupil is as constantly commended in recitation, and thus encouraged in idleness and mischief, the greater part of his time: this method gives ample opportunity for the teacher to commend the slow and backward pupil, for his industry and faithful effort; while the active and sharp pupils will be held to continual application, by writing the lessons and pursuing their investigations, as they never can be on the whizza-whizza plan.

4. The pupil is constantly learning to think independently, and voluntarily to use his dictionary and other reference books in the preparation of his lessons, in order to secure the most exhaustive reports on any subject assigned.

Remark.—The objections to the writing method of study may be numerous, but they all disappear or become real advantages under proper management. The plan, as I have before said, must be modified to meet the demands of every different branch, and to suit the different powers of pupils of different ages; and when so modified with any degree of skill or good judgment, every objection is removed, and the objects are secured, viz: the habit of critical, thorough investigation, and the habit of continuous, cheerful, earnest labor.

Artifice 2. For promoting thorough investigation, I would secure such an arrangement of the processes of recitation, as will make the principle of emulation the most effective on the most backward in a class, rather than on the most forward.

In a subsequent lecture, I shall explain such an order, and describe some of the various processes by which emulation may be made a healthy stimulus to all in a class, rather than, as it too often is, an evil and an evil only, by inciting the forward, those only who do not need the stimulus, and discouraging the backward, the only ones who do need it.

3. The Habit of Systematic Arrangement and Methodic Action.

The habit of good order, as opposed to carelessness, slovenliness, shiftlessness, is one of vital importance in school training. The natural depravity of man is in no other particular so universally exhibited as in this. While the love of order and system is instinctive with every child, his natural laziness or carelessness is averse to the restraints and the efforts to secure the benefit of good order in his own case, however much he may admire it in others. Hence, here is where the teacher can exert his most needed and most salutary influence in molding the character of his pupils.

To excite the love of order so vigorously, to exhibit its necessity and advantages so constantly and beautifully, as to induce in the heart of his pupils a decided preference for systematic arrangement, and to establish it in his actions as a controlling usage, in other words, a fixed habit, is a work no less than any other that a conscientious teacher should strive to accomplish. Such a habit, controlling personal, mental, business, and religious activities, will obviously be worth more than all other school acquisitions; in fact, is the very essence of the first and overtopping *habit of a love of work*, without which life soon becomes a barren waste, or a living hell.

Besides the other Normal methods of securing order, by the love of it, which will be explained hereafter—and tho systematic disposition of time in school hours for study, as well as for recitation, provided for on the general school programme, I shall give a brief view of the plan of using outlines to stimulate methodic study and systematic thought. 1. Outlines supplied by the teacher; 2. Outlines made by the pupils.

Arranging Subjects in Outline.—Normal Artifice.

(Method by the Teacher.)

1. An outline can be given on the blackboard for the study of any successive lesson in a given branch.

Example.—I will take a lesson in geography, and will assume that the subject of the next lesson is Massachusetts. After having attended to the recitation of the previous lesson, I write on the blackboard, a list of topics by which the class are to study the subject. Rather, I ask some member of the class to transfer to the blackboard the outline, or list of topics which I have previously prepared on paper. This outline may be more or less extensive, according to the advancement of the class, and the facilities which they can reach to meet the demands of the outline. The outline may be divided into two sections to meet the capabilities of two different sections of the same class; for there is great advantage in combining two classes in geography, not too unlike in advancement, and taking the time of both classes for the combined recitation. The less advanced portion of the class may be limited in their study to the topics in the first section of the outline, and they will be expected to recite only on these topics; while the more advanced pupils, forming the second section of the class, will be expected to investigate all the topics on the list, and will be permitted and encouraged to add other topics to the list. The inquiry for these additional topics will be made at the beginning of each recitation; then the first section will recite, on the first section of the outline, the second section being always called on if all the members of the first section fail in any particular. Then the second section are called on to report on the second section of topics in the outline.

Remark 1.—This method of exciting diligent study and thorough investigation will give splendid results, if managed with any degree of skill on the part of the teacher. The interest of the class will never flag; the only trouble will be that the pupils will be inclined to take time from other branches to give the branch so managed. But *all* the branches must be managed in some such way, to make them equally attractive. Thus study becomes a delight, instead of a burden, the laggards are soon reached, and their lazy bones are seen to move in spite of themselves.

Remark 2.—Any pupil of the first section will be permitted to pass into the second section, whenever in the judgment of the teacher he can sustain himself there; and thus a healthy emulation is sustained in the first section. Pupils of the first section are also permitted to criticise the pupils of the second section, always, of course, in the established order of the class.

(Methods, with outlines by the pupils, in regular study and recitation.)

1. Enlarging any outline given by the teacher.
2. Applying an outline given for one subject to another designated by the teacher, and making the appropriate modifications.
3. After sufficient drill in previous methods, the pupils may be requested to make outlines of a subject or chapter already gone over in the regular study and recitation, during several previous days. These outlines are, of course, examined by the teacher, and can be graded, 1, as to business appearance; 2, as to exhaustive investigation; 3, as to logical arrangement of the matter contained. These outlines on paper may be attached by the several pupils to the wall, and opportunity thus given for each pupil to complete his outline by examining the rest. A high degree of emulation is thus excited by exhibiting each outline to the whole class. The class are then called on individually, to report orally on any subordinate topic contained in the general review; and

thus a most thorough and interesting review is accomplished.

Remark.—It may be thought by those teachers who have not used this *outline* method of study and review, that it will make superficial students, and that in working on outlines they will know nothing else. My experience has been quite the reverse. The exhaustiveness or completeness ever being an object of emulation in the class, the result is a general thoroughness and mastery of the subject, which can be obtained by no other means that I have ever known tried.

Outlines in composition writing,

4. Pupils for composition writing, after previous practice, 1, in writing letters; 2, in writing stories narrated by the teacher, or read by the teacher from a book to which the pupils have not access; 3, in simple descriptions of material objects, etc., may be requested to make each an outline of some miscellaneous topic. It will be well for the teacher to give an outline on the blackboard of some kindred topic first, as a guide to the effort.

After the general theme has thus been investigated and partitioned by the class, and the results of the investigation of each have been systematically arranged in an outline, and these outlines have been examined, compared and graded by the teacher, as before mentioned, in the particulars of, 1, appearance; 2, thoroughness; and 3, methodical arrangement; the teacher can distribute the subordinate topics of the same general subject to different pupils, to outline again; and as themes for short essays. These essays will, of course, be read at the regular time set apart once a week for the composition exercises. The essays then will be taken and criticised, and managed in the manner described on pages 31–33 NATIONAL NORMAL.

Remark 1.—Composition writing, managed in this manner, will cease to be a humbug, a bore, and a nuisance, in the nomenclature of the pupil; a bugbear, a drag, a sham, a fizzle, in the vocabulary of the teacher.

Concluding Remarks on the Use of Outlines.

By these and other similar uses of outlines in regular studies, as well as in essay writing on miscellaneous topics, the heart and will are trained to the habit of order:

1. In methodical study in spite of books.
2. In methodical arrangement of all facts, principles, and applications of every subject studied.
3. In the immensely greater ease and satisfaction with which the memory stores up practical knowledge for future use; and in the wonderful facility and certainty with which the memory furnishes such stores when needed for further progress in study, or for actual life use in conversation, in business, or in public discussion.

Explanation of the term Habit.

Before entering on the discussion of the last topic of the general theme of this lecture, I shall give you my idea of the term, and of the actuality, habit.

As I have used the term, and as I have found the actuality in the human constitution (see Outline, p. 360), habit is the susceptibility of doing, thinking, and feeling, the more readily, the more pleasurably, and more persistently, from frequent repetition and continued use.

While the aid and influence of this susceptibility in school training is hardly recognized by the majority of school teachers and superintendents, college professors and presidents, it is really that element in our nature which makes training of any advantage, and education a possibility.

Then, I am ready to affirm that it is the true educator's first and only business, to help the pupil to establish correct habits of feeling, thinking, working; not so much to watch for bad habits, that they may be checked and repressed, as to forestall them by establishing good habits. I have before shown how habits of laziness, dishonesty, self-indulgence, involving a hatred of work, and impossibility of any continued course of useful effort, are to a great extent the direct results of ordinary school and college training, that all the scolding, coercing, watching, spying, offering of prizes, and awarding of honors to the few, are only direct and sure methods of introducing and establishing vicious habits, in the many, if not in all.

It is manifest then, that any plan of education, any course of training, to be what it claims to be, what it ought to be, must be brought into working harmony with the faculties, susceptibilities, and true ends of our being, as revealed by the teachings of experience and the light of the gospel, before it will with any certainty establish good habits, such as will enable the possessor *to work from choice*, rather than necessity; and will give him the highest satisfaction and success in any calling he may decide to adopt; will make his life a joy to himself and his family, a blessing to the community in which he lives, an honor to his country and his race.

NOTE 1. THE SUBJECT CONCLUDED IN NEXT LECTURE. The discussion of the theme, 'Formation of Habits' in school, will be concluded in next lecture.

NOTE 2. EXPLANATION. The first lecture of this course was printed from a phonographic report, the remaining lectures have been rewritten, with the bestowal of much time and labor, as the pressure of multiform duties and cares otherwise would permit.

NOTE 3. METHOD OF USING THESE LECTURES. This course of lectures is substantially the same as I have been accustomed to deliver to classes of pupil teachers for several years. It has been our custom to spend the lecture hour of every alternate day, in discussing points of difficulty or interest, involved in, or suggested by the lecture last delivered. Such discussions are carried on chiefly by the pupil teachers. Almost any inquires as to the practical working of any method, or any phase of any method can be elucidated by pupil teachers present, who have at some previous time attended the training class, and have reduced these methods to practice in their own schools. Thus my general statement, that I propose no methods, of teaching or management, which I have not tried myself, and tried successfully, finds confirmation in the experience of returned Normal Teachers, who gladly avail themselves of the training class, the second and in some cases, the third time, to improve their 'Theory and Practice.' These returned students are in this manner invaluable aids in these discussions, and the discussions are immensely more useful to the classes than the lectures themselves possibly could be.

It has been the practice of the teachers of several public schools, on receiving their copies of the NATIONAL NORMAL, to meet together, read and discuss the lecture. This has also been done by some township and county associations, at their regular meetings.

LECTURE ON SCHOOL MANAGEMENT.

LECTURE XI.

SCHOOL MANAGEMENT IN CLASS MANAGEMENT.

THE HABIT OF UTILIZATION: USEFULNESS AND BENEVOLENCE.

Methods of Training.

1. The pupil should enable himself to interest his class.

Aside from and beyond the motives already proposed as proper incentives to diligence and order in school management, (more closely in class management), which are 1, the desire to know; 2, the love of order; and 3, the desire of power or superiority which emulation strives for; there is a much higher order of motives found in the higher ends, *Usefulness* and *Benevolence.* As they should never be separated in life, I do not see how they can well be separated in school training.

The low and selfish end of making a good recitation to avoid demerit marks, or to obtain high per cents, so often the *only* end relied on, as having any power with a class in compelling them to study, while by some college authorities it is confessed to be the only means by which the professor can secure decent treatment from the students during recitation, falls entirely out of consideration under the more effective stimulus of these higher ends. These ends can never be applied by force, nor while the pupil is under coercive restraint; they can only be brought to bear on the free. Pupils must act, if they act at all from such motives, of their own choice, in the pure and invigorating atmosphere of liberty, such liberty as has for its essential elements faith, hope, and love.

If, then, in the class exercise, each pupil is incited to make such effort as will interest his class, and even instruct them, and the teacher will so far as time will permit, keep this end in view, pupils will find a healthy glow invigorating their efforts in preparation for class drill, higher, purer, more stimulating than from merely studying to avoid bad marks, or to obtain good ones.

This motive comes in play more effectively in preparing special reports, and yet more in writing essays on miscellaneous topics, but it should be brought to bear in every ordinary recitation, and arrangements made for it by the teacher; that is, by permitting the pupil to go beyond the narrow limits of his text-book in preparing his lesson.

2. The pupil should enable himself to interest his friends in conversation, and by correspondence.

There is no place so favorable for the cultivation of the social faculties, for their healthy development, as a mixed school. The topics of ordinary regular school study, the topics of debating clubs, of essays, besides the ever fresh and varying current of scientific, educational, political and religious news, of these stirring times, furnish continual and ample material for conversation and social discussion, excluding the foolish, frivolous, flirtation nonsense or pruriency of most other social intercourse. I am well aware that any teacher engaged in a separate school will turn up his snuffing nose at these statements. I pity his blindness and ignorance, but let him snuff on. The power to converse on topics of Science, Literature, and Art, should ever be held up as a noble and beautiful end, which class preparation and class drill should ever have in view.

How many of the graduates of female seminaries, for instance, that you ever saw, could bring a single valuable idea, obtained from the study of school books, or from recitations of book lessons, into subsequent social life. "Oh, they don't go to those institutions to get science, they go to get polish," you say. Well, so let it be understood. But how is it with the graduates of male colleges? They generally treat ladies as simpletons, and if they find any lady otherwise, not a few of them will speedily "beat a retreat from the strong minded." It is not congenial atmosphere for these college gentlemen.

3. The student should be trained to make constant connection of the ideas obtained from books and class discussion with the facts and phenomena observed in nature, and in the common experience and observation of every-day life.

It has often seemed to me in witnessing the recitations of many different schools and colleges, that the object is to detach and draw off the mind of the student from every useful application of ideas obtained from books, as it were to sublimate the mind from all base contact with sordid things of real existence, real life. The result of this unnatural course is, that marks of merit and demerit must be used to stimulate the student to any effort, and generally that effort will be the least possible, with close calculation, which will exempt him from public disgrace. But if by this plan of management the student is made to hate study and all real effort in any good direction, how does he or she fill up the long unoccupied hours of school and college life? Let the accounts which all such students, when out of school, give of their mischief, their plots, their intrigues, their tricks played on the teachers, their midnight revels, answer. Who ever heard any thing else of college life, either of male or female college, that seemed to the graduate to be worth relating? And let the general want of success of college graduates for several years after leaving college, to which fact there are some noble exceptions; let the frequent self-abandonment to vicious habits acquired in the unoccupied hours of college life, tell the sad story.

I say then, the teacher can hardly with too much care and earnestness hold up to the mind of the pupil the connection of every book statement with the facts and phenomena of nature and common life, and strive to excite him to observe these facts and phenomena for himself—to form cabinets, to store his *Index Rerum*; also in the same spirit of remunerative industry every effort in preparation for recitation, and in recitation should be made with constant and direct reference to securing greater power and more speedy success in future life. Nor should any common school teacher excuse himself from this course of action in school management, claiming that his brief connection with any one set of pupils can have but little influence either way. Such a teacher, by his lazy, shirking spirit, turns the most delightful of labors into the most burdensome for himself. A succession of such teachers make our common schools the moral pest-houses we so often find them.

In many instances I have known one good Normal teacher to change the character of a school entirely, open the eyes of directors and parents to the advantages of a good school, so that they were unwilling afterward to employ any irresponsible vagabond, or frivolous flirt, that could show a county examiner's certificate, as they had been before, provided such a person did not demand too much wages.

4. The student should be trained to propriety of expression and cogency of thought in writing.

To this end are directed the reporting of one or two pupils daily on some special topics in every branch, as well as to incite them to thorough investigation and cheerful industry. But the essays written on miscellaneous topics, read and criticized semi-monthly, weekly, or daily, are the exercises most relied on to accomplish this object. Every such class or section should have the opportunity, as often as once a quarter, to read or declaim their essays before the whole school, a public audience being also invited. It may also be proposed to a class to write an essay on some subject of public interest, such as setting out shade-trees, laying side-walks, repairing or enlarging the school building, building a lyceum hall, etc., with the promise that the best essays on the subject will be published in the village paper; or that several of the essays will be read before a public meeting, perhaps subsequently called, for the same object. Even though such essays are not published in a newspaper, or read before a public meeting, such a subject, in which all pupils must be interested, is much more exciting for the time than any other, and of course so much the more effective in training the class, the school, to useful and benevolent effort; the end proposed in this division of my lecture.

Normal Method with Advanced Classes.

With more advanced classes in the college course, it would be immensely more effective as a means of training for the pupils to prepare and read theses or lectures, on the several subjects studied, than to listen to lectures from the professor.

Take even the most difficult and abstruse of all subjects, Psychology; it has been found here by the experience of several years with successive classes, that the members of the Senior year, who had had the advantage of the training of the Junior year, could so investigate any topic assigned in Psychology—so describe the phenomena of any faculty, and its relations—so analyze their own consciousness with the aid of the various authors, as to produce theses quite as original and experimental as any of those in any of the more recent books compared with others previously published.

But of how much more, incalculably more, value, in every point of view, is this preparation and reading of lectures by the students, with the accompanying criticism and discussion of fellow-pupils and teacher, than the course pursued at present in the so-called best colleges and universities, which is substantially this: the professor prepares a course of lectures on Psychology; he delivers these lectures to the Senior class; they listen, take notes, consult the prescribed text-book, are examined at each lecture hour, on the subject-matter of the preceding lecture, in expectation of being examined at the end of the course for honors, or at least to escape dishonor.

This course, it is claimed, imparts a thorough knowledge of the subjects so treated. To this I reply, that even in this particular, the acquisition of knowledge, it is far inferior to the plan of having the students prepare their own lectures.

But the acquisition of knowledge is a very low end comparatively, and should so be held always. The accumulation of power for the higher ends of business, of usefulness, of benevolence, ought to be held as the true aim of every school effort and exercise; and in this respect I affirm, with no fear of successful contradiction, that the normal method of training advanced classes is immeasurably superior to the present college method. I have tried both.

5. The pupil should be trained to fluency and impressiveness in speaking.

While the teacher will have clearly in his mind that the management of his school, of every class in his school, is to fit his pupils for their several vocations in coming life, he must not fail to keep this end before the minds of his pupils, and show that in every request, in every plan, in every exercise, he has some one or more distinctive, useful ends in view for the higher success of his pupil in his business or profession, in his social standing and in his general influence.

(1.) *The oral exercises of a recitation* may most assuredly be so managed as to improve every pupil in ready expression of well defined thought.

But the almost universal practice of requiring memoriter answers to printed questions, the answers to be memorized being in many cases included in pencil marks made by the teacher, or copied by the pupil from some book on which he has made them; or the somewhat improved method of the pupils giving the ideas of the text-book in his own language, in answer to questions improvised by the teacher, who must ever have the text-book in hand during recitation, is, neither of them, well calculated to make independent thinkers, nor good talkers, inasmuch as the pupils so managed are unable to say any thing on the subject so studied and recited, unless plied with questions; and this never will be, outside of the class-room, save on examination occasions. But school recitations and county examinations are not all of these pupils' future life.

Now, instead of asking the questions printed in the book, or improvising questions from the page before the eye, let the teacher first master the subject of a lesson, by the aid of reference books, better than any pupil possibly can; let him have the subject-matter of a given recitation well systematized on paper, and thoroughly imbedded in his own mind; let him feel himself independent of his text-book and entirely superior to it; then he can propose appropriate topics, embraced in the lesson to each pupil for discussion. These topics will be given to the several pupils according to their several capacities, and the management of each pupil while discussing his topic must be according to the pupil's ability. The teacher will not follow any regular order or routine in calling on the pupils for their exercises in a recitation.

A topic having been given to a pupil, that pupil will rise in his place and proceed with the discussion. If the pupil decline to discuss the topic, being unprepared, the same topic may be assigned to another. In some cases it will be best to help the beginner in this kind of class drill with some suggestions, and to aid him in the prosecution of his discussion; but generally it will be better to ask no leading questions, give no suggestions, but let the pupil learn to depend entirely on himself, on his own memory, on the thoroughness of his preparation, rather than on the teacher's aid in recitation. Provided any pupil declines or fails in the management of a topic assigned him, he should always be permitted to redeem himself on another topic, of less difficult character, during the same recitation.

When a pupil has finished his discussion of a topic, the class is called on for criticisms on the manner and matter of this pupil's discussion; and the teacher will also *briefly* add his own views, so far as he can not draw them out of the class.

To this method of conducting a recitation, the machine-teacher, the stupid teacher, the lazy teacher, if any such should ever happen to hear of such a method, would raise numerous objections, no doubt. The objections all lie in their laziness or stupidity, and not in the plan. It has been used here, and by hundreds of our pupil teachers in their more advanced classes the country over for years, and with the highest success in most cases.

Remark. Let me state here that every plan which I have recommended, or shall recommend, has undergone the ordeal of continued trial by myself and numerous others, who have been trained in these Normal Methods, and have adopted and made them work, generally with marked success

(2.) *By giving oral reports on special topics,* connected with the subject-matter of a lesson, or growing out of the class discussions, pupils may be trained to coherent and continued discourse. It is generally best, at first, for the pupil to place an outline of his report on the blackboard, and then, with pointer in hand, give his elaboration of the outline orally, relying on his own power, obtained from previous preparation, for the necessary ideas, and the appropriate words to express them.

After some little practice, in this manner, the outline may be omitted, and the pupil thus trained will soon learn to depend on his mastery of the subject and on himself for a creditable and interesting oral report on any topic assigned him by the teacher.

REMARK. This method of giving reports is treated of in the article, "Books, and how to use them," on pages 197–204, NATIONAL NORMAL.

3. *In debating clubs* the advanced pupils, of many ungraded schools, even, may be trained to ready and forcible speaking. The Normal Method of organizing and managing debating clubs in school, is given by Mr. Carver, on pages 94–97, NATIONAL NORMAL.

The only modification that I would suggest is that the teacher meet the older pupils in the evening for his part in the exercise, in drilling the clubs for their management of themselves and of their questions.

4. *Declaiming written essays* before the school, or before an invited audience, is an excellent introduction to public debate. It is, of course, understood that each pupil declaim his own essay, written on a topic assigned by the teacher. The teacher may or may not examine and criticise the essay before its public delivery, according to his confidence in the pupil's judgment and good feeling.

5. *Public debating* on questions proposed by the teacher. It is better, perhaps, to have the several questions discussed by the pupils in pairs, and when practicable, a lady on one side and a gentleman on the other.

6. *Public speaking on living issues* by pupils who have

succeeded best in the previous methods of training, may be expected as a spontaneous outgrowth and necessary result of such school training, whether it be in a College, Normal School, Academy, Graded or Ungraded School.

7. Religious students so trained will feel it their privilege and a part of their training to visit and address Sabbath-schools, and organize Sabbath-schools in destitute neighborhoods; and when authorized and invited, to fill vacant pulpits, occasionally or regularly.

Concluding Remarks.

1. In these lectures on School Management, as accomplished chiefly in Class Management, I have endeavored, by presenting the real aims and ends of school training, *the formation and fixation of correct habits*, and by giving some of the methods by which these aims and ends can be reached, to show, by contrast, the utter inadequacy of the views entertained by most college professors, school superintendents, and teachers, in reference to their daily work.

2. It is plain, in the light of this discussion, why college and school life is so often abortive, or rather why male colleges and female seminaries so seldom produce vigorous *working* alumni.

3. It is encouraging to know that several colleges are *partially* adopting the freedom of the sexes. They will never make the plan work well, till the young people in school are thrown entirely on their own responsibility, unrestrained by any laws, save the ten commandments, and the ordinary usages of good society. Those individuals in any school or college who transgress should be dealt with individually, rather than that the whole school should be made antagonistic to authority, by the enacting and enforcing of laws entirely unnecessary for the large majority, and more than useless for the few, for whom they are thought to be necessary.

4. If it is objected to some of these methods, that all pupils do not expect to become public writers or speakers, and especially the females, in very few, if any cases, ought to be fitting themselves for public life, I reply—1, that there is

nothing in any of the methods proposed in this or other of these lectures but what is supposed to be subject to modification to suit the particular case; it is chiefly the SPIRIT of these methods that I wish to set forth and recommend; 2, that I would use these methods so far as they reach out to public observation, as healthy stimulants to incite to *diligent and earnest industry*, as a habit, and to establish this and other good habits in the life, in the soul of every pupil. These incentives are infinitely more effective, when properly managed, than watching, scolding, and coercion can ever be, for any good purpose whatever; 3, that young ladies are necessarily and properly feeling more and more that they owe it to themselves to prepare to take care of themselves, as so large a proportion of the talented young men become hopelessly abandoned—either in college or out. The matrimonial prospect for good girls seems less and less inviting; so much so, that there is too little hope in marrying, but to find the necessity of enduring a sot or a fool—and raising and supporting a family, in spite of the incumbrance.

5. It was my purpose to speak of works of usefulness and benevolence in school—distinctively as such, but I shall defer this topic to another occasion. It has, I trust, been noticed however, that the entire spirit of these Normal Methods is diametrically opposed to the selfish, short-sighted practices of most schools, in the working of the few to win honors and prizes, and of the many to avoid disgrace and penalties; and that these methods find their effectiveness and success in appealing to the nobler feelings and better purposes of pupils, and inspiring them with a true ambition to do life's work well.

LECTURE ON SCHOOL MANAGEMENT.

LECTURE XII.

SCHOOL MANAGEMENT IN CLASS MANAGEMENT.

A Class in Mental Arithmetic.

Ladies and Gentlemen :—As you have seen and experienced, most of you, in my Training Class, the method of managing a class of younger pupils, including those who are just able to read fluently, and as I have endeavored, in that drill, to put in practice the principles which underlie all really good and successful management of children in school, I shall here attempt to arrange and describe the same processes, and show the adaptation of each to the mental and moral constitution of children, and their connection with the true ends of school management, viz: the formation of correct habits in the happy and efficient use and development of their mental and moral capabilities; not so much for the school-room and its per cents, as for life, its responsibilities and rewards. I claim that such ends ought to be reached with more or less certainty and success, according to the skill and faithfulness of the teacher whether in common schools or in colleges. Yet we all know that such habits are seldom thought of, much less worked for, by the great majority of teachers in any class of institutions.

As this lecture will deal with numerous details, various special arrangements and complicated class maneuvers (complicated in description but very simple in evolution), it may need some patience, as well as continued attention, to follow me and keep my bearings; especially from those present who have not participated in the exercises of the training class. I trust I may be able, however, to show that these maneuvers and artifices are such in their very spirit as are calculated to initiate and establish the good habits before mentioned in the younger classes of children, as the plans proposed in the two preceding lectures were more especially adapted to the more advanced classes in common schools, and to all classes in academies and colleges. It will also appear, in the course of this discussion, if I mistake not, that nearly all the usages of our common schools, with the younger children, now in vogue, tend to fix habits of laziness, shiftlessness and worthlessness, generally; and to produce tardiness, absenteeism and disorder, hatred of study, aversion to school, love of mischief and longing for holidays and vacations, and that these evils are the direct result of the management pursued.

In order to make the description intelligible I shall place it under several heads, which, though successive in description, are to some extent simultaneous in practice.

ORGANIZATION OF THE CLASS.

I am supposing that you, as a teacher, are in your school for the first time, and that you do not know the pupils by their names, even.

I. Then, first, take the names of the pupils on paper, or if the class is large, request some older pupil to do so. When the names are written, call them and determine the pupil that answers to each name. This list of names may afterward be transferred to your class register, and you can use it in calling the names of pupils in recitation, until you know them all, thus avoiding the embarrassment and disorder incident to calling pupils by wrong names.

II. Examine by concert exercise in counting in units, in tens, in hundreds, the advancement of the class in counting. The most advanced will hold out the longest. Requesting these to remain silent, try the rest of the class, and so on until you ascertain the ability of every one. Furnish books and slates, so far as needed. It is generally best to use the books of which there are the most copies already in the class. Since it is exceedingly desirable that all the pupils have books to commence with, I should furnish the books myself, and let the children pay for them afterward. If it is objected that I shall lose by it, I reply that I shall gain more in starting my class right than I can possibly lose in the value of the books. I would furnish slates and pencils, and own them myself. The patent slates are preferable to the stone slates, for many reasons.

III. Preliminary Drill. Write the operation for the first example on the blackboard yourself; describe this operation (2+1=3) in all its points. In order to do this,it will be well to draw the outline of a slate on the blackboard as many times larger than a slate as your figures on the blackboard are larger than those to be made on the slates. Then place your operation economically and evenly in the outline, and number it, as numbered in the book; direct the pupils to do the same on their slates; aid them to do so till all have succeeded passably well. Place the operation of the second example in the outline on the board; request the children to copy it; aid them again, if necessary. Now request the class to write the operation of the third example themselves, directly from the book; and so on, till you are sure that they will all be able to work at least a few examples for the first recitation. The lesson may now be assigned; and the class having the hour given in the general programme for studying this lesson will be requested to work at it only during that time.

Reasons for Studying Mental Arithmetic on Slates

1. It helps the child to be industrious. With proper preliminary drill, children from seven years of age to ten, can be so much interested that they will work out on their slates the simple solutions of these examples with eagerness and continuous application for as long a time as is prudent for health; thus freeing the teacher from watching and scolding them for idleness and mischief; thus forming the habit of industry,

and breaking up their old habits of idleness and mischief, the direct results of previous training.

2. We help the child to think by himself, independently of his teacher. Abstract thinking is difficult enough for adults, and simply studying a book, and working out examples mentally with book in hand, is next to an impossibility with most children; at least, it is so repulsive that it takes frequent and special stimulants of watching, punishing or purchasing, to keep it up for any length of time. The operations of the fingers, and the attention of the eye to the mechanical part of the work on the slate, are aids to study and diligence in continuous application. Thus the habit of patient study is formed, with immeasurably more certainty than by simply studying, or pretending to study, on the *whizza whizza* plan, or in any object-lesson drills that I have ever known practiced. In fact, object-lesson teaching subverts all true and independent study on the part of the pupil, and throws the labor on the teacher.

3. It gives the teacher opportunity to encourage the dull and slow for their industry, at least; rather than to stimulate the quick and mischievous in their mischief, by approving of their correct recitations, when they have scarcely looked at their lessons during the study hour.

4. It helps the child in learning to write. The younger members may have to *print* their letters at first, but very soon they learn the script hand, especially if they are permitted to write from copies with the rest of the school.

5. It helps the child to learn how to spell, capitalize and punctuate.

6. It is the beginning of composition writing, as we shall see from the fuller development of the plan.

7. It helps the teacher to make the school attractive or this class of children by furnishing them something useful to do, that they will like to do. The teacher is thus spared the necessity of watching and scolding, threatening and punishing. He is not pronounced a "cross old teacher," but "a real pleasant teacher."

Objection. If it is objected that this kind of study on slates or paper, is written arithmetic, not mental; I reply that by this method, immensely more independent mental activity and mental power are evoked than ever can be by the sticklers for the whizza whizza method of studying, or by the object-lesson method of not studying. The drill in the recitation, in giving some new example for solution, in calling for better solutions of questions, is the means by which ready apprehension, tenacious grasp, and close reasoning are obtained.

Remark. Many teachers permit their pupils to recite with book in hand. This is not even written arithmetic, it is *printed* arithmetic; rather, it is more laziness than arithmetic of any kind, both on the part of teacher and pupil.

ORDER OF PROCEDURE IN RECITATION.

1. Examine work on slates or papers. This is done by passing around the class, or by gathering all the slates and papers, and examining them by calling the pupil, if necessary, from the recitation seat to the desk to look over his own slate or paper, while under examination. It is generally better to pass around the class.

2. Deposit slates and books. These may be laid on the floor, if no better place can be found, by five words of direction to the class: (1.) Rise; (2.) Forward one step; (3.) Deposit books on slates; (4.) Back; (5.) Be Seated.

3. Drill the class on the examples of the lesson by mental solutions of some questions in the lesson, and with some not in the lesson.

METHOD OF DRILL.

(1.) Read an example for the whole class to solve mentally. (2.) Request each pupil to raise his hand as soon as he has solved the example. When nearly all hands have been raised, ask: (3.) "How many have the result?" Hands of all who have succeeded are again raised. (4.) "John, you may give the result." John gives the result. (5.) "How many have a different result?" Samuel raises his hand. (6.) "Samuel, what is your result?" He gives it. (7.) "How many agree with Samuel?" Hands are raised, possibly. "How many agree with John?" Possibly no hands are raised. (8.) "Mary, you may give the solution."

If this is the first recitation Mary will not know what I mean by a solution, and she will give the result. Here then comes the fourth operation of the class procedure, and always the most important of all.

4. *Preliminary Drill for Next Recitation.*—In this case the children will be made familiar with the four-step method of solution. These steps are: (1.) The Question; (2.) The Theory; (3.) The Process; (4.) The Conclusion

The names of these steps may be written on the blackboard to aid the pupil, somewhat; but with a beginning class it will be necessary for a teacher to give a solution himself, and request some pupil to give the same solution of the same question; then some other to give the same, till the formulæ of the steps are mastered. To make these steps intelligible to any teachers present, who are not already familiar with them, I will give an example in addition. The pupil gives the steps thus, in the solution of this example, supposed to have been read by the teacher from the lesson assigned.

(*Question.*)

Pupil.—1. Seven and five are how many

(*Theory.*)

2. As many as the sum of seven and five,

(*Process.*)

3. Which is twelve.

(*Conclusion.*)

4. Therefore, seven and five are twelve.

It is not to be supposed that all in a class will master the steps of this solution at once. Some days will pass, possibly, before this will be accomplished.

I will here give several solutions of different examples, to show how clearness of thought and accuracy of expression may be attained by children in this study, if the teacher is clear-headed and accurate himself.

I will take the concrete example:

If Henry gave 5 cents for an orange and 2 cents for a lemon, *what* did he give for both?

1. *Correct.*

2d Step. As many cents as the sum of 5 and 2,

3d Step. Which is 7.

2. *Correct.*

2d Step. As much as the sum of 5 cents and 2 cents,

3d Step. Which is 7 cents.

1. *Incorrect.*

2d Step. As much as the sum of 5 and 2.

Criticism. 5 and 2 are not much, they are many.

2. *Incorrect.*

2d Step. As many as the sum of 5 cents and 2 cents, which are 7 cents. Criticism. 5 cents and 2 cents are not many, they are much, and the word, sum, the antecedent of *which*, is singular.

Thus the pupil should be taught to distinguish in his language between much and many; rather, between magnitude and multitude; also to notice the plainest syntactical agreements. These are only given as examples of one or two of the points in accurate thought and correct expression.

The last process for the teacher in the solution of a question by the class, is to call on the class for criticisms on the solution as given by the pupil.

Any pupils who have criticisms to offer, can raise the hand; and the teacher receives the criticisms in order, and decides, or calls on the class to decide by vote, on the propriety of the criticism. He finally, in every case, gives his own decision.

Points of Criticism.

1. Mathematical accuracy.
2. Grammatical correctness.
3. Rhetorical beauty.
4. Logical coherency.

While these *terms* need not be used with a class of children, violations of any one of these principles may be clearly shown to any class, and their wits sharpened by mutual criticism, so that they will readily detect any errors, under any head.

Faults to be Avoided by the Teacher.

1. Want of order and of certainty in class management.

2. Routine, such as enables any pupil to judge he will not be called on, at any moment.

3. Talk, talk, talk.

4. Scolding, snubbing, repressing, discouraging.

5. Overlooking or neglecting any slow or backward pupil.

6. Failure on the part of the teacher to give his decision on any point of criticism, or in case of difference of opinion in the class.

Remark.—In any case in which the teacher feels unprepared to give an opinion at the time, he will do well to lay it over for investigation. Then he must be sure to bring it up at the beginning of the next recitation, or it will be forgotten, and the class will lose confidence, both in his ability and in his honesty.

7. Want of interest in the class, or in the study. Every class and every branch must arouse every faculty and every energy. In short, the teacher must do his very best every time; and every time excel his own efforts in any previous recitation, not in the exhibition of his own powers and gifts, especially the gift of gab, but in interesting the laziest, or most mischievous, or most stubborn and sulky pupil; not by doing his work for him, but by giving every such pupil such work to do as he will be interested in, as will draw out his powers and as will merit the teacher's approbation and good will. Fault-finding, scolding and punishing will make bad scholars out of good; but will never make good scholars out of bad ones.

PARTIALITY MUST BE USED, not to good scholars, not to smart scholars, not to attractive scholars; but to vicious pupils, dull pupils, repulsive pupils. How? By kindly keeping them occupied and interested, and bestowing on them a cordial attention inversely as they seem disposed to give attention to their duties and privileges. This course is better than returning evil for evil, in any manner that you can devise. It will win, sooner or later. The other brings defeat, both sooner and later.

THE STANDING OF EVERY PUPIL, IN EVERY RECITATION, MUST BE RECORDED. This may be done in the general register, but better in a class register, in which every class is enrolled by itself; and in this the grade of every pupil should be recorded daily. Some pupils may be graded more particularly for industry, some for skill, some for independent effort, some for neatness and propriety; but each pupil should know for what he is graded, and that his grade is so given for his encouragement, where he most needs it. Again, it may be well to grade the whole class, sometimes on some special object, in which you wish to excite special interest; as neatness of work on slate or paper, or accuracy of verbal solution during recitation.

GENERAL APPLICATION.

The processes described thus far in this lecture can, with suitable modifications, be applied to the management of any class in any branch, from a class in the alphabet to a class in civil engineering or metaphysics as you have all witnessed, I suppose, in the various classes in daily operation in this institution. I have taken mental arithmetic as being the subject, perhaps, most generally worst abused, and that in which I think it requires as much skill to arouse and sustain interest and self-propelling industry, as in any other.

I have likewise taken this particular subject through which to develop the normal plan of class management, as it could hardly have been done abstractly, that is, without concreting it in *some* particular branch and class.

Though, as I forewarned you at the commencement of the lecture, the description of the various processes is, perhaps, complicated and tedious, the working of the plan is simple, effective and certain, when conducted with any kind of skill, or with any proper degree of enthusiasm, and yet in the spirit of kindness and sympathy.

OBJECTS TO BE AIMED AT.

The objects to be aimed at constantly in the management of every class, whether in mental arithmetic or in any other branch, I shall discuss under the following heads: I. Immediate; II. Mediate; III. Ultimate.

I. Immediate objects to be aimed at in class management.

1. *Attention of all the class all the time during recitation.* Not merely the attention of the best pupils, but of the dullest and worst, is the object, first, last and always during a recitation.

The plan of hearing a class recite from head to foot, or in any course of rotation, is abominable. It is making a reptile of a class. While you are at work with the head, the body is squirming and the tail is wriggling and twisting, ready to sting you; but while you are at work with the tail, the head is, most probably, ready to strike you with its fangs. Do away with the head and tail arrangements. Let the class be a body with a soul, yourself the spirit, every part and member inspired by your energy and enthusiasm. If any member lacks animation, kindly address yourself to enliven it; if any member is excited, what other member does not always sympathize with it? So hold your class, teacher, that every pupil feels himself a participator in every operation either as operative or critic, ready and anxious to be called on, eager to perform his or her part.

If it is found that the solution of a problem or the performance of any other duty assigned to one pupil is so long that some member of the class loses his interest and falls into inattention or mischief, the pupil who is reciting can be excused, and that inattentive pupil called on to perform the remainder of the work especially in hand. But if criticism (not of the pupil, but by the pupils,) is managed properly, this will seldom be necessary or desirable. If any pupil fails in the exercise assigned him, always give him an opportunity to retrieve his character, by affording him another opportunity on another question or exercise, before the recitation closes.

2. *Interested, earnest study in preparation for the recitation.*

This, of course, will depend on class management, while in recitation; and any class management which does not of itself secure it, is essentially wrong. In the preliminary drill, which is really the most important part of teaching, there must be enough of explanation of the next lesson, to awaken curiosity, to arouse ambition, to excite emulation; and yet labor and difficulty enough must be left to be performed and overcome to employ the study-time fully, and tax the energies adequately; otherwise discouragement will deter some from effort, or want of employment will almost force others into mischief and disorder, in their study seats.

The writing method of study, before described, answers a better purpose for securing diligent and equal study from *every pupil* than any other that I have ever known tried. If the class is very unequal; it may be divided into two sections, and a part of the lesson, comprising the more simple problems, may be given to the first section. Where, in any case, this division of the lesson is impracticable, the more advanced section can work examples in some more advanced portion of the text-book, or examples which you can give on the blackboard, to occupy their time, and to stimulate their ambition.

Caution.—I may say here, in connection with these first two immediate objects of the teacher's class work, it is necessary that *communication between pupils*, either on recitation seats or on study seats, should be entirely precluded; and there can be very little hope of true success in the attainment of either object, if communication is tolerated in any of the ten thousand forms in which it can be practised. In a subsequent lecture on school discipline, I shall show how whispering, and other forms of communication may best be prevented.

10

3. *Self-reliance in continued speech.*—The common method of recitation, that of requiring memoriter answers to definite questions, or the monosyllabic answers, yes or no, to direct questions, is the very means to train the pupil to feebleness of thought and utter inability to express any consecutive ideas on any worthy subject; and it is no wonder that so few persons are able to converse with any degree of satisfaction to themselves or others on subjects they have studied at school, or any other subject except the latest case of scandal, gossip or tattle afloat. This is the direct result of the prevalent method of conducting recitations in nearly all schools, seminaries, and colleges of the present time.

Mental arithmetic is as little favorable to the cultivation of coherent expression, of independent thought as any branch, and yet this always ought to be kept in view. The four-step method, although a series of verbal formulæ is still susceptible of such variations; and, in fact, often demands such variations as may aid young pupils very much in this self-reliance, in the clear, accurate, coherent deliverance of critical, incisive thought. But success here will depend on the interest aroused in mutual criticism.

Direction.—*It is necessary that the pupil rise in his place and stand while he recites*

Reasons for standing in recitation: (1.) It cultivates self-reliance. (2.) The class can hear better, and the class interest is better sustained. (3.) It prevents "looking on the book" while reciting, and prompting from other pupils.

4. *Quickness of apprehension and grasp of memory.*—To this end the teacher should read or speak the question but once, and so cut off the carelessness and mental feebleness resulting from the practice of giving a problem several times

Caution.—Permit no pupil to use his book in recitation, save in preliminary drill for next recitation.

5. *Power of analysis.*—This implies sharp, thorough critical, energetic thought, just such thought as constitutes business tact, and professional skill in any direction. If this power is kept constantly in view, in every exercise of solu-

tion or criticism, it will surely be more likely to be attained than if never thought of, as is too generally the case, with most teachers.

6. *Mathematical skill.*—That which is generally thought to be the *only* object in the study of mental arithmetic, I will not entirely ignore. It will surely be acquired if the other objects are attained.

7. *Orderly self-management.*—Without this as an immediate and constant object of class training, all others are comparatively futile. Parliamentary rule, in a very simple form, should be maintained in every recitation, and in the management of the whole school, also. The teacher is the chairman; the class, the "assembly." All pupils must address "the chairman," though not by this formal title; and never address each other. No member may address the chairman without his permission, as having "obtained the floor." The pupil obtains permission by raising the hand. In most cases the member occupying the floor will stand while speaking. In order to secure attention of all the class, all problems and definite questions must *first* be addressed by the teacher to the class, when those prepared to answer will raise the hand; thus indicating a desire "to speak to the question," in other words, to give the "*result*," which the question demands; or the solution, or a criticism, as the case may be. This formality may seem, at first, as tending to retard progress, but with any skill on the part of the chairman, it "facilitates business," just as much as in any other constituted assembly.

Orderly self management, *in study hours*, is also to be provided for in class recitation as well as in the general school programme.

II. Mediate Objects.

These were given in order, and somewhat at length, in the two previous lectures. It will hardly be necessary to dwell here. The same considerations which hold in one branch, for the *formation of correct school habits*, surely must hold in all, or the work of one recitation would neutral ize the work of another in this regard. I will merely recapitulate the mediate objects as before discussed.

1. Love of work. 2. Thoroughness. 3. Promptness and order. 4. Utilization, or making connection constantly between book knowledge and life's labors, implements and utilities; nature's phenomena, machinery and laws, as experienced and observed by the pupil himself. These, all, are object-lessons of some force, which the drivelling object-lesson teaching, so called, seems almost entirely to neglect or ignore in its meager, one-sided view of isolated objects, and their individual properties.

III. Ultimate Objects

No class of children is so immature that each pupil in it is not preparing, in each recitation, ill or well, for life's work, for eternity's destiny. How seldom, teachers, is this, apparently, thought of in the school-room work. I shall here simply enumerate the objects, which I denominate *ultimate*, because they are *ends desirable in themselves*; demanding the most earnest consideration, and most unremitting effort, on the part of every teacher and every pupil, every day in every recitation:

1. Success in business; 2. Position in society; 3. Usefulness in life, involving, (1.) the approbation of one's own conscience; (2.) the approbation of all good men; (3.) the approbation of God, the supreme end of all action and aspiration.

Model Solutions in Mental Arithmetic.

I shall close this lecture by giving several solutions, and several different methods of solution required by different classes of examples. The written forms of solution to which a class will be trained are those ordinarily given in practical or written arithmetic.

Examples of verbal solutions in addition have already been given.

Model Solution in Subtraction—Abstract Example

TEACHER.—4 less 2 are how many ?
Solution by the pupil during recitation
(1st step, *Question.*)
PUPIL.—4 less 2 are how many?
(2d step, *Theory.*)
As many as the difference between 4 and 2,
3d step, *Process.*)
Which is 2.
(4th step, *Conclusion.*)
Therefore, 4 less 2 are 2.

Model Solution in Subtraction—Concrete Example.

(1st step, *Question.*)
PUPIL.—If James had 6 cents and spent 2 how many had he then?
(2d step, *Theory.*)
As many cents as the difference between 6 and 2,
(3d step, *Process.*)
Which is 4.
(4th step, *Conclusion.*)
'herefore, if James had 6 cents and spent 2, he then had 4

Errors likely to be Made in the Solution

1. Repeating the first step in the second. Redundancy. 2. Repeating the word cents in the second, thus :

As many cents as the difference between 6 *cents* and 2 *cents*. Tautology

3. Giving the plural verb *are*, in 3d step. The antecedent of *which*, difference, is singular.

4. Giving a part of the 2d step in the 4th, and using wrong auxiliary verb; thus :

Therefore, if James had 6 cents and spent 2, he *would have as much as the difference of* 2 *and* 6, *which are* 4.

Compare this expression, in italics, with the model: there are six errors in it

Model Solution in Multiplication—Abstract Example.

PUPIL.—4 times 5 are how many?
As many as the product of 5 by 4
Which is 20.
Therefore, 4 times 5 are 20.

Model Solutions in Multiplication—Concrete Examples.

Solution First—Correct.

PUPIL.—At 10 cents each, what will 2 lead-pencils cost?
As many cents as the product of 10 by 2,
Which is 20.
Therefore, at 10 cents each 2 lead-pencils will cost 20 cents

Errors.

1. Repeating the first step in the second. Redundancy. 2. Repeating the word cents in second step, thus:

As many cents as the product of 10 cents by 2. Tautology

3. Using plural verb *are* in third step. The antecedent of *which* is *product.*

4. Repeating the second step or a part of it in fourth step.

Solution Second—Correct.

Pupil.—At 10 cents apiece what will 2 lead-pencils cost?
As much as the product of 10 cents by 2,
Which is 20 cents.
Therefore, at 10 cents apiece 2 lead-pencils will cost 20 cents.

Errors.

2. As much as the product of 10 by 2, which is 20 cents.
As much as the product of 2 by 10 (or 10 cents) which is 20 cents.

Analysis.

Definition. Analysis in Mathematics is any method of reasoning by means of a unit value, known or unknown.

Solution Third, Analytic—Correct.

Pupil.—What will 2 lead-pencils cost at 10 cents apiece?
If one lead-pencil costs 10 cents, 2 lead-pencils will cost twice 10 cents,
Which are 20 cents.
Therefore, 2 lead-pencils will cost 20 cents, at 10 cents apiece.

Model Solutions in Division-Abstract Example.

Pupil.—12 are how many times 2?
As many times 2 as the quotient of 12 by 2,
Which is 6.
Therefore, 12 are 6 times 2.

Model Solutions in Division—Concrete Examples.

Solution First—Correct.

Pupil.—At 10 cents apiece how many oranges can be bought for 20 cents?
As many as the quotient of 20 by 10
Which is 2.
Therefore, at 10 cents apiece 2 oranges can be bought for 20 cents.

Solution Second—Correct

Pupil.—How many oranges at 10 cents each can be bought for 20 cents?
As many as 10 cents are contained times in 20 cents,
Which are twice,
Therefore, 2 oranges, at 10 cents each, can be bought for 20 cents.

Solution Third, Analytic—Correct

Pupil.—At 2 cents each how many apples can be bought for 10 cents?

If 1 apple costs 2 cents as many apples can be bought for 10 cents as 2 are contained times in 10,

Which are 5 times.

Therefore, at 2 cents each 5 apples can be bought for 10 cents

Model Solutions in Complex questions, Involving Multiplication and Division.

(1st Step, *Question.*)

PUPIL.—If 3 slates cost 30 cents what will 12 cost?

(2d Step, *Analysis, Separation, or reasoning from many to one.*)

If 3 slates cost 30 cents 1 slate costs ⅓ of 30 cents which is 10 cents.

(3d Step, *Synthesis, Combination, or reasoning from one to many.*)

If 1 slate costs 10 cents 12 slates cost 12 times 10 cents, which are 120 cents, or one dollar and twenty cents.

(4th Step, *Conclusion.*)

Therefore, if 3 slates cost 30 cents 12 slates will cost one dollar and twenty

SHORTER ANALYSIS, (BY CANCELLATION)

Model Solution of a Compound Complex Example.

(1st Step, *Question.*)

PUPIL.—If 45 men in 8 weeks, working 5½ days per week, and 10 hours per day, build a road 3½ miles long, and 4 rods wide, how many weeks will 63 men require, working 4½ days per week and 11 hours per day, to build a road 12⅔ miles long and 3 rods wide?

(2d Step, *Analysis.*)

8 weeks is the base term, because it is the same kind as required in the answer. If 45 men require 8 weeks, 1 man will require more; hence multiply 8 weeks by 45: if 5½ days require 8 weeks, 1 day will require more; hence multiply by 5½: if 10 hours require 8 weeks, 1 hour will require more; hence multiply by 10: if 3½ miles require 8 weeks, 1 mile will require less; hence divide by 3½: if 4 rods require 8 weeks, 1 rod will require less; hence divide by 4. This resulting compound fraction:

$$\frac{8w.\times 45\times 5\tfrac{1}{2}\times 10}{3\tfrac{1}{2}\times 4}$$

gives the number of weeks required by 1 man, working 1 day per week, 1 hour per day, to build 1 mile of road, 1 rod wide.

(3d Step, *Synthesis.*)

If 1 man require the number of weeks expressed by this fraction, 63 men will require less; hence divide: if one day require the number of weeks expressed, etc., 4½ days will require less; hence divide: if 1 hour require the number of weeks, etc.,

11 hours will require less: hence divide: if 1 mile require the number of weeks, etc., $12\frac{2}{3}$ miles will require more; hence multiply: if 1 rod require, etc., 3 rods will require more; hence multiply. Placing each of these multipliers above and divisors below the vinculum of the fraction resulting from the analysis before given, it becomes,

$$\frac{8w\times45\times5\frac{1}{2}\times10+12\frac{2}{3}\times3}{3\frac{1}{2}\times4\times63\times4\frac{1}{2}\times11}=\frac{7{,}600 \text{ weeks}}{441}=17\tfrac{103}{441} \text{ weeks.}$$

The pupil using the blackboard should place each number in the numerator, or denominator, as he determines it by his reasoning to be a multiplier or a divisor. If it is objected that examples of this kind involve written arithmetic, I reply as before, that I am more anxious to make clear and accurate reasoners of my pupils, than I am to keep them in *mental* arithmetic exclusively. There is no particular sanctity in mental arithmetic. In fact, that course is the best in *mental* arithmetic, which will best train the mind; not that which most rigidly carries the pupil in some thoroughly worn rut.

In questions involving unknown quantities, I have found that the introduction of a simple symbol for the unknown quantity aids and encourages the pupil very much in studying his lessons; thus:

Example. A horse cost 4 times as much as a cow and $5 more; the cow cost 10 times as much as a sheep; and the horse, cow and 5 sheep together cost $170. What was the cost of each animal?

Written statement. Let the unknown quantity, the price of a sheep, be represented by O, and let this symbol be called the unknown quantity, or the unknown unit of the example.

$\bigcirc$=Price of a sheep.

$\textcircled{5}+\textcircled{10}+\textcircled{40}+\$5=\$170$, by the conditions of the question.

$\textcircled{55}+\$5=\$170$, by adding terms.

$\textcircled{55}=\$165$ by subtracting $5 from both members.

$\bigcirc=\$3$=the price of a sheep.

The verification should also be worked out by the pupil thus:

$\textcircled{5}+\textcircled{10}+\textcircled{40}+\$5=\$170$; statement.

$\$15+\$30+\$120+\$5=\$170$ verification.

The distinct steps in this solution for the pupil at his study seat with which he should be made familiar in the preliminary drill, are: 1. Determine which unknown quantity you will use as *the unknown quantity.* 2. From the conditions of the question find two equal values, or two expressions for the same value, one of which, at least, must contain *the* unknown quantity. The statement is then made with the use of the unknown symbol and the signs. 3. By adding or subtracting equals, or by multiplying or dividing by equals determine the value of the unknown quantity, or unit. 4 Verify by substituting the value of the unknown quantity in the original statement. If any teacher prefers to use x, the algebraic symbol, he will only find it somewhat more puzzling to the child than the symbol I have proposed, while no particular advantage is gained. If any one objects, "this is teaching algebra, and not mental arithmetic," I reply that I am much more solicitous that my pupils learn to study with zeal and interest, and form good habits, than I am to have them pursue any prescribed course of study, whatever; and especially any such course as I find is discouraging to the majority of a class, and thus tends to laziness and continued failure, hatred of study, and of school.

The spirit of EAGER INDUSTRY must be fostered and sustained whatever else may have to yield. There can be no genuine THOROUGHNESS in a discouraged, lazy class; no METHODIC ACTIVITY, no spirit of UTILIZING THRIFT; and just these are the HABITS which distinguish every successful and useful man, in every department of life, and make him such. I will add here, that in the recitations of any examples in mental arithmetic, I would have no book used by the pupil, nor slate, but would have the pupil give a verbal solution, bringing into use, of course, the study bestowed on the solution previously accomolished on the slate.

It will be well in the PRELIMINARY DRILLS for verbal solutions in the four-step method, to require the whole class, from the first drill, to write out on their slates the verbal solution of the same examples. Then, in criticising these written, verbal solutions three additional points will be noticed, viz:

5. Spelling.
6. Capitalizing.
7. Punctuation.

If the blackboards are capacious enough, it is much more convenient for criticism to have these verbal solutions in preliminary drill written by the whole class, simultaneously, on the black-board. In the recitation, however, these verbal solutions are given orally, unless a majority of the class fail to master them, when it may be well to request all the class again to write a verbal solution on their slates, or on the blackboards.

Additional Remarks.

Object of this Lecture.

This lecture is written out so fully, and the process described so elaborately to show the working character, if possible, of some of the Normal Methods in class management by which the habits discussed in sections X. and XI. can be established in the spirit and power of truth and love.

2. *Anti-Rote; Anti-Force.*

It is not claimed that these methods are all new, or that they are the only normal methods, that can be devised or used by ingenious and energetic teachers *to establish good habits.* They are given as the simplest to describe, and the easiest to adopt, and reduce to practice by any who may desire to do so, without special training. It is hoped, at least, these descriptions will show that *rote* and *force* can be displaced by ingenuity, enterprise, and benevolence, in any kind of school or college, and even in that branch in which these two elements, laziness and tyranny are generally the most odious and oppressive.

3. Discussion of this Lecture.

For the discussion of this lecture, on the day following its delivery, I requested the class of pupil teachers each to make an outline of the matter contained, as it had been taken in his notes. The result was very satisfactory, and the practical ability to bring into use the various points made in the "Training Class," during the drill, and recapitulated in the lecture, was obviously largely increased.

4. *How to Use this Lecture.*

It is hoped that a careful reading, and perhaps many re-readings of this lecture or parts of it in connection with the daily instruction of a class in mental arithmetic, will introduce a SPIRIT of eager, earnest work, to the displacement of all shirking and laziness, and that the teacher will apply the same methods, with suitable modifications, to classes in other branches.

If any teacher should attempt these methods as described in this lecture, and should measurably fail, I can only say that hundreds and thousands of *trained* teachers have used them with entire success and thus have revolutionized themselves as teachers.

The compound complex question given above for "Shorter Analysis," by Cancellation, is such as is ordinarily solved by Compound Proportion in "written arithmetic"; but I have been accustomed to introduce such questions in mental arithmetic at a proper stage of advancement, to give the pupils a sharper analytic power in the solution of all complex questions. Since there are no such problems found in mental arithmetics, I have them transferred from a written arithmetic to the blackboard by older pupils, both for preliminary drill, and for the study hour

It will be found that this drill in the shorter analysis of complex questions, will enable children from seven to ten years of age to solve questions in compound proportion with ease and certainty, which are ordinarily considered difficult for persons of any age.

There are five different errors to which pupils are inclined, in giving the verbal form of the Shorter Analysis. I shall leave them to the teacher to discover and correct, as the pupils fall into them.

LECTURE ON SCHOOL MANAGEMENT.

(COPYRIGHT SECURED.)

LECTURE XIII.

PRELIMINARIES TO ORGANIZATION.

INTRODUCTORY REMARKS.

Having given in the first five lectures of this course the teacher's leading qualifications, and in the next three brought to view the principal difficulties which those qualifications must meet and overcome, having also in the ninth lecture given an outline of the Human Constitution as the material to be wrought and embellished by the teacher's art, and in the tenth the Objects and Aims of the true teacher in his school work, I endeavored in the twelfth, to give a pen sketch of the management of one school class, showing how these qualifications before described, can be applied in class management to constitute the soul of school management.

I shall now proceed to develop the more general arrangements necessary to give a true class management a fair opportunity to work out its legitimate results, in the prosperity and progress of a school in all its operations, bearings and interests.

In this lecture I shall present the necessary arrangements immediately preliminary to the opening and organization of a school.

So many teachers, and those who are least prepared, too, simply engage to teach a school at so much a quarter, and learn nothing about the character of the school or its facilities or want of them, till they find themselves in the midst of a turbulent, boisterous crew of children and youth, that I have found it necessary in my training exercises to dwell with particular earnestness and minuteness, on these necessary preliminary arrangements, in immediate preparation for opening and organizing a school, in order to insure any fair prospect of success. I shall now proceed to enumerate these necessary preliminary arrangements.

I. Arrangements with Directors.

1. *You should consult the School Laws*, a copy of which you can find in the possession of any Justice of the Peace or other State Officer, and learn the legal powers and authority of School Directors, as well as the duties enjoined on yourself, by legal enactment.

(1.) You will find that their power over a school is almost absolute, limited only by the amount of money they can control for its support.

(2.) Contracts with Directors in order to be binding, must be made before other witnesses than the parties immediately interested, or they must be drawn in writing, and properly signed.

(3.) You will discover that the Statute Law empowers the Directors to make repairs and improvements on school buildings and surroundings within certain limits of expenditure, and that they can raise this amount by a special tax, without taking a vote of the district.

(4.) You should know that you have no authority in the school save that which you derive from the Directors by explicit contract, or continued assent.

(5.) And lastly you should understand that if you transcend this authority so derived in any particular, in any direction, you can be held as having violated your contract and are liable for damages, and can thus, as you perceive, be dismissed almost at pleasure by a disaffected board. Common Law and general usage will sustain the Directors in almost any course they may choose to adopt, in your case.

2. *You will do well to be definite and specific in your contract with Directors.*

Items in Contract with Directors.

(1.) *It is better to engage by the day* than by the month or term, for at least four good reasons. (a) Since you are liable to be dismissed any day, as I have already shown, you will thus be able to leave any day, and demand wages up to the time at which you leave. Otherwise, not having taught the time you agreed, you can not enforce payment for the time you have taught. (b.) It gives the teacher opportunity to look out for a better position, and stimulates him to work for a reputation that will call him to a better position and higher wages. (c.) It makes every day's work a distinct responsibility, for a definite amount of money. And this fact being recognized by Directors and teacher is more likely to energize the teacher in his every day's work, and make it worth the wages he is to be paid. (d.) It makes the Directors more watchful over the interests of their school, to know daily that the teacher is faithfully fulfilling his contract and earning his stipulated wages. "Short accounts make long friends."

(2.) Agree definitely as to the number of days the school is to be taught in a week.

(3.) *Agree definitely as to the number of hours* you are to teach for a day's work; otherwise, you may teach eight or nine hours and then "you will do no more than you ought; you are only sitting in the house by the fire and hearing the children read and spell; the hired man works out doors at hard work, a great deal longer, and he only gets half as much as you do." By all means, then, agree to teach six hours for a day's work, and only six hours; thus you will know when your day's work is done. But if you think the school or any class demands more time, you can *give* it, and get the credit for your generosity. In the one case you are a 'lazy school master,' however much you may do; in the other, its being known by the older and leading pupils, who of course will form this extra class, that you are *giving* them your time and labor, will aid you much in waking up a like generous spirit in them towards you; and this will enable you the better to carry out any desirable plans for the benefit of the school; for instance, composition writing or declamation.

(4.) *Agree as to the number of extra branches.*—Show the Directors that the common legal branches will more than occupy your time, if properly attended to and that every extra branch must take time from these common branches.

You can make the proposition, that if they will agree that there shall be only one extra branch taught, that you will take your own time beyond the six hours, to attend to this class.

Without such a definite agreement in this matter, you will not unlikely find as you are an extra teacher, paid extra wages, that the older pupils, children of the Directors too, will wish to study a half a dozen different extra branches, and no one will be willing to give up, "It's this branch that I want to study, and pa agreed to pay the teacher such high wages so that I could study it, and he would not have to send me away to school." So argue the several children of the different Directors. Now, previous agreement cuts off all this difficulty and changes it into the advantage of giving you an opportunity to show your generosity, instead of failing to satisfy any one in trying to manage this otherwise unmanageable difficulty.

You will do well to agree on the extra branch you shall teach. I advise Book Keeping, provided you are competent to teach it. You will find it the best means of securing diligent, interested study from overgrown young men. Such 'privileged characters' and 'hard cases,' will give you no trouble, if you can furnish them something to do, that they think pays better than mischief or hoggishness. In fact the hard cases of former teachers may thus prove your best pupils and your firmest friends.

(5.) *Agree that fuel shall be supplied, well prepared*, and if not, the school may be dismissed till it is; but you receive wages for time thus lost from want of fuel, or from any other cause, for which you are not properly responsible.

Do not rest satisfied with the usage of providing green unchopped wood, and especially request that the pupils may not be under the necessity of chopping the wood during school days. It is a great evil and adds very much to the difficulty of securing good feeling from the larger pupils; and without this, you cannot expect to manage a school well. It is just as bad as a failure in a school, to be under the necessity of sending out boys to chop wood when all their time is needed to accomplish their regular work in the school room. No regular programme can be maintained, if this arrangement is forced upon you, and yet unless you make it a matter of special agreement that good fuel and well prepared be provided, you will probably find that long usage in that district has made this interruption of the boys' study hours a law.

(6.) *An understanding should be had as to janitorship.* If you receive four dollars a day, or more, the Directors will in all probability hire a janitor for you and pay him from the school funds. If you receive less, you will be expected to pay for sweeping and dusting the house, building the fires, etc., or to do this work yourself. "To him that hath shall be given," you know.

It will be well to speak of this matter, and assure the

Directors, if you are a lady teacher, that you will not be obliged to call on them to build fires, every cold morning.

This janitor's business is easily managed, however, even if you do have to pay for it from your wages. A little contrivance and foresight will give a good warm room on the coldest morning, and without this foresight any janitor that can be hired, almost, will fail to build a fire in time on the coldest mornings.

(7.) *Inquire for the number of pupils that you may expect.* The Directors will give the number that attended last session, and it will be about one-third, probably, of those legally entitled to public money. Inquire, then, for the number enumerated in the district, and state that you hope to have nearly all in attendance. This you may fairly expect if you obtain higher wages than any former teacher, and if you succeed in impressing the Directors with your ability and determination to make a good school.

(8.) *Agree as to the admission of extra pupils, i. e.*, any over twenty one years of age, or any from other districts. Propose that the tuition of all such be not less than fifty cents per week, and that one half go to the district, and one half to increase the teacher's wages. This arrangement can be shown to be reasonable, and it can hardly fail to work well, every way.

(9.) *The Power of Suspension should be secured by contract.* Since there will, in all probability, be pupils too old and too large to control by physical force, even if you think this admissible in any case, it will be well for you to provide for the worst before hand. This very provision to meet any exigency will be the best safeguard against the occurrence of that exigency. I would, therefore, ask of the Directors the power of referring any unmanageable case to them, and the power of suspending a pupil, when necessary, until a meeting of the Directors could be called to consider such a case. If, then, the Directors are of the opinion, on examining the merits of the case, by hearing both sides, that I am incapable of managing the school, it will be for their interest and for mine that I abandon the school; but if they decide that the pupil, whose case is brought before them, is in the fault, and that the school can go on successfully, provided this pupil be expelled, they can expel him till such a time as he is willing to make proper acknowledgement, when the teacher ought to be willing to receive him back, on trial.

To such an arrangement, many boards of Directors will not accede at first. They will object: "We don't want to be bothered with governing our school; we hire a teacher to do it, and we want him (or her) to do it. We can't be running to the school, every day or two, to settle difficulties between the teacher and the scholars. We expect the teacher to be able to settle his (or her) own difficulties, and manage the school to suit himself (or herself) or give it up, and let some other teacher take it, that can manage it."

To this I would reply:

"It is not my intention, gentlemen, to make you trouble, or throw any responsibility on you which I can possibly avoid, and it is for this very reason that I ask this power of suspending an unmanageable pupil.

If any vicious boy should stand out and resist every influence I could bring to bear upon him, becoming still more troublesome, and defeating his own true ends in stubbornly trying to defeat mine, it is plain that if I can refer his case to you, and he knows it, that I shall have an amount of authority and power which he will hardly be willing to brook. Thus yielding to a necessity, he may come under more kindly influences, while otherwise he would continue to set all influences at defiance. It is true, I might expel him from school, but I prefer not to take such responsibility. In fact it will do such pupil or pupils much more good, and be much more likely to save them to the school, and to themselves to have their case decided by disinterested parties."

Caution.—Provided the Directors are persuaded to grant you this power of suspension, it will be necessary for you to hold it in reserve as the very last resort, acknowledging to yourself, even then, that if you possessed more power in your own personal influence, such extraneous aid would be unnecessary. So you can not but consider that every time such aid is appealed to, or indeed a resort to it is threatened, it is only betraying your own weakness. Still, it is better to use such means than to be defeated in every plan and effort, you can devise and put forth for the good of the school by one or two brutish pupils. In other lectures I have spoken and shall speak of special measures to be pursued with such hard cases before referring them to the Directors.

(10.) *Ask the Directors to visit the school house with you.* No doubt you may find some reluctance; but before you conclude your contract, by all means, examine the school house, its grounds, its out houses, its well, its seats and desks, its windows, blackboards, etc., etc., and report to the Directors. Now you will be able to get the Directors to visit the school house, I think.

Possibly, there will be some expression of surprise at the state of affairs, a dirty floor, (possibly hogs or sheep have lodged on it, since the close of the last term), broken window panes, rickety desks, demolished benches, fragments of a chair, an old burnt out, cracked stove with dislocated pipe are the promising prospect for the 'new teacher' to commence school with.

It will be well now to suggest or rather to win the suggestion from the Directors, that there shall be a thorough renovation of the whole affair. The Directors have the power to do whatever is necessary to be done within certain limits of expense. The rest can be done by a general gathering of the young people of the District. The floor can be scrubbed, the windows washed and the broken panes restored, the walls can be whitewashed, the desks repaired or possibly new ones obtained, the stove can be repaired and the pipe replaced or a new stove and pipe purchased, a rostrum provided with a suitable teacher's desk and chair: lastly, recitation seats are a necessity, and must be obtained if possible.

(11.) *But what of the apparatus?* viz., The blackboards, the bell, the clock; a globe, geometrical forms and solids, wall maps and charts?

If you dare, Teacher, if the interest now excited will warrant the probability of success in carrying through such arrangements, it will be well to suggest to the Directors that most graded schools have such facilities, where the teacher has much less to do, having only two grades in a room; whereas there must be at least four grades in any good country ungraded school, so called.

Remark.—Let me caution you here, my young friend, against leaving all or any of these proposed improvements to be accomplished by the school board, before the time agreed upon for your school to commence. In nine cases out of ten there will nothing be done, without your presence, inspiration and supervision of the whole matter. So you may as well assume the responsibility at once, by volunteering to come on as soon as practicable, and to go to work with the Directors and any others that can be enlisted and do what is necessary or desirable to be done. This is the only safe course to take in the premises. And thoroughness and energy in this matter will pay, I assure you.

(12.) *It is well to have an understanding about text books,* how they are to be supplied, and what kinds are to be used. You can thus forestall the objection, so often raised against new teachers, by so many fathers who spend enough every week, if not every day, in tobacco and whisky, to furnish their children with an entire outfit of new books; "That's just the way, every new teacher must have a lot of new books; just speculation, nothing else; I'm not agoing to stand it."

To enable the Directors to answer this objection when you call for additional books it will be well for you to state that you can get along with the *kinds* of text books now used in the school without change: all you want is that each pupil be supplied with his own books, so that there will be no necessity for two or more pupils using the same book, thus creating disorder by communicating, or preventing any one from working under a regular school programme.

3. *Do not fail to enlist the interest of the Directors in their school and in your plans.*

All these arrangements in your contract will aid you in doing this, if you suggest them in the spirit of deference to the proper legal authority vested in the Directors and with suitable personal respect to the gentlemen themselves. An earnest desire evinced on your part to make suitable arrangements for a good school with the ability to point out what is necessary or desirable can hardly fail to win the respect and confidence of any board of Directors that you will be willing to work under, and to arouse in them an interest that they have never before felt in the prosperity and success of their school.

It requires more 'common sense," knowledge of human nature and tact to win Directors over to their own interests, and to the interests of their children than to manage the children. Ladies, we must admit, if gifted with any degree of personal attraction, can succeed in this direction better than gentlemen teachers. But the interest and co-operation of the Directors must be secured, in order to a large and true success. I would be unwilling to engage to work for any board of Directors that I could not in some way influence to make some personal effort and sacrifice for their school. In your novelties and innovations in methods of teaching, for instance, in teaching geography by drawing maps, or in using the word method, or phonetic method in teaching the alphabet, you will very likely need the Directors to stand between you and fault-finding parents; but still more, in the matter of government, as for instance, if you should think it necessary to deny a pupil the privilege of reciting in a certain class, in case he was tardy or otherwise troublesome.

By securing the friendship and confidence of one or more of the Directors, you can proceed under his or their advice with much more confidence in adopting any measures which you feel are desirable for the good of the school.

II. Arrangements for One's Self.

1. *You must secure the sole occupancy of a comfortable room*, at your boarding place. For how can you otherwise have the use of your time for study and preparation for classes?

2. *You will own such reference books as are necessary for the several branches* you expect to teach. You will need an unabridged Dictionary, and a Brand's Encyclopedia, as books for general reference. Besides these you must purchase the best books on the extra branch that you expect to teach; also several practical works on methods of teaching and school management. You ought also to subscribe for one or more of the best Educational periodicals, and thus keep up interest in professional friends and current professional topics of discussion.

3. You should not put off coming to your school till the morning on which you expect to commence the term; but be on hand some days before, and see that all the arrangements in the school house and for your own comfort are completed. You will thus begin the new term with a pleasant room, well arranged, newly whitewashed, sweet and clean. So dispose of your apparatus, maps, charts, clock, and pictures if you have them, as to present an attractive appearance. The very atmosphere of such a room, even though it be the same old place where disorder and misrule so long held sway,—may by such a transformation become inspiring with the elements of cleanliness, neatness, order, moral purity, and mental energy. You may use your school room for your own study, if you can find no more convenient room at your boarding place.

Remark.—The most important feature, after all, in these preliminary arrangements, though they are all essential to a high success in teaching any common country school, is that they impress your pupils and your patrons with a new appreciation of the value of their school; and it is scarcely possible that the teacher who enters upon his work with such a spirit of earnestness and enterprise, can fail of making as much better school than ever was known in that district before as his efforts and plans are nobler and more self sacrificing.

Such a Teacher can 'have everything his own way,' in most cases; at least, after he has demonstrated that he is able to carry out his plans; because the Directors must feel and know that his every purpose and effort is designed and is well calculated to promote the real and permanent interest of the school and community.

LECTURE ON SCHOOL MANAGEMENT,

(COPYRIGHT SECURED.)

LECTURE XIV.

ORGANIZATION OF AN UNGRADED SCHOOL.

INTRODUCTORY REMARKS.

Ladies and Gentlemen, Teachers:

It is supposed that the arrangements enumerated in my last lecture have been made, and that you, any one of you, are to begin your operations as a teacher in a new room, new in its appearance, attractiveness and facilities. Yes, the very atmosphere and light of that school room are renovated. Purity, vigor and honor are the pervading elements and so impress themselves on the feelings of every one entering.

You will be sure to be there, at your school room, at least an hour before time for the school to begin. See that the room is comfortable, and all charts, wall-maps, cards, mottoes, and recitation seats, are properly arranged for making the most pleasant impression. So of your globe, and any other articles of apparatus, let them be properly displayed.

Now, ladies and gentlemen, if there is one here, more winning and capable than the rest, to whom this preliminary work is not necessary and he or she can succeed any where under the most unpromising circumstances, such a teacher will avail himself of these suggestions and secure the manifest advantage of such preliminary arrangements as I described in my last lecture. But if there is any one here entirely inexperienced, possessing little working or winning power, and who needs every favoring circumstance to prevent utter failure and an inglorious fizzle in his first attempt at teaching, he is the one who will give no attention to these directions. He will simply agree to teach for so much per quarter, learn nothing about the character of his Directors, patrons or pupils, ascertain nothing of the condition of the school-house, not even whether it is tenable or not. He will find himself late on the morning of commencing school, and most probably a noisy crew of semi-savages to face, made so by his own neglect and inefficiency. The sooner he leaves the school in discouragement and disgust, the better for all parties.

I remember once, when a child, waiting at a school-house an hour or more with fifty other boys and girls for the teacher who was to open the school that morning. All the hootings and howlings, the bawling and screaming, the stamping and dancing, the running in and running out, the upsetting of tables, desks and benches that could be done, were done as thoroughly and heartily as twenty big boys and little boys intermingling with coy great girls and screaming little girls could do it. In the midst of such a Babel we heard a squeaky little voice, crying "Boys, boys, stop your noise. Take your seats." The new teacher had come, a slender, maiden-faced young man, "right from Yale College." He thought we were the worst set of children he ever saw, and so we were, but it was his own fault. The Directors dismissed him from the school at the end of two weeks. Whether he had any better success any where else, I never learned; but the Directors provided an old gentleman, who by free use of the rod subdued that school into apparent decency though we did little but spell columns, and 'do sums,' that winter. It was the only district school I ever attended, and I endeavored to make good use of it when I came to teach by doing everything as differently as possible from everything Dr. Goodson did as a teacher.

But in order to prevent such proceedings, or the formation of leagues against you, or the power of an unorganized combination of sulky or defiant rowdyism, find yourself early at the school-room and prepared to take all such qualities out of your pupils by infusing better ones.

Take every pupil by the hand as he or she enters, and interesting yourself in his or her studies or wishes, make him or her your friend by showing an earnest friendly spirit and a real desire to promote the interests of each pupil. You can inquire about studies and books, the wishes and expectations, etc., etc., of every one, nearly, while the school is assembling. Thus, when the proper time arrives, a stroke of the bell will enable you to call the school to order, and a kindly request will be sufficient to seat the pupils.

Let the pupils arrange themselves as they desire on the seats. They will for the most part take such seats as are suitable. If not, a suggestion or request will be sufficient. In case of any previous claims, however, which can not be reconciled, a drawing for seats may be advisable. The seats being arranged, it may be well to state definitely your purposes and aims with regard to your term's work; and in so doing, a few pertinent, kindly sentences will be better than any amount of gasconade or bluster.

In prosecuting a course of examination for classifying the pupils, you will observe these three directions, as closely as may be practible.

(1.) Furnish something interesting for every pupil to do, from the commencement, and all day long.

(2.) Forestall disorder by establishing order at every movement.

(3.) You will more readily interest the younger classes by engaging with the older classes first, than by pursuing the opposite course.

Classification in Arithmetic. Investigation in Reading.

In order to become acquainted with the pupils as speedily as possible, their general culture, or want of it, their peculiar personal habits of thought and expression, an exercise in reading will prove the most satisfactory as a commencing exercise. If conducted with any skill and vivacity it will not only reveal the literary advancement of the older pupils who engage in it, but the criticisms and re-readings of the teacher will enlist the attention and interest of all the younger classes. It may be well to ask all to join this advanced class who have been accustomed to read in the two higher classes before. Before dismissing the class from the recitation seats you will make provisions for occupying their time, by proposing to them the formation of an advanced class in Arithmetic, to include all those pupils who can add and subtract 'Common Fractions,' with any degree of certainty.

You will say. "It is my wish to form at least three classes in Arithmetic, and all who can add and subtract any simple fractions, as two-thirds and three-fourths, four-fifths and seven eigths, I would like to have join the advanced class. Some, I have no doubt, have gone farther in the arithmetic, but we will begin our operations in arithmetic this term with a thorough review and mastery of fractions. How many of this reading class have worked examples in fractions? "Well, as many of you as wish to do so, may look over this subject, work out as many examples by the rules in the book, as you are able, and I will try your ability in adding and subtracting fractions, as soon as I have heard the other classes read."

Calling Pupils to Recitation Seats and Excusing Them.

You will establish order in this matter at once. While you can not call individuals, in the first instance, to the recitation seats, not knowing definitely who belong to any particular class, you will use all diligence in bringing every pupil to the first exercise of the class who properly belongs in it. As the exercise proceeds you will ask some older pupil to write the names of the members of the class on a piece of paper which you will furnish. As soon as the names are written you will call them, and thus fix more definitely in your mind the name of every individual in the class, and save yourself from the embarrassment of calling wrong names, and the disorder and laughter at your expense which such mistakes will necessarily occasion.

When the exercise is concluded, you will not excuse the class in a mass, but individually, calling the name of a boy and a girl alternately as far as this is practicable; it being supposed that the sexes occupy separate seats during recitations, as also, of course, during study hours.

This easy, kindly, introduction of orderly movement, at the very outset, will, if managed with any skill, impress all pupils with a respect for the school room, and all its evolution and exercises. While so much military precision as to be burdensome, may not be required, yet just enough of orderly movement to avoid confusion will secure a good natured compliance from all, and the very atmosphere of the school room will seem pervaded with cheerfulness, kindness and respect.

Having assigned business for the most advanced class, in preparing for an informal examination in Arithmetic, you can now call for those who are accustomed to read in the second and third readers; and after an exercise of about thirty minutes, during which their names shall have been taken, you may state that you intend to form another class in Written Arithmetic. If any are able to add and subtract Fractions they may belong to the highest class; if not, and they can perform examples in Long Division, they may belong to the second class. Then you can mention some example by which you will be likely to test the class, as 1565 by 35. This definite example with a few others placed on the blackboard will give more point and energy to the effort than the simple announcement of an intended examination. Thus you provide interesting work for this class, while you are attending to the class in the first reader, and to the abcdarians.

You will carefully dismiss the pupils of the several classes in order, by name, from the recitation seats, and secure quiet and respectful movements to and from recitation seats.

Numbering the pupils in the classes may be deferred until their formal adjustment in their respective classes. Still the requisite order may be sustained by dismissing pupils by name, a girl and a boy alternately, rather than dismissing a class in a mass. The classes of small children may be furnished with slates for drawing when not engaged in their class drill.

Recess

By the time that the reading classes are examined, it will be proper to give a recess. It may be well to ask the pupils to arrange their books and slates so that they will not be thrown on the floor during recess. It will now be necessary to excuse pupils by rows or tiers of seats, rather than to pronounce the word, Recess, and thus initiate general disorder and misrule, by permitting forty, sixty or more to bound pell mell towards the door, out of which there goes an explosion of noises hideous, as if all Pandemonium had broken loose on an unoffending world. Convert all such occasions for disorder into pleasant orderly movements; then you will not be compelled to give disagreeable scolding lectures against rowdyism and ruffianism. You will find in nineteen cases out of every twenty where you are inclined to scold the pupils, that you are more in fault, than they, for not having foreseen the difficulty and for not having made such arrangements as would have prevented it, or converted it into a decided instance of good order and kindly management.

Examination in Arithmetic.

As your school will in all probability be graded best on the basis of Arithmetic, and as you can not well make more than four grades, I will suggest that the grades may first be established according to the following plan:

The A grade will include all who can add and subtract fractions.

The B grade will include all below the A grade who can work ordinary examples in Long Division.

The C grade will include all below the B grade who can read simple sentences.

The D grade will include all below the C grade.

The examination in Arithmetic should be conducted with reference to locating every pupil in his proper grade. It will be objected to this plan of grading a country school, that some pupils who can not manage fractions will be found much more advanced in other studies than some that can. To this, I reply that while I would not hold every pupil inflexibly to the grade to which his advancement in Arithmetic would assign him or her, I would adhere to this plan of grading as closely as possible, for reasons that will soon appear, in constructing an ideal programme.

The examination of the Arithmetic classes may occupy the rest of the forenoon, save that one more exercise must be given to the abcdarians: they must not be overlooked nor neglected.

Afternoon Exercises.

Classes may be organized in English Grammar by assigning a definite sentence for all who are sufficiently advanced to study grammar to parse with reference to an examination for the purpose of forming two classes. Those who can parse the sentence with some degree of correctness may form the advanced class, all the rest included in the A and B grades can begin in a primary class. While theA grade is preparing for examination in Grammar, the B grade can be examined in Geography, also the C grade in primary Geography, and such directions for the first recitation may be given as may incite to some effort for the preparation of the first lesson.

The a, b, c, pupils must now receive attention, after which the Grammar class may be examined by being called on individually to parse any words in the sentence assigned. If it is found that few if any can parse common constructions correctly, and are unable to distinguish parts of speech, it will be well to have but one class in Grammar.

Recess.

Be careful to maintain good order in excusing pupils for recess, again also in their resuming their study seats. A writing class may now be arranged for, and you will carefully state what kind of paper, pens and ink, you prefer, and ascertain what facilities there are for obtaining them. It is understood that you give your entire time to Penmanship during the practice hour, and that all the pupils who write copies attend to it at the same time, and at no other time during the day.

When the Reading and Spelling classes also are provided for, you will be ready to decide on the arrangements for the extra class. (1.) What branch it shall be in. (2.) What text-book the class shall use. (3.) At what time the class shall meet.

As to the branch, I advise Book-keeking,if you are competent to teach it. No branch can be made so useful and interesting to an ordinary class of boys and young men, and no study will help so much to win their respect for the school, provide you know how to teach it, and no branch will prove so heavy a drag,if you do not understand teaching it. The individual plan pursued in Commercial Colleges will prove a failure in every sense.

These arrangements having been satisfactorily made and such provisions for a good supply of books and slates for to-morrow's work as shall seem to be satisfactory, you are now ready to engage in the closing exercises of the day. They may consist of a speech of congratulation as to the very favorable prospects for a good and interesting school; your determination to lay yourself out to do your best to please your pupils and benefit them; your expectations that there will be so much of interest in the recitations and in the preparation for the recitations on plans which you shall propose that there will be no necessity for any rules save the rule of right; but if there is, you intend to propose a rule only when the last necessity demands it, and then you expect that every pupil for the good of the school, for the better improvement of its privileges, and for the higher advantage that can be derived from them, every pupil will try to sustain any such rule or regulation as may be seen to be imperatively necessary, but just so soon as the rule is found unnecessary it will be laid aside. But still it is your desire rather that so much interest and good feeling shall be manifested that no positive rules will be necessary. It is so much more pleasant and noble to feel that every one, teacher and pupil, is trying so hard to do right and is so busy in his regular work that he has no time nor disposition to do wrong and make trouble. It is in fact your feeling, and you are persuaded that it is the feeling of every pupil, that the school is to be a grand success.

I have thus, teachers, given you a few leading thoughts

for a closing speech just such as several similar occasions in my early experience inspired me with. In every case, my hopes and purposes were more than realized, and my experiences in my country District Schools are remembered as among the dearest and happiest of my life.

Now, it does seem to me with such feelings in your own heart, earnestly expressed, that there can not fail to be a more than corresponding feeling and determination on the part of your pupils to avail themselves of the arrangements which are being made for their benefit, and that every one will leave the school-house that evening with a new purpose aroused in his soul to try and do something for himself, and to make something of himself, if he has never had such a feeling before. Earnestness begets earnestness, kindness begets kindness, enthusiasm begets enthusiasm, pure motives and high aims beget noble resolutions and determined effort.

After such a hearty, earnest speech and the cheerful responsive countenances answering in smiles or tears to its sentiments, is a most fitting time to introduce the singing of a hymn, the reading of a few verses in the Testament, and a brief prayer for the guidance of divine wisdom in carrying out the plans and purposes of the term. Teacher, if you have never prayed before, how can you deny yourself so high and blessed a privilege now?

I will not here contrast the common way of spending the first day of a term in a country school; its want of systematic procedure; its consequent embarrassment, disorder and confusion in trying to find out what is to be done; the noise and turbulence of the occasion, the sharp words, and the sour looks of the teacher; the ill restrained boisterousness of the pupils, ever ready to break out into a brutish laugh at the teacher's expense; in short, the general disgust of both teacher and pupils for each other, and for the school; the noisy, defiant or contemptuous talk of pupils on their way home, including threats of barring out, and all sorts of mischief and wickedness, if the teacher don't carry himself pretty straight. Such scenes are too common and too well understood to call for any description here.

Organization Proper.

I pass now to the construction of a programme to guide and control the labors of the school.

Remarks.

(1.) Nothing can be done well without an orderly disposition of time, and a well arranged system of labor, both for the teacher and every pupil during every moment of school time.

(2.) It will be necessary to make as few classes as possible, in order that more time may be secured for those recitations which require some considerable time in order to excite an interest in the subjects of study.

(3.) It may be well to condense reading and spelling classes, making only half as many as has been the custom before. The reason for this course must be carefully explained to the school.

(4.) Before beginning the construction of the Programme, it will be necessary to make out a list of the recitations for each grade, annexing to each the amount of time desirable for the recitation, also the number of recitations or exercises of any one kind to be held with any class in a day.

I will give such a list here as may be supposed to be applicable to almost any of your prospective schools:

	ALLOTMENTS.	
	Trial. Minutes.	Corrected Minutes
Arithmetic, advanced class	40	35
Arithmetic, intermediate class	30	25
Arithmetic, primary class	25	15
Grammar, advanced class	40	30
Grammar, primary class	25	15
Geography, advanced and intermediate classes	50	35
Geography, primary class	20	15
Reading and Spelling, advanced class	40	25
Reading and Spelling, intermediate class	30	15
2 Reading and Spelling, primary class, each 20	40	30
4 A, B, C, exercises, each 10	40	40
Book-keeping or Algebra	50	40
Recess	40	40
General Exercises	10	10
Penmanship	30	30
	8h:40m.	6h:40m.

I find in adding the column of trial allotments of time, all of which are too meagre, the programme will require eight hours and forty minutes. I cannot work over seven hours per day in the school room without loss of animal vigor and spiritual vivacity. So I shall have to cut down the several allotments and reduce my entire time including Religious Exercises, General Exercises and Extra Class to seven hours.

I have given in the second column the corrected allotments and reduce the time to six hours and forty minutes. Now I am ready to make a programme. It will be better to arrange the several recitations and drills first; and afterwards, arrange the times of study.

If I could have an assistant how much better work I could do. But I must submit to the circumstances and make the best of them.

This programme which I give here will not be adapted precisely to any school, probably; but with some slight modifications it will be suitable for almost any *ungraded* school with only one teacher, provided the pupils are all well supplied with text-books.

This ungraded school, so called, thrown into four grades, A, B, C, and D Grades as before explained in this lecture; and my programme must provide for the constant employment of every grade and every pupil in every grade, during every moment of the school hours, save recess.

PROGRAMME.

TIME. From.	To.	A Grade.	B Grade.	C Grade.	D Grade.	Time of con-tin'ce.
8:45	9:00	Religious	Exercises.	General	Exercises.	15
9:00	9:02		Roll	Call.		2
9:02	9:30	***Geog'y.***	***Geog'y.***	Ment. Arith.	Blocks.	28
9:30	9:45	Book-keep'g	Geography.	***Ment. Arith.***	Blocks.	15
9:45	10:00	Book keep'g.	***Grammar.***	Ment. Arith.	Blocks.	15
10:00	10:10		Rec	ess.		10
10:10	10:20	Book-keep'g.	Grammar.	Ment. Arith.	***Reading.***	10
10:20	10:45	Book-keep'g.	***Arith'tic.***	Read & Spell.	Slates.	25
10:45	11:00	Arithmetic.	Arithmetic.	***Read & Spell.***	Slates.	15
11:00	11:10		Rec	ess.		10
11:10	11:20	Arithmetic.	Arithmetic.	Geography.	***Reading.***	10
11:20	12:00	***Arith'tic.***	Arithmetic.	Geography.	Dismissed.	40
1:00	1:30	***Pen'p.***	***Pen'p.***	***Pen'p.***	***Slates.***	30
1:30	1:45	Arithmetic.	Read & Spell.	***Geog'y.***	Blocks.	15
1:45	2:00	Grammar.	***Read & Spell.***	Geography.	Blocks.	15
2:00	2:10		Rec	ess.		10
2:10	2:20	Grammar.	Grammar.	Read & Spell.	***Reading.***	10
2:20	2:45	***Grammar.***	Grammar.	Read & Spell.	Slates.	25
2:45	3:00	Grammar.	Grammar.	***Read & Spell.***	Slates.	15
3:00	3:10		Rec	ess.		10
3:10	3:20	Read & Spell.	Geography.	Ment. Arith.	***Reading.***	10
3:20	3:45	***Read & Spell.***	Geography.	Ment. Arith.	Dismissed.	35
3:55	4:09		Roll Call	and Singing.		5
4:00	4:50	***Book-keep'g.***	Dismissed.	Dismissed.	Dismissed.	50

EXPLANATIONS OF THE PROGRAMME.

(1.) The consecutive exercises of each grade are given in the appropriate column.

(2.) The recitations are given in *bold-faced type.*

(3.) The study hours are given in common type

(4.) All general exercises are given in capitals.

(5.) The times of beginning and ending each exercise and its continuance are given in the time columns.

REMARKS ON THE PROGRAMME.

(1.) It will be noticed that the study times of every pupil are as carefully provided for as the recitations.

(2.) In order that every class may make immediate use of the preliminary drill given in every recitation to enable the pupil to work at his next lesson with interest and success, some time for studying every branch is allotted as soon *after* every recitation as is practicable, with the exception of the Reading and Spelling Exercises, and the Geography for the A grade.

(3.) It is supposed that the A grade will study their Geography lesson at home. If this is impracticable in any case the pupil may be excused from the study of Geography or from the study of the extra branch, Book-keeping, as given here.

(4.) If the teacher finds that a change of time is needed in order to give more time to any particular subject he can generally make the change on the programme for any one grade without disturbing other grades. But he ought always to make the change clearly on the programme, at the time he orders it, for any class.

(5.) It will be found necessary to write out for the use of the school on the second day two programmes at least; one for the teacher and one for the monitor. It will be well also for each pupil, to copy the programme for his own grade, with the exception of the D grade.

5. The Teacher will find it imperatively necessary to *work closely* by his programme. The temptation will be, continually, to hold on to recitations too long, and thus, some recitations, or some recess will have to be omitted, or the school detained beyond the hour of dismission, all of which will work very badly, every way, as the teacher will soon discover.

6. The teacher will find it a great relief to appoint a MONITOR for every half day, whose duty it shall be to announce the time either five minutes or ten minutes before closing each of the longer recitations. This is in order to give the teacher time for preliminary drill, or to announce the extent and character of the next lesson for the class within the time prescribed for this present recitation. The choice of monitors may be made as a matter of honor; no one being com-

pelled to serve; or the pupils of the A and B graaes may be appointed in regular rotation, each to act only for a half day at one time.

An earnest enthusiastic teacher will find this kind of monitorial system almost a necessity. It will operate infinitely better in keeping order and preventing whispering, though the monitor is expected to give his entire attention to the time of the programme and his own studies, and know nothing of the diligence or order of other pupils, than that of appointing a monitor to watch offenders and record their names. It is seen that the Normal monitor is no spy on the actions of his fellow pupils, his duty is to keep the teacher in order, and if the teacher comply closely with the monitor's announcements, the very spirit of good order is established in that school room and scarcely any other rules and regulations will be found necessary. The respect which the teacher shows for the programme can hardly fail to inspire the school with like respect and with a love of good order generally.

7. It will require some attention of the teacher for the first few days, to keep the different grades at their appropriate work, according to the programme, during their study hours, but the proper use of time during study hours is more important for the pupil if possible than during recitation. Very few, if any, variations from the regular programme should be granted to individual pupils.

8. No studying together from the same book should be tolerated. It is an open gate for all irregularity. Every pupil should have his own full supply of books to use for himself, at the time assigned to his grade on the programme.

9. If pupils do not master their lessons during the time assigned, do not let that be given or taken as a reason why the time of some other branch should be used, in any individual case, but rather modify the next lesson, or make a change in the programme for the whole grade.

10. It will be objected to such a programme, that some are more apt in one study, and some in others; and hence some pupil in a given grade will require much more time, for instance, in Arithmetic, than another, while he requires much less in Grammar perhaps, and thus it would be doing that individual a wrong in such a case to keep all to the same precise programme. Now, there, are several ways to manage such a difficulty, without breaking up the power of a regular programme by yielding to every individual caprice and demand for special deviations from the general programme.

(1.) The pupil can study that branch in which he finds himself behind his class, at home, out of school hours.

(2.) He must be encouraged to think that, considering his previous opportunities and advancement, he is doing well, even if he does not master the whole lesson; and the next time he goes over the subject he will in all probability lead the class.

(3.) He can be assigned to a lower grade, at least, in the particular branch in which he is most defective.

(4.) He can be permitted to omit one of the studies of his grade and thus be allowed the time of the omitted study for the branch in which he is deficient.

(5.) The proper arrangement of the recitation, in the matter of preliminary drill, and in dividing the class into a *more advanced* and *less advanced section*, thus requiring no more of each pupil than he can well do, is the proper remedy for this difficulty, and can hardly fail if well managed to convert the difficulty into a real advantage both for the backward pupil, and for his class. But he can be assigned extra duty in the subject in which he is more advanced.

11. The introduction and explanation of this programme on the second morning of school will consume some time; opportunity must be given for each pupil to copy his part of the programme for his own guidance, and the proper arrangement for monitors may be made at once.

It will be well then, to set aside that part of the programme for this day whose time is consumed in general arrangements, and commence at that part of the programme which the time of day has reached. Lessons must be assigned, in making general arrangements, for those *studies* in the programme whose recitations have been omitted. Thus careful provision must be made for full employment of every pupil on this most trying day of school, or disorder will make such headway as will be difficult to overcome in many days.

12. The reading and spelling exercises have been condensed into one exercise, through the entire programme. The time may be divided at each exercise or one exercise may be given to reading and the next to spelling and so on alternately.

LECTURE ON SCHOOL MANAGEMENT.

(COPYRIGHT SECURED.)

LECTURE XV.

NORMAL METHODS OF INCITING TO DILIGENCE AND ORDER.

PRELIMINARY REMARKS.

There are various courses pursued by different classes of teachers who use the force methods, for introducing and establishing order and compelling diligent study. I shall notice one or two.

1. The Directors draw up a set of rules, and require the teacher to enforce them, as a part of his contract.

Any such system of rules or regulations, however good in themselves, will,in most cases, in a great measure defeat the ends they are intended to secure,when introduced simply by the authority of Directors and enforced by the watchfulness and coercion of the teacher. Out of prison, no laws that are not appreciated and sustained by the governed, can be enforced to any good moral effect.

And any endeavors that seem to be successful in any degree in carrying out a code of school laws that do not receive the full and hearty sanction of the pupils, only seem so, because that school is a prison, in its discipline.

2. Another plan is for the teacher to draw up a set of rules with or without the consent of the Directors, to read them at the opening of the school, and demand strict obedi-

ence from every pupil, under the penalties of flogging, imprisonment, or expulsion. This plan generally works better than the first, as the teacher is probably more careful in constructing a code of laws, the enforcement of which he feels will be difficult enough at the best.

3. The more common course is for the teacher to begin school with no well defined plan of procedure, trusting to luck or some other equally reliable power for the government of his school. This teacher, not unfrequently, promulgates half a dozen laws in a day for days in succession, and presently finds that his laws and his own personal authority are both treated with contempt and ridicule. Such a teacher is generally blamed for "not beginning right; for not putting down the laws at the start. He was too easy, he let the school get ahead of him," say the Directors. The pupils all say that "He was too cross, he was scolding all the time, he couldn't find time to do any thing else." I might continue this enumeration of futile and mischievous plans or want of plans in establishing order and diligence, indefinitely; but these will suffice, I think, to show that all such measures are abnormal, and defeat the true objects and aims of school management, which are the promoting of the GOOD HABITS of cheerful industry, all-conquering thoroughness, orderly disposition of time and labor and the practice of useful activity.

Who cannot see that any plan of school government with any system of laws or no system of laws, carried out mainly by authority and coercion, will most surely defeat every one of these ends, and of necessity fix the opposite class of habits, viz.: hatred of work, shallowness and shirking in study, love of mischief, and increasing delight in tricks and meanness at the expense of the teacher.

Now, if any teacher who is pursuing any such plan and is feeling more and more that teaching is a very wearing and disagreeable business, and that he intends to get out of it just as soon as he can find anything else to do; let me ask him, if I can reach his ear or his eye, whether, if he were a pupil under just such government as he is attempting to administer, he would not himself be one of the worst and most troublesome. He will answer, if he is candid, "Of course I would. I always used to keep up my end, when I attended school." And yet that same teacher pursues that same course, which nearly ruined him, and made most of the schools he ever attended failures. It has been my purpose in these lectures to break up this line of hereditary descent, in which each successive teacher becomes more pernicious than his predecessor; and I may express my thankfulness, that so many hundreds and thousands have gone forth from these training exercises with the spirit of these lectures, and reported ere long that they *enjoy teaching*, and not a few, every year, declare, by letter or otherwise, each for himself, or for herself, "I have the best school I ever saw; I am just perfectly delighted with my school, I have the best scholars, I love every one of them."

Now, friends, I wish you to contrast the declarations of the abnormal teachers with those of the genuine Normal Teacher. Nor do I assume that every one that attends here a term or more and goes forth to teach, is able or willing to adopt Normal methods and principles. Some haven't the natural ability, or, in other words, the qualification of common sense. Very many do not remain here long enough to obtain the requisite knowledge of the branches or of the methods. Some are too far gone in vicious physical or moral habits to receive, or even to appreciate Normal methods, or to drink in the genial spirit of good will and earnest application, which so generally pervades this school. I do not claim, by any means, that every Normal Student will make a good Normal Teacher, or that every person even of fair natural abilities *can* adopt Normal methods in his own self-management, or in the management of others. It would be worse than vain and foolish in me to do so, it would be criminal.

But this I do claim, that multitudes (and large numbers, too, possessing no extraordinary mental capacity) who have been trained here, and elsewhere, in genuine Normal methods, have been revolutionized in all their ideas and practices of school management, and so far from feeling that teaching is a burden and a drag, have learned to feel that the business is their pride and their delight.

I. Some Normal Methods of Introducing Diligence and Order.

1. Working by a Programme.

There will undoubtedly be some difficulty in bringing all the pupils in a school to see the advantages of studying by a programme, such having been the loose, careless usages in this matter, that every one has studied any lesson when he felt like it, or when he was especially urged to do so, by the teacher. More frequently, if there has been any study of a lesson, it has been just before recitation; whereas, a lesson should be studied as soon as possible after a recitation, in order that every pupil may avail himself, in the best possible manner, of the instruction and directions given in the preliminary drill.

To overcome this difficulty of getting all the pupils to study by the programme, the time of the first recitation in each branch must be given in part to such explanations of the method of conducting the recitations, as will show the necessity and advantage of the plan proposed.

(1.) It should be stated that as the time of the teacher is fully occupied in the several recitations, it will be impossible for him to give any aid to pupils during study hours, in getting their lesson. The preliminary drill, if properly attended to by the pupil will enable him to master his lesson without further aid from the teacher; and it is not expected that pupils will study with each other, or get help from each other. Every pupil needs all his time to accomplish his own work, and may not be interrupted by giving or seeking aid from another: besides, studying together is incompatible with good order and truly independent and self-reliant development.

(2.) Then, a preliminary drill on some part of the branch under consideration should be given; such as will arouse interest, excite curiosity, and make it easy for every pupil to engage in the study of the branch at the time prescribed on the programme. Nay, if a preliminary drill is conducted with any skill and spirit in any branch, the difficulty will be in keeping the pupils from working at the lesson before the prescribed time, but this can be managed.

2. Training the WILL into Good Habits.

I feel compelled to dwell here for a moment on the Normal method of training the will. The will as an educational force is too often lost sight of, or it is viciously assumed, as in breaking (not training) colts, that the will must be broken. Now, I affirm, that a broken will makes a spiritless or a vicious animal, whether it be a colt or a boy.

The will is *trained* by a skillful horseman, not broken. So the true teacher can never lose sight of the fact, that the will is *the* force which is to be guided and determined, incited and energized to choose, to prefer, and to work in correct and useful action, rather than to be roused to resist and then crushed; and no teacher should feel satisfied with his own influence on a pupil, while he sees that the pupil's will is not won, and it is not his choice *to work*, and to work with laudable aims and real satisfaction in the school plans. Some few teachers, very few, seem to have an intuitive gift in this regard. Their pupils seem, at once, to prefer to do anything they may request; but the majority of us, teachers, find it necessary to study HUMAN NATURE in the boys and girls, that we may know how to determine their choice for the true, beautiful, and good, as involved in our plans, as worked out in our methods, and as aimed at in all our arrangements.

In my opinion, the first lesson we have to learn is not to excite antagonism, but to forestall it, and bring its energy, in other words the will power of the individual, to work in our favor instead of against us. To this end we must present stronger inducements for virtuous action in carrying out our plans, than possibly can exist in the minds and habits of the pupils against them.

(1.) Now, in avoiding the senseless repulsive routine of memorizing and repeating lessons, and of *requiring* such useless and tedious labor, one chief difficulty is removed, that is so often effectual in exciting antagonism, or at least in producing listlessness and indifference to school work, and decided aversion to the school itself.

(2.) In avoiding the assigning of *any* lesson without sufficient explanation and previous drill to enable every pupil to accomplish the work assigned without discouragement and consequent idleness and mischief, another very prevalent difficulty is removed.

(3.) In exciting so much interest and enterprise in every pupil, for the work assigned, that he is as eager to get at it as if it were any game or play is indeed carrying the will where you desire, teacher, and this must for the most part, be relied on to convert the *Will Power* from indifference or antagonism to *decided preference* and energetic action in the study and labor you prescribe for the pupil's pleasure and progress. That which is first done by special excitement and dominant attraction, sooner or later becomes a matter of habit, and thus in a measure moves itself. Thus by careful foresight, by ingenious contrivance, by patient labor and continued effort, teacher, you or I may accomplish the transformation of a mind, a heart, yes, a life, from habits of laziness, opposition to all good and noble action, into habits of thrift, energy, and benevolence. What true teacher can aim at, or desire less? But no one else can reach many of these young persons, and save them, but the teacher in his school work.

Caution in Training Will.

Let me give one caution, here. There is no worse way to train a will to determined evil action, than to demand, exact and compel good action. No really good act can be performed under compulsion. Every one knows it, feels it in his own case. Every one is ready to declare in any particular case of exaction made upon him or her. "I would do it, and do it willingly, if he didn't try to *make* me do it. Now I won't do it if I can help it." So, Teacher, let us *always* try to *work* by attraction, *never* by compulsion.

Another Caution in Training the Will.

Whenever you have shown the propriety of any particular course that you have requested or required; and much more, when you have shown that the opposite course is morally wrong, do not by any means, in a single case yield your claims to parleying, teasing or coaxing. Demonstrate, establish your firmness, your immoveable fixedness in your regard for your own convictions of right. Show your pupils in all such cases that your conscience is a sovereign power, and though they may not yield to your arguments or persuasions, do not, I beg, make yourself a partaker in any course of action that you have felt is wrong, and that you have characterized as such. One such case, however trivial, or however well explained away, diminishes the confidence of all in your moral integrity; and your moral and religious influence is very much weakened, if not entirely destroyed. How many a mother has ruined her wayward child by first forbidding, then arguing, then consenting, then apologizing for an act, rather, a long series of acts that the boy well knows his mother's judgment and conscience utterly condemn. His will gains increased energy for wrong every time he wins in such a conflict, and that mother can devise no more effectual method of training her darling's will to resist all reason and right, and make him the bound slave of appetite, than the one she is pursuing.

Now, Teacher, every time you win with a child, in helping him to assert the *power of will* in any right action, or course of action, that will is being more or less effectively trained into the habit of right action, and the easier will every successive victory become in the conflict with laziness or lust, not in school only, but in after life.

By a beautiful provision in our natures, the control of the will becomes less and less difficult in every effort till all difficulty is at length lost in a fixed habit of virtuous action in any given direction.

A Precaution in Training the Will.

You will never succeed in managing a bad boy if he has any suspicion that you are afraid of him, You *must* have his respect. If he thinks you are weak, or are a coward, you can not. Almost any such boy or young man is very likely, too, to interpret every act of conciliation on your part, into an admission of fear, or an exhibition of cowardice. This fact must be met decisively, or you will never succeed in subduing a rebel, and winning him to friendship.

Any such bad boy or young man is a bully, and of course a coward. He is easily intimidated, if not in a combination with others who are backing him; but he is not very easily won to anything that he thinks is tainted with right, and especially that kind of right which shows submission to a "school master." His only boast is in his meanness and hoggishness. This will continue as long as he can find anybody to listen to him and laugh at him. You discover, teacher, or very probably you will quite soon enough, that you have to break up the confederacy of bullyism in your school before you can have success with any particular ruffian, bully, coward or hog, for the same individual is all of these, and glories in it; and it's all the pride or ambition that he knows or feels.

The management of such cases is generally easy enough by the Normal method of commencing and organizing a school as given in the last lecture. This method in fact forestalls all such difficulties. They seldom or never make their appearance. The fact that you have the power of suspending any such hard cases until action of the Directors can be had, if judiciously used, will be one means to hold such dastardly spirits in check until you can win them by better measures.

II. How Shall Laws be Introduced?

They can *not* be well introduced, (1.) by authority of Directors; nor (2.) by authority and coercive power of the teacher. (3.) No law should be introduced when the teacher is in a special excitement from the disorder or insubordination of any particular pupil or pupils. Such a law could hardly have the assent or support of the majority of the governed, without which any law will prove an evil by provoking a general spirit of insubordination and rebellion. (4.) No law should be introduced till the majority of the school can see that it is necessary, and that their comfort and progress in the school can be improved by its enactment. (5.) The teacher must admit that the necessity for the introduction of any law as law, with its penalty, (for no law is of any force without its penalty) is but a confession at least to himself that he lacks the requisite personal influence and mental activity to control his school without law. Some other person might do it, but he can not. Still that teacher will prefer to secure order and good feeling by means of one or more definite laws and the enforcement of their penalties, than to permit disorder and lawlessness to prevail, thus losing the respect and confidence of his school altogether.

To illustrate a wrong and a right way of introducing a law, I shall give two examples of establishing a law against whispering or communication between pupils on study and recitation seats.

Example 1. *Establishing a Law.*

The teacher is engaged in the recitation of the primary Geography class, we will suppose. He is compelled frequently during the recitation to check the whispering of some of the older pupils in their study seats. They are studying together, or otherwise communicating, and some of the most influential pupils, are engaged in this form of disorder, regardless of the repeated request of the teacher that the pupils would each study by himself or herself, and not communicate even about their studies during study hours.

The recitation is at length laid aside, and the teacher, feeling very much annoyed, attempts to present the necessity of a law against whispering; speaks of the manner in which he has been interrupted, and says "the evil is increasing to such an extent that very much of the time and energy is diverted from the recitation, and thus no recitation is as interesting as it might be, if he were permitted to attend to it uninterruptedly." Now, is it not plain, that even if the teacher should without exhibiting any particular irritation, try to win the general assent of the school to such a law under such circumstances he would be likely to fail, at least, in arousing a general and hearty determination to stand by it, and carry it through? Why? Because some of the most influential pupils can not but feel that they are chargeable with the necessity of the law; they have provoked the teacher to say that he can not work any longer with so much interruption. Hence the co-operation of those whom you most desire to win, is but feeble, if given at all. Here is want of tact.

Example 2.—Establishing a Law.

Let us suppose the teacher is engaged in the recitation of the advanced Grammar class, that he is frequently interrupted by the communication and disorder of pupils in inferior grades, and thus he is compelled to stop his recitation over and over again, and give his attention to disorderly pupils in the study seats, and request them to be quiet, and each attend to his own study.

Now, if there has been any degree of interest excited in that branch, the members of the class will feel annoyed at these frequent interruptions. They see that their privileges are very much abridged, and they are sustaining a real and heavy loss by these interruptions. Now, if for the protection of this class of leading pupils in their recitation, as well as for the greater interest which may be imparted to the recitations of all the classes, provided they can go on without interruption, the necessity and advantage of a law against communication be presented, the hearty co-operation of all the more influential pupils can readily be secured. They do not now feel that the law is aimed particularly at them, and made for their especial restraint.

Under such circumstances, and with such management I have never found any difficulty in winning the vote of a large majority in favor of such a law.

Fixing a Penalty.

But the next thing is the penalty; for no prohibitory law can be effective without a penalty. In fact, a prohibitory law without a penalty is worse than no law, for it soon brings itself and all other law into contempt.

The penalty should be as light and as gentle as can be selected, and yet be recognized as a penalty. A severe penalty is difficult to enforce, and when enforced always excites the sympathy of the governed towards the offender rather than feeling against him for breaking the law.

Neither will it answer for the teacher to use his discretion in imposing or withholding the penalty. It must work with inevitable certainty, or the hope of escape is but an incitement to infraction of the law. The best general penalty I have been able to devise for violation of school law is privation of recess, by the pupil's retaining his seat and communicating with no one during recess.

I would secure a full and hearty vote if practicable for this penalty, while the matter of the law is under discussion, and I would also state that "any pupil who is deprived of his recess can be out if he desire it two minutes after the recess, but only one pupil can be out at a time." I can readily see, Teachers, that you can raise various objections to this plan so briefly stated for introducing a law or a series of laws. But the necessity of having the full and hearty assent and co-operation of the large majority of a school in sustaining any law or code of laws, is manifest if you would have a Normal method of government. To my mind any government based on force and executed without the consent of the large majority of the governed is abnormal, is tyranny; and so far as school or college government is concerned can work nothing but evil. If any have lived as pupils under such law and have derived advantage from the school or college whose government was carried on by force and suspicion, the advantage was derived in spite of the government and not as a result of it.

Enacted Law an Alternative, and the Least of two Evils.

I have said that the necessity for law or a code of laws, is an admission of personal and strategic weakness; and even if any school or college is held in subjection by law, and good order is maintained by the vigorous executive ability of the Principal or President; and the rigorous imposition of penalties does crush down all disorder and insubordination; and even though this course produces high per cents in lessons for the time being; still, any such government is with the majority of students pernicious in its moral influence, and just so far as vigilance is exercised in ferreting out offenders and penalties applied to correct offences, just so far is any such government feeble and inoperative in fixing good principles and good habits in the hearts and lives of the governed, whether offenders or not. In every such instance force is used for want of personal influence and moral power, but in no case is it an equivalent.

Some years since a change of Principals occurred in the Baldwin Institute. Some two or three months after the change, the wife of one of the trustees, coming to the Founder, John Baldwin, says, "Bro. Baldwin, don't you think it was a mercy that we secured Bro. Harris when we did; the Teacher that resigned would never have been able to govern these bad boys, and high-strung young men that are here now. It takes Bro. Harris to control them. They are afraid of him, and they have to behave. He puts his foot on their necks and they daren't say a word. By expelling the three that he did he has made the rest a good deal more orderly and decent." Bro. Baldwin replied, "Our former Principal was here nine years and built up our school. He never had any bad scholars all the time he was here, and if he had remained nine years longer he never would have had any occasion to punish any wicked young men, or expel them from his school."

In about a year that former teacher was offered an increased salary to resume his place in the school by a unanimous vote of the Trustees.

Co-operation of Directors.

In my last lecture I urged the necessity of securing the consent of the Directors to decide the case of any pupil that you were unable to manage.

If the promise of such co-operation be obtained, and the power thus secured be judiciously made known to a school, it will in most cases prevent any necessity for its use. But if you are compelled, Teacher, to acknowledge to yourself that your own resources are insufficient, it will be better that you avail yourself of the aid of your Directors, in deciding whether the rebellious pupil shall prevail, or your own authority.

I would never call the Directors, nor any one of them into the school-house during school hours, to settle any difficulty, nor would I threaten anything of the kind. If you call the Directors once, you will soon find it necessary to call them again. Your own authority is at an end.

But when every expedient has failed and you feel that you can no longer exercise patience and kindness, toward the wayward pupil or pupils, and that to do so would imperil the farther progress, and final success of the school, it will then be necessary to suspend the pupil till a meeting of the Directors can be called to decide the case. If the pupil should refuse to comply with my decision of suspension I should proceed as if he were not present; if he should undertake to make disturbance, I should quell it or dismiss the school until the matter could be settled. If the Directors after a fair hearing of the case from both parties with witnesses and parents should decide me incompetent to carry on the school, of course this would end the matter. But if they should decide otherwise, and expel the disorderly pupil, I should request the pupil to return and make proper acknowledgements, and assure him that I was willing and anxious to aid him in studies and to do him any favor in my power.

This in my opinion is the only legitimate method of using the personal and legal authority of the Directors. But while a resort to the Directors is better than the use of personal violence on pupils, and is now the only alternative by which you can retain any order or decency in the school, it would be a self degradation that any truly noble and generous nature would resort to as a terrible necessity, and the very last expedient.

Sympathy of Pupils for or against a Law.

When a law has been enacted, the administration of that law must be carried on with certainty and yet with moderation. It is a very easy thing to make a good law odious by any rigor that may seem unnecessary to the majority; it is still easier to make a law inoperative and a butt of ridicule by setting aside the penalty from any plea or pretext that may be offered by the offender. I would take no excuses. The teacher has no time to weigh excuses. In fact it is to be understood, so far as possible, that every violation of school law is a matter of thoughtlessness rather than evil design, and is thus the pupil's misfortune rather than his crime; but that the penalty is annexed to train the individual to better habits of care and thoughtfulness, rather than to extort damages. Taking this view, a penalty is suffered with much better effect on the individual, and without arousing the antagonism or exciting the sympathy of his school fellows. Any spirit of vindictiveness in carrying out a law, will most surely make the law a source of increasing evil.

Suppose the teacher, when he had secured a law by a unanimous vote of all interested, should virtually take this course in its administration, and his actions if not his words should seem to say to his pupils, "Now I've got you; you have made me trouble enough, and now you are cornered, and I am going to straighten out the last one of you."

The power that made the law can easily unmake it, at least, in effect, and the teacher thus applying the law as a seeming means of obtaining revenge would soon find that the law would make his vindictiveness more obnoxious to criticism and resistance than if he had not resorted to a vote of the pupils for the enactment of a law. The pupils would have reason to feel that they had been entrapped, and that they had just cause for indignation and rebellion.

The great and prevalent error, however, in school and college management is the enactment of various laws, which being necessary for a few, place uncalled-for restraint on the many, and thus most surely arouse the sympathy of the better class of pupils towards the worst offenders, whenever they fall under rebuke. Such unnecessary laws, then, not only do no good in restraining the vicious, but, in many cases, they positively excite the good to violate them and thus bring all law into disrepute; and the offenders are generally considered and treated by their fellow pupils as martyrs and heroes. In no particular, do these remarks hold true more disastrously on the morals and habits of students, than in that of rigid laws to prevent social intercourse between the sexes.

Thus, these most energetic forces for mental and moral improvement, the very means provided by nature and society for making our educational establishments most effective instrumentalities for cultivating the chivalry of manhood and the graces of womanhood, are so perverted by this spirit of barbarism and monasticism still clinging to the management of nearly all our colleges and academies as to make them the constant theatres of repressed disorder or open lawlessness, and the very training schools for iniquitous indulgence of every appetite, passion and lust.

Is it any wonder that so many young men graduated or expelled from colleges, make speedy final wrecks of themselves, trained as they are by such a system to view law and order as their natural enemies, and the gratification of their passions as their chief boast and their only desirable aim?

Teachers, beware that your well meant efforts to check and subdue evil practices do not train the will irrecoverably into determined resistance to every principle of right, simply because it is right.

III. Normal Methods for Introducing and Sustaining the Law of Right.

1. *Exciting Interest in Studies.*

The first general idea in sustaining the law of right, in other words, living free from all positive enacted laws, save the general arrangements proposed and explained by the teacher at the organization of the school, and modified from time to time as the progress of the school shall seem to require, is that the interest excited in the recitations and carried through the study hours must furnish full and attractive employment for all the pupils, and that they will be so much absorbed in the legitimate business of their studies and recitations, that idleness, mischief and disorder find no time or place in the school. It may also be added that in order to excite and sustain this interest, the most earnest devotion of the teacher to his work is indispensable; and yet more, a decided and positive personal regard and affection for every pupil must be evinced both in class work and in social intercourse, and especially whenever remonstrance or reproof is found to be necessary. These should, if possible, always be given in private, in order to show the pupil that you regard his feelings, and take that course in correcting an evil which shall give him the least annoyance and pain.

2. *Exciting Enterprise for Higher Excellence.*

In the great disparity that must always exist in every class, both in natural and acquired ability, it becomes necessary to provide full occupation for the most willing and the most capable. This is done by assigning special topics, in addition to the regular lesson, as has before been explained. It will be found a valuable aid to the pupil if you can discriminate in regard to the excellence of his recitation, not merely as to his knowledge of the lesson, but as to his power of explaining or demonstrating any principle, proposition or rule.

I am accustomed, as you well know, to distinguish the different degrees of explaining power by recognizing three grades, thus:

Grades of Explaining Power.

(1.) That degree of clearness which convinces the teacher that the pupil has studied the particular subject in hand thoroughly, and has mastered it so far as patient study of the text-book would enable him to do it.

(2.) That degree of clearness and energy of expression which will make the subject matter plain to any of the best pupils who have not studied the same matter.

(3.) That degree of clearness and tact in explaining any point, that will make it plain to the dullest member of the class, and impart to him a thorough understanding of the matter.

The full and hearty recognition of these different degrees of power, (*a*) in analysis, (*b*) in synthesis, (*c*) in expression, (*d*) in illustration, as evinced by every pupil in his recitation, will arouse a growing spirit of enterprise for higher excellence and more beautiful results, (1.) in thoroughness in mastering subjects, (2) in fluency and propriety, (3) in the expression of ideas, (4) in aptitude of illustration (5) in winning and holding attention, that will prove highly exciting to leading pupils, and very profitable to the entire class.

The ambition of the pupils will be stimulated to relieve the teacher from the necessity of taking up time in explanation, and so giving the entire opportunity and advantages of the recitation to the pupils, both as learners and teachers. That teacher who can thus make himself the least needed for explanation and demonstration, in other words who can contrive to teach the least, is really the teacher who teaches the most and best. He is the nearest approach to my ideal of the Model Teacher.

3. *Requiring no More nor Less of Any Class or of any Pupil in a Class than it or he can Cheerfully Accomplish.*

It requires no small amount of watchfulness and tact to meet the different degrees of ability, advancement and energy of the different pupils in a class, Perhaps the best plan for accomplishing this is to section a class, giving different labor in the same lesson to each section. To one who has never tried this plan, nor ever seen it work, I confess it may seem beset with difficulties, but we are accustomed to make the plan work here, in all our classes, where we choose to apply it, with entire success; and I first began working on this plan in my geography classes in the first school I ever taught. It was a country district school. I will not here describe the plan nor the workings of a sectioned class, but will close this lecture in giving a little of my experience in that school which may be pertinent to this division of my subject, viz: not to require more nor less than pupils can do cheerfully, and yet with full employment.

I had an Arithmetic class of, perhaps, twelve pupils from thirteen to fifteen years of age. They were, as to ability, an average class of boys and girls. They had been as badly taught as most such classes are. They were unable to give a single reason for any process required in Arithmetic, or in any other subject.

I thought I would try to have them understand the rules of Arithmetic, at least. So I commenced with that determination; and as I thought gave very good and very clear demonstrations of every point in every rule, and then in turn required them to give the reasons for the several processes. But the class instead of becoming interested, were more and more restive and disinclined to study or recite. After two weeks of pretty thorough discouragement on my part, I concluded something must be wrong. In reflecting on the matter, I said to myself, "The fault is not in the subject; Arithmetic can surely be made interesting if any thing can; the fault is not in the class; it is as good a class as is often found in a common school. The fault must be in me, and in my management. It is just this, I am *forcing* reasons upon the children. I will try another plan to-morrow." The next day as the class were engaged in Division of Compound Numbers, I requested them to work the examples by the rule, and carefully withheld all explanations. This went on till the class succeeded in following the rule, and working the examples by it.

At the next recitation, as the class were occupied with one of the most difficult examples given under that rule in Adams' Arithmetic, and at a certain point, they had failed to follow the rule, a little, black-eyed Helen earnestly inquired: "Why do we have to bring that down there? I don't understand it." "O, never mind," said I, "the book says so." "But you told us we ought to understand why we do it." "Well, it will get the answer, wont it, if you do as the rule tells you?" "Yes, sir; I suppose so, but I don't understand it." "Perhaps you will, after a while, if you work the example correctly by the rule." Here a curly-headed fellow, turning his head around back of the class, whispered to the one that sat near him, "I don't believe he understands it himself."

I thought it about time, now, as the spirit of inquiry was aroused, and somewhat at my expense, to give the explanation of the point in question. I had learned how to manage my class, and thenceforth had no difficulty in securing all the attention and study desirable.

Teachers, never force your wares on the market, but make a demand for them, if possible; then you can sell them at your own price.

LECTURE ON SCHOOL MANAGEMENT.

LECTURE XVI.

DISCIPLINE.—INCENTIVES.

PRELIMINARY REMARKS.

1. *The Term Discipline Explained.*

The term Discipline is often taken in a broad sense, including all the appliances, studies and exercises of the student's life. In its more contracted sense, it is applied to the *correction* of particular errors and faults. I use the term here more in the sense of preventing and correcting bad habits, than of correcting and punishing special delinquencies in diligence and order. In this lecture I shall give an enumeration and brief description of the regular and definite means to be kept in constant daily operation to secure diligent and earnest study, as well as interesting and profitable recitations. These means to be discussed in this lecture I denominate Incentives, as their entire design is to act in harmony with the desires of the pupil, to excite and energize his will to pleasurable effort, to healthful and determined exertion.

2. *Tendencies to be Guarded Against.*

(1) It is not my purpose to give you any school machinery that will go itself; and I wish to guard you against presuming that I claim any such power for Normal methods of discipline. No, if I knew of any such machinery that you could put to work in the school-room thinking it would exempt you from hard work and earnest endeavor, I would reject it as worse than useless. You can never obtain good work from pupils, and establish good habits in their characters without yourself leading in the work, in obedience to the habits you desire to establish in them.

(2) You must guard against the tendency to routine; the best means and methods conceivable lose all force and excellence when gone through with mechanically, by rote. The means which I propose are of such a character, designedly, as to require constant inspiration in carrying them out. Any thing like rote in their application will convert them into a nuisance. Why? Rote is laziness; but laziness and Normal methods are contradictory to each other.

(3) You must guard against too great rigor, oppressive precision and exacting demand, with well-meaning, kindly-disposed, yet careless and thoughtless children. It is very easy to convert thoughtlessness into willfulness. If you are not particularly watchful in your anxiety to secure perfect order, and industrious application, you will interpret some thoughtless neglect, or heedless act, as intentional disregard of your wishes, and thus make that child your enemy. Better interpret ten intentional misdeeds as instances of thoughtlessness, than one thoughtless act as designedly wicked. Your error in the former case is recognized as that of charity and good will; in the latter case of harshness and spite.

(4) You must guard against too great laxness, such as will be attributed to indifference or want of sufficient discrimination; or, again, that easy, slip shod kind of good-nature which lets every thing take its own way, and everybody do as he pleases. Above all things, you must keep up to your programme, especially in Recesses and Dismissions.

Do not permit yourself to use the time of recess for purposes of discipline; take the time rather from recitations. I would like to have you tell me three reasons why this latter course is the best. How many can give them?

3. *Sine Qua Non.*

The Normal methods of school management require first, last and always, a spirit of thrift, of satisfaction and pride in the work, an unflagging desire to please and be pleased, on the part of the teacher. This spirit is the very soul of all incentives; yes, of all penalties also, and without it nothing can be done NORMALLY in the way of School Discipline.

INCENTIVES, AND HOW TO APPLY THEM.

I. PROPER INCENTIVES.

1. For Pupils Who are Sufficiently Advanced to Study Their Lessons.

1. In Recitations.

(1) *Preliminary Drill.*—In previous lectures I have described and exemplified preliminary drill and characterized it as the most necessary part of a recitation, and as that which requires more skill than all else. It is too generally neglected altogether.

(2) *Approbation in Recitation.*—If the teacher seek for every opportunity to find something to approve in the performance of every backward and dull pupil, he can not fail to win the confidence of that pupil, and he will soon be found doing his best, since he has found some one who does not think him a dunce or a brute. He has found in you a friend, and your partiality, in spite of his awkwardness, backwardness and many defects can not fail to win his gratitude and affection. He will try to please you as he never tried to do any good thing before. On the other hand, how easy it is to discourage and alienate even a good pupil, to make him indifferent and contrary, if he once feels that you are watching for opportunities to find fault, and to be sharp at his expense.

(3.) *Marking the Standing.* I am aware that the "marking system" as it is called, is decried by some of our leading teachers, that it was recently voted out of Williams College by the students. But the objections lie against the abuse of the system rather than against the system itself. If marking is used *chiefly* as punishment and as a means of checking rowdyism, and intimidating roughs in school or college, it ought to be squelched as a nuisance, for it can only increase these evils. But if the Teacher grades his pupils *chiefly* for their encouragement, and they really feel that this is his design, they accept of it as a worthy and effective stimulus, and heartily avail themselves of its power, to hold them to a good purpose, to help them in fixing good habits. In large classes it becomes necessary to mark each pupil called on for an exercise in recitation, that none may be slighted, unless the teacher pursues the same order at every recitation, which ought not to be done, of course. Hence, marking the character of the effort made by each pupil, with regard to thoroughness of preparation, readiness of utterance, skill of explication, facility of illustration, or any other point that he may wish to make prominent at any given time, or with any particular individual, is a matter of no additional labor or inconvenience. The class or the individual should of course be previously apprised of the particular point or points on which the grading is to be given.

Grading bestowed in this manner, and always with the purpose of encouragement, I have ever found to give excellent results, especially with the more backward or indolent, in study, in recitation, in good feeling; last not least. Nor have I ever known pupils to object to the plan, and in but very few instances has any pupil objected to his own grade.

2. In Roll-calling.

In many large schools the labor and time required for roll-call are abridged by various contrivances. I prefer to take time to call a roll every morning, and in most cases, every evening. The advantages of calling a roll more than compensate for the time, if the thing is managed well.

(1.) *Without Enacted Law.* The kindly respectful tone of

voice used by a Normal teacher in calling each pupil by name, and the corresponding feeling evinced in the responses more than compensate. Then, if you wish to have pupils give the number of minutes tardy, or any other special report in their responses, as a means of helping themselves and each other in any specified direction, roll-calling may be made especially serviceable in obviating the necessity of any positive law.

(2.) *With Enacted Law.* When any law is enacted, as that of 'no communication,' roll-calling at evening as well as morning becomes almost a necessity, in order that each pupil may give his own report of his compliance or non-compliance with the law or laws established.

3. In Self-reporting at each Recess or at Dismission.

No point in school discipline has been so much discussed, and yet with such utter variance of opinion as that of self-reporting. Its opponents aver that it puts a premium on lying, and trains children to deceit; that it is evil, only evil, and evil continually. Its advocates as confidently affirm that the practice, when well managed,is the most effective means to break up the habit of falsehood, and to establish the love of truth, and the habit of fair dealing, not only in the school government, but in the very heart and life of the large majority of the pupils.

It is not difficult for me to account for this striking discrepancy of opinion. I have noticed that those who favor the plan of self-reporting, are in their management kind, genial, hopeful, confiding and honest; and those who most denounce the plan are better known as *rigid* disciplinarians, and of course, they are exacting, suspicious, and cold-hearted. Such teachers will train children to hypocrisy by any method, and I am not slow to admit that self-reporting is the worst *they* can adopt.

Normal Method of Self-reporting Described.

The pupils are supposed to be called on at regular periods, each to report his own compliance with the established law or laws, or the violation of it or them. I will assume that the law established is that of 'no communication.' It is understood that the law has been successfully inaugurated by a vote of a large majority of the school. Now, to make this law work successfully, and win popular favor, till *all* shall cheerfully comply with it, is the object. I shall endeavor to show, as briefly as may be, how this can be done; rather, how it has been done, in numerous instances.

The law is, no communication by any conceivable means; *i. e.*, no intentional communication of thought or feeling among the pupils. All communication must go on through the teacher. If the law only forbids whispering, there is the writing of notes; and if it excludes this also, then there are innumerable other methods of communication which take more contrivance and time. So, the only rule that will do any good is

NO INTENTIONAL COMMUNICATION BETWEEN PUPILS.

In order to make the law work as pleasantly as possible, it is well to give the pupils an opportunity to report frequently. I have found that reporting every hour works the best. To this end, and for many other reasons, I prefer to have short recesses at the end of every hour, rather than one longer recess every half day. I wish you would report to-morrow three good and sufficient reasons why short recesses every hour are preferable to one longer recess each half day.

When the signal is given, by the bell, for books to be laid aside, and arranged on the desks; and this has been accomplished, I inquire, "How many perfect?" As many as are raise the hand. It is understood by previous explanation that all who have not violated the law, will report "perfect." Then I inquire, "How many imperfect." Any one who has violated, then raises his hand. Thus, in a moment, the report is taken. If I choose to record the vote, I can do it on my general register, as I shall describe hereafter, almost before the report is given. It is understood that all who report perfect are entitled to their recess, and those who report imperfect will sit at their desks during recess, and hold communication with no one, unless the teacher should require it. The teacher has no time to hear excuses, nor to deliberate on them. Excuses form no part of the programme, either in the violation of this rule or in the matter of tardiness. If you tolerate excuses either verbal or written you will have little time for anything else. Excuses are the bane of good action, and the pupil who is good at excuses is good for nothing else. As I have before said, let every violation of rule or instance of tardiness be considered rather in the light of a misfortune or accident; and thus the penalty is not regarded so much designed to punish the vicious, as a gentle stimulus, intended to quicken the watchfulness and foresight of the good, in order that such misfortunes and accidents may occur as rarely as possible. Thus the operation of this law, managed in this manner will contribute most effectually to the breaking up of the bad habits of carelessness, thoughtlessness and excuses, and to the establishing of the permanent habits of foresight and promptitude, honest work and cheerful endeavor, worthy ambition and noble aspiration.

Caution in Carrying out the Rule of Non-communication.

You will be plied with the request, 'May I speak,' from every quarter, as soon as this rule is adopted. My caution is, do not permit yourself to yield to the request under any circumstances, do not even tolerate the request, "May I speak." It is the utter defeat of all good order and diligence in a school. It is death to all honest effort. Out with the nuisance. Rather, forestall its entrance.

But in order that a pupil may not suffer from want of a pencil, or a book, or from not knowing what his lesson is, introduce this practice thus:

Any scholar may call the attention of the teacher at any time by raising his hand. Let the pupil then state his want definitely, and the teacher will give his whole attention to the matter until the want or desire is properly met. This of course is done at the expense of the class engaged in recitation, but the very fact that the recitation is interrupted in all such cases, is the best preventive to the too frequent recurrence of the causes of such interruption.

The honor and generosity of every pupil are thus appealed to, and interruptions of this kind will happen less and less frequently. Pupils will suffer considerable inconvenience and loss rather than call on the teacher to provide paper, pencil, book, or anything of the kind. Rather, they will learn to see beforehand that they have all these things in readiness, and they learn thus to cultivate the *habits* of care, foresight and generosity.

In case of violations of law during the last hour of forenoon or afternoon sessions, the offender remains seated two minutes after the dismission, as the penalty for the violation.

In case of reporting for tardiness, the number of minutes tardy in the morning may be given at noon, and the number of minutes tardy in the afternoon may be given at roll-calling at night.

4. In Daily Reporting.

Pupils also report at night on their compliance with enacted law during the day, thus: if a pupil's hourly reports have been 'perfect' for the entire six hours of the day he reports 'five,' if he has been 'imperfect' one hour during the day he reports 'four,' and diminishes one for every hourly imperfect report. The report 'one' or 'zero' will then denote an unfortunate day, indeed; and the frequent recurrence of such misfortunes in the case of any pupil may call for additional ways and means in his behalf. But of this hereafter. Then reports as given by the pupils in answer to roll-call are of course recorded, when given, on the general register.

If disorder is somewhat prevalent, and the teacher thinks it necessary, he can make a record of the hourly reports of imperfect, by a pencil dot in the day's space for the pupil on the register. But this will seldom be necessary. The teacher can generally remember the hourly reports well enough to determine the accuracy or honesty of the daily report any individual pupil may give.

5. Encouragement by Weekly Reports.

Weekly reports of each pupil may be given, (*a*) orally, at the close of the week, to the school; or (*b*) on Monday, they may be sent on Weekly Report Cards to the parents for their examination and signature.

These weekly reports are the sums or averages of the daily reports, recorded on the general register. Some teachers may prefer to keep special class registers for each class, or grade register for each grade; but I have always made the general register answer all purposes. I will show you by a diagram how this is effected, with the use of any common School Register. I give in the diagram a week's record for four boys.

		Mon.		Tues.		Wed.		Thu.		Fri.	
		— 2		4 3	— 10	—	—	3	9 0	5 4	13
Samuel Smith.	Gr. Ge.			2	1			2	1	2	1
	Ar. Sp.	1	2					3	7		2
		5		5		5		5		5	
Jesse Holden!	Gr. Ge.	4	5	4	5	1	3	3	4	4	2
	Ar. Sp.	5	5	5	5	5	2	4	5	6	5
		5		$\overline{4}$		5		4		4	
John Harris!	Gr. Bk.	4	4	4	4	5	5	5	5	5	6
	Ar. Sp.	4	3	3	$\overline{4}$	5	5	5	5	5	5
		5		5		5		5		5	
Alfred Holmes.	Gr. Bk.	5	5	5	5	5	5	5	5	5	5
	Ar. Sp.	5	5	5	5	5	5	5	5	5	5

This record includes (1) number of half days absent; (2) number of times tardy; (3) number of minutes tardy; (4) Deportment; (5) grades in four studies.

You will notice, I give two horizontal lines to each pupil. In the upper parallelogram I keep the record ot presence or absence, by drawing with my pencil a line from the left side to the center, for absence in the forenoon; and from the center to the right side, for absence in the afternoon; and a line through the center from side to side for absence all day. The number of minutes tardy is recorded in the upper half of the upper parallelogram. The reports for decorum or compliance with established law or laws is recorded in the lower half of the upper parallelogram. These reports are the same as given by the pupils as before described in daily reports.

Thus the upper parallelogram contains the record of the the first four items as given in the enumeration, while the lower parallelogram is used for grading in four studies. The wide space immediately after the names is used as a key to the marking of each pupil's standing in his several studies. The four corners of the lower parallelogram of each pupil for each day are used as the corresponding four corners indicate in the key, or large parallelogram marked as before mentioned. In case any pupil is absent one or more half days in a week, he is allowed merit marks in decorum and recitations in making up his weekly report equal to his average in the same particulars during the days present. I give on the following page a copy of a weekly report card:

It is designed that each self-reporting pupil shall have a card. Each card is enclosed in an envelope with the pupil's name superscribed. The Teacher fills up these cards each Saturday, writing the sums of the daily reports in their respective places on the card.

These cards, properly filled out, are handed to the pupils on Monday evening. It is expected that they will take them home, that the parents will examine them, and one of them will affix his or her name in the appropriate space. The cards will be returned the first time the pupil comes to school.

If any card is dropped by the way, a new envelope can be furnished; if any card is lost, a new card can be made out.

Advantages of Weekly Report Cards.

(1.) They secure *co-operation of parents*, as no other plan can.

(2.) They *prevent false reports* from scholars to parents, and untruthful statements of detentions by the parents.

(3.) They thus secure *regular attendance;*

(4.) And aid in *preventing tardiness.*

(5.) They aid in inciting to *earnest study;*

(6.) And in securing *good behavior* in school.

(7.) If successful otherwise, they are found to excite a healthy spirit of emulation in all the different exercises of school.

*TEACHER'S WEEKLY REPORT

OF THE SCHOLARSHIP AND DEPORTMENT OF

....

Commencing..., 18............

Weeks.	½ days ab sent.	Times Tardy.	Minutes Tardy.	Deport-ment.					Parents will aid the teacher much by visiting the school often. Please come often.
1									
2									
3									
4									
5									
6									
7									
8									
9									
10									
11									
12									
13									

In the teacher's daily record of grade for deportment, and for each study, 5=perfect, 4=good, 3=fair, 2=poor, 1=bad, 0 signifies a misdemeanor or failure. Hence, the highest grade for deportment, or for only one study, is 25. The 0's in the upper part of the spaces, signify the number of failures or misdemeanors for the week.

☞The parent will please examine this report and sign his or her name in the blank space opposite to the last report given.

....Teacher.

*The form of card here given is much wider than the card really used, as that is the size of an ordinary envelope.

Objections to the Use of Weekly Report Cards.

(1.) They cost two cents for each pupil.

(2.) It takes time and labor to make them out every Saturday.

(3.) Parents may refuse to sign them, or, indeed, may be unable to sign them, and thus they may excite opposition to the teacher.

(4.) Pupils may not show them to their parents, and get some other person to sign the parent's name.

(5.) Some of the pupils may think themselves too old to report to parents, and, indeed, it may not be best to require it.

I leave it to the ingenious and faithful teacher to overcome these objections and others that may arise. They are used in hundreds, thousands of schools and are made to work well, though I do not claim that they will prove a success in all hands. Nothing else will.

No teacher should rely on weekly report cards for his success. There must be industry, earnestness, foresight, contrivance, tact, superadded to all the other qualifications described in the first five lectures of this course; then weekly report cards for a time at least will pay, and pay well.

Incentives for Pupils who do not Study Lessons. D Grade.

As this method of hourly, daily, and weekly reporting would be inappropriate and useless for children who can not yet interest themselves in studying lessons, it will be better to adopt the 'reward of merit' system with the abcdarians, and, perhaps, also with those reading in the first reader.

The Atwater tickets work very well with this class of children; but I prefer the plan which I introduced in the first school I ever taught, over thirty years ago. It is simply this, and I shall denominate it

Normal Method of Inciting Abcdarians to Good Conduct and Love of school.

Procure some good thick fools-cap paper, also a blue, and a red pencil, or crayons. You can now with some little ingenuity and taste make any number of pretty tickets, with blue borders and red fillings, of such words as, 'excellent,' 'meritorious,' etc. One of these tickets may be given to each pupil of the D grade every night, provided he merits it by good behavior; in other words, has given the teacher no special trouble during the day. By the way, I would not insist on 'non-communication' for this class of pupils, and yet a certain kind and degree of order must be preserved, so much as that they do not interrupt the recitations and study of older pupils. The only penalty such pupils will ever need, if the teacher has any skill in teaching them is to deprive them of the privilege of "saying their lessons," and thus, in course, of their tickets to take home at night.

When any child has received five of these reward tickets, he can bring them back, and the teacher will give him a little primer, to keep for his own. The teacher will write on it or in it the name of the pupil, the number of the prize, and the date. The child will be able to read that primer through, in most cases, before he comes to school next morning. Such primers can be bought by the gross for about a half a cent each. When a pupil has received five of these small primers, he may be entitled to a larger or two cent primer. Thus it is possible for every child to win two large primers in one session of three months.

You will perhaps foresee a difficulty in dividing the school for these two methods of management, the self-reporting and reward of merit plans. The following suggestion may be serviceable. The first reader class or C grade, (see programme, last lecture), may be placed in either system as you may think best, or as they may prefer. They will generally prefer to be ranked among the self-reporters. If any pupil in the C grade, gives too much trouble on this plan, for a few days, he may be placed under the lower plan. That is, since he is unable to take care of himself in the self-reporting system, the teacher will have to take care of him as he does of the other little fellows, and he will probably need a special seat to make the care of the teacher over him more convenient.

Rolls of Honor.

It is very helpful, sometimes, as a stimulus to good order and promptitude, to have a roll of honor for all who comply with the law or laws through a given time—say a week. This roll of honor may be placed in a frame with a glass front, and, if it is somewhat embellished, all the better. The effect is much heightened if pupils are consulted before it is introduced. There can hardly be any opposition to the plan from any one. On the other hand, the whole school will welcome the plan, if proposed with any degree of kindness and skill. It may also be proposed that the names of all who are thus enrolled nine-tenths of the weeks during a longer period—say a term or a year—shall be inscribed on a permanent Roll of Honor, in a fine gilt frame, to be left hanging in the school-room, or in any other place that the pupils may designate.

Several teachers have reported that this plan has worked well in connection with other incentives. It is generally applied to the rules of no communication and no tardiness, and is well calculated to promote an honorable regard for these essentials in good management, and a cheerful and earnest desire on the part of *all* to maintain these laws.

If there is a paper published in the village, it may be well to have the roll of honor published once a month, or once a term.

II. Improper Incentives.

1. *Prizes.*

Though the prize system is almost universal, especially in colleges, I can see nothing but evil in it.

The first wrong it inflicts is on those who are superior by nature or by previous training, and who, of course need no such stimulus. All such are incited to use their advantage, and that which is of itself an act of meanness, is sanctioned and sanctified by the fact that the prize is offered by the highest authorities.

All such as are superior to others *ought in honor* to withdraw from the contest.

Is it not mean for a six-footer to crush a five-footer, or in any way to provoke a personal conflict?

Thus, any one can see that a very mean pride is excited in those who consciously have a decided advantage in contending for any school prize.

The second wrong is inflicted on those who are consciously inferior. All such need the stimulus,perhaps, but instead of the prize acting as an incentive, it most thoroughly discourages them. They soon abandon all effort, not only to win the prize but to attain to any degree of excellence. They are disgusted, and well they may be.

The 'head and foot' arrangement in the management of a class works the same way, and should never be tolerated under any circumstances in any study, recitation or exercise whatever.

There is one exception to this general statement,that prizes are improper incentives. This is in a penmanship class. By offering a prize to the one who improves the most, and not to the one who writes the best, the evils before mentioned may be avoided. The poorest writers are most stimulated because they obviously have the best opportunity to make the most improvement. This plan of managing a penmanship class will be given at some other time and place.

2. *Exemption from Study.*

While I consider the imposition of extra study, as the silliest and wickedest of all penalties, the offer of exemption from study as a reward is so nearly akin to the penalty in its effects, that it comes under the same condemnation.

The effect of it is to impress on the mind and character of the pupil, the idea that work is a burden and an evil, and that the highest honor and enjoyment is in avoiding it.

How does this tally with a purpose to make work attractive and industry honorable? How can *any* desirable *habit* be established in the school room, while such practices make work odious, by imposing it as a punishment, and idleness honorable by offering it as a reward for extra exertion.?

I would rather strive to reverse this order of affairs and give extra work as an incentive, and impose privation of work as a penalty.

Teacher, with the true spirit of your calling, this can be done. It has been done. You will at least aim for such a state of feeling and habit, in your school. Do not be satisfied till you attain it.

With these views, I deprecate half holidays, holidays, and believe that vacations are a nuisance, and should be abated as far as possible.

It grieves me when I find my pupils are counting the number of days before the term expires. Rather would I have them express regrets that the term or the school is so soon to end. Such a state of feeling, Teacher, is worth working for, and may be held as a *proper incentive* to incite you to the utmost kindness and efficiency in your school management.

3. *Monitors and Spies.*

If the use of monitors or spies has ever been resorted to as a stimulus to promote good conduct or diligent study, it is its own condemnation. Nothing in the whole range of human contrivance could be better calculated to promote determined and habitual shirking and shamming, mean expedients and shallow pretexts, than the knowledge that one is watched and treated as a knave and a wretch beyond the pale of confidence or hope.

Is it any wonder, that tricks on the teacher or professor are the order of the day—of the night rather—that hazing and cutting, are beyond control, in colleges and academies, when spies are employed and *proctors* or '*governors*' are watching round to keep order?

The teacher who resorts to such a method of school government ought to have his chair legs sawn nearly in two, ought to be 'barred out' most effectually. Such a teacher will do immensely more hurt than good in any school.

4. *Excuses.*

I hardly suppose you would place excuses in the category of incentives, at all; but I have found they may operate when received or tolerated as the worst form of incentive to miserable habits of lying and laziness, unthrift and depravity.

I would not receive excuses in any form oral or written. In any shape, they are an abomination, and can work only evil results to the pupil who offers them, to the general workings of the school, and to your character as a teacher. So, I beg, that you make no provision for excuses; give them no countenance, no toleration.

LECTURE ON SCHOOL MANAGEMENT.

LECTURE XVII.

DISCIPLINE.—PENALTIES.

PRELIMINARY REMARKS.

MY FRIENDS:

The subject for our consideration this morning, Penalties, I approach with more reluctance and, possibly, misgiving than any other in the whole range of our school work. Yet, as God has established a system of punishments as well as of rewards in his all-fatherly government, we may not expect with our limited capacities to be able to lay aside that which the Infinite has deemed necessary for the well being of all his children.

But our Heavenly Father always punishes in love, to save the offender, and, through the suffering of any one, to make better many more and thus protect from injury themselves and others. Here, then, is our Key Note.

Precautions.

(1.) We will not punish in haste, but with all long suffer ing, will win if possible, by gentler means.

(2.) We will not punish in anger, and thus more effectually alienate those whom we have failed to win by incentives.

(3.) We will not use such methods of punishment as will give unnecessary physical pain or mental distress.

(4.) We will not punish, expecting to *force* pupils into good conduct, but if at all, to restrain them from bad conduct.

(5.) We will not punish by imposing any school duty or exercise, as a punishment; and by this means make that duty or exercise and all others burdensome and hateful.

(6.) We will not punish by making the school-house a prison and ourselves the jailors.

(7.) We will not punish simply to vindicate our own consistency. It is better to violate our word when we find ourselves wrong, than to demonstrate our regard for the truth by committing a greater wrong.

General Tenor of Judicious Punishment.

(1.) Copying, as far as we are able, the great Original we will adapt the penalty to the offence.

In the human constitution if the eyes are abused they suffer, if the stomach is gorged it is compelled to rest. The nerves of the skin are not made to smart for every misuse of every other part of the system.

(2.) We will delay punishment until the majority of the school shall consider the teacher the suffering party, and sympathy shall be on his side, rather than on that of the offender.

(3.) We will so administer the punishment as not to turn the tide of sympathy in favor of the offender, and thus render the punishment a greater bar to our success than the offence it is designed to remedy.

For the convenience of discussion I shall classify Penalties into Proper and Improper.

I. PROPER PENALTIES.

1. *Privation of Recitations.*

If a teacher hasn't the power of making every recitation attractive, he should strive to obtain this power. Some of the ways and means to accomplish this necessary end, I have given in Lecture II, in showing how a love of any branch may be obtained; in Lecture III, in discussing the 'Teaching Power;' also in Lecture V, in demonstrating that a love of the Work is a necessary qualification, and in presenting the methods by which it can be obtained.

If, then, the teacher has not the skill and interest in teaching any branch which shall make it possible for him to use the privation of recitation in that branch as a penalty, his first business is to secure the necessary ability. If he can not, he is abusing not only that branch of study, but the minds of the pupils. He is, moreover, fixing the habit of disrelish for study, so far as that branch is concerned, and it will not help the matter to compel the class or any pupil in the class to make up for any remissness by extra study in that branch, This course, so generally pursued,is only making bad, worse. It is the teacher's fault, that the class are not interested, and why should he punish the class for his malfeasance by the imposition of a still larger amount of the same evil.

Again, if some pupil, when deprived of a recitation, should seem to say in his actions, "That is just what I like, I didn't want to recite, I didn't know any thing about my lesson, and I don't intend to," it will be found, if the teacher will hold on his course patiently, that such a pupil will presently come round, and be willing to make a good effort. The laugh of the class will be against him, and he can't stand it. He may also be informed that unless he can sustain himself in this class, or at least make some proper effort to do so,he will be unable to retain his place in the class, and will thus be compelled to join a lower class.

2. *Privation of Recess.*

I have shown in Lecture XV, how this penalty may be introduced by a vote of the school, for the violation of any enacted rule, or law.

The teacher should strive to bring about such a state of feeling among the pupils, in regard to the law or laws established, that their conscientious self-reporting may permit him to stand in their defence, by showing that the penalty is *not deserved*, as for a willful act, but is suffered as a means of aiding the pupil to more care and watchfulness in sustaining the law. So it will be seen that the teacher can be inflexible in the administration of the law and its penalty, and yet charitable in attributing motives to the violators, and kindly disposed in interpreting their purposes and intentions.

The propriety of this penalty is found in the fact, that if the pupil takes the time of his study hour for communication or play, it is no more than right that he should be deprived of his play time, as a compensation.

In every case when a pupil is deprived of recess, he should be permitted to "go out" two minutes, after recess. But only one should be out at a time.

3. *Private Reproof.*

The first object of every true teacher will be in every case, to retain or win the good will of his erring pupil. Any unnecessary exposure or uncalled for severity in reproof does not exhibit a friendly spirit, nor will it win friendship. Hence tongue castigations, before a school, can not do the offender any good, but worse than that, they turn the sympathy of the school against the teacher and in favor of the offender; thus every scolding makes the state of the case worse, and increases the demand for more of the same article.

But if, on the other hand, the pupil realizes that the teacher regards his feelings, and it is only from the necessity of the case, that the reproof is offered at all, and yet it is done so as to annoy the pupil the least possible, that pupil will thank the teacher for his kindness in the matter, and make a good effort for amendment; whereas, in the former case, he would only be alienated or enraged, and declare to his school mates, that he hated the teacher and would make him all the trouble he possibly could.

4. *Reproof Before a Class, or Before the School.*

I do not deny that there may be cases, in which public reproof or remonstrance may be necessary, but even in any such cases, it is better to make the remarks general rather than personal, unless in case of open impudence or insolence.

5. *Privation of Position in a Class.*

If a pupil fail through carelessness, continual idleness, or absence, to keep up with his class, it is immeasurably better to remove him from the class, than to compel him to study to "catch up with the class." By the former plan, his study and his class position are held as desirable objects of which he is deprived; by the latter course, coercion makes study hateful, and puts idleness at a premium. Who can not see it? Why will teachers continue to take that course which more than any other makes their occupation a tread-mill and life a burden? But worse than this, why do the great majority of teachers in all schools and colleges persist in making their pupils consider shirking and shamming as honorable, and industrious application as only the part of a menial or a soft pate? It is this course which has given occasion for so many opprobrious epithets, ready to be applied to any student who shall resist the general current of college life, and really make good use of the advantages which the institution affords. The more common epithet for the diligent student, one who prefers industry to idleness or wickedness, is that of 'Dig.' To this is not unfrequently added Spoon, Spooney, Scrub, Spy, Boot-licker, Bore, Blue, Blue-light, Blue-skin, etc., each of which is applied according to circumstances.

Who ever heard any of these epithets used here?

6. *Daily and Weekly Reports.*

Such reports given, as described in my last lecture, mainly for the purpose of incentives, may of course become effective as penalties, and the more so, as the general character of the reports improve, under a kindly and successful management. A poor report under such circumstances will of itself be all the correction that a pupil may need, for any remissness whatever.

7. *Notes to Parents.*

Notes to parents by safe hands, stating facts of absence, tardiness, or any bad habit or act, may under suitable circumstances be very thankfully received by parents, and may be made very helpful in restraining the pupil, or in helping him to restrain himself from indulgence in some careless habit or vicious propensity. But it is one of those helps which must be used with discretion or it will only increase the evil. The parents are very likely to array themselves against the teacher, and thus confirm the child in the wrong.

8. *Suspension.*

It is understood that the power of suspending a pupil has been derived from the Directors, by contract, as was described in Lecture XIII. The teacher will hold this power in reserve as the last to which he can resort. He will always confess to himself that it is only for want of sufficient personal attraction, or adequate strategic ability that he finds himself compelled to fall back on the Directors. Taking this view, he will be strongly incited to more patience, more contrivance, still one more expedient, one more trial of the pupil, before he gives him over to the Directors as beyond his power to manage. And even then it is the teacher that is under trial as much as the pupil.

9. *Expulsion.*

I ought hardly to include this penalty among those pertaining to the teacher's school management. The Directors, I conceive, are the only authority empowered to deprive a pupil of his school privileges. Yet as a probable result of a hearing of the case before the Board of Directors—this may perhaps be made use of in argument with an incorrigible pupil, not so much in the way of threatening, as an inevitable result to be dreaded by both teacher and pupil.

10. *Corporal Punishment.*

It is not my purpose to discuss the propriety or necessity of corporal punishment here. Notwithstanding it is a prominent object in this system of 'Normal School Management' to enable the teacher to govern his school without degrading himself by the use of any form of corporal punishment,

I would not advise any teacher to take the position before his school or elsewhere that he will never use the rod. It may be necessary, and is much more likely to become so, if the teacher shall declare that he will not use any form of physical punishment.

I know of several instances where young men have avowed such a purpose on opening their schools, and were compelled to abandon their school or take back their avowal In every one of these cases the declaration appeared to me very unfortunate, inasmuch as, if it had not been made I thought from the character of the young men they would have succeeded without the necessity of corporal punishment.

11. *Withholding Friendship.*

The true teacher of the highest grade only, can resort to this form of punishment with good effect. Where an ordinary, or even a tolerably good teacher, would make his denial of the ordinary kindly intercourse a means of provoking still greater wrongs, and perhaps personal insult on the part of the pupil, that teacher who knows and feels that his smile is the life and power of his school may with the very best effect withhold such kindly expression from some individual who has thoughtlessly or wantonly trespassed on the law of kindness in regard to some other pupil. I only mention this as one of the occasions where such a penalty may be proper and very effective.

12. *Special Penalties.*

There is no class of general penalties which will afford the best correction for the ten thousand special evils arising incidentally from the ever varying peculiarities of dispositions, and the endless novelties of circumstances. The ingenious teacher will often better resort to special penalties growing out of the special character of the offense rather than apply any general penalty, whatever. I can, perhaps, illustrate by an example or two:

John has a new jack-knife, the first he ever owned. He

must snap the blade, even after requested several times not to do so. He can not help it. Now, it will be better to ask him to place the knife on your table, than to inflict any punishment recognized as such. The smile of the pupils at his expense will be all the correction the case requires. The knife will of course soon be returned to him, and will give no more trouble.

Sarah will keep combing and "fixing" her hair. Even after being requested not to spend so much of her school time on her toilet, she still persists. Now, if after requesting her repeatedly not to waste so much time, and she still continues in the practice, it may be well to request her to stand up every time she feels it necessary to rearrange her hair. It might help her to understand how much time she bestows on her hair, and thus calling the attention of the school to the matter in a kindly way, enable her to overcome the difficulty. Probably in such a case, however, a private conversation with Sarah would have a better effect in checking the evil, and in holding her good will.

Samuel, in his uneasiness, has discovered that his desk can be made to creak and the temptation is too strong for him to resist. Now the better way,perhaps,in this case would be to set him, during a recess or intermission, to remedying the evil by repairing the desk. If this is impracticable, a change of seat with some more quiet pupil would be better than any more common or general penalty.

William brings apples and nuts to school and is inclined to eat them during study time. Of course a general request has been made that pupils will not eat or chew any thing while engaged in study. But William disregards the request, and is noticed eating or chewing somewhat furtively, even after being requested to eat only in time of recess. It may be well to propose to set apart a special time by the clock each hour for William to do up the business of eating, which seems so necessary for his well-being. You may inquire of him how much time he wishes to devote to it, as it will be better to do one thing at a time, and do it well, rather than attempt to study at a difficult lesson and have his mind more than half engaged in a different direction, on something more attractive.

Concluding Remarks on Proper Penalties.

There is no penalty nor class of penalties enumerated here, which may not become entirely improper by misapplication, or by being inflicted in a bad spirit. The spirit and feeling of the teacher in carrying out any plan of school management, whether by incentives or by penalties, is of much more importance than the kind of penalty or incentive used in the particular case of Discipline.

And most especially would I urge, again and again, that the teacher do not permit himself by impatience or petulance, and thus by seeming ill feeling toward the offender, to turn the tide of sympathy in the school against himself and his mode and degree of punishment as vindictive or spiteful. No punishment with the exhibition of such a feeling can do any good. but will, in every case, make more punishments necessary, till the school shall become a very prison or bedlam.

II. IMPROPER PENALTIES.

I shall only enumerate some of the more common improper penalties, and shall leave the discussion of their evils or benefits, if they have any, to yourselves:

1. Threatening individual or general punishment.
2. Scolding at individuals or at the school.
3. Asking for excuses either written or oral.
4. Whipping as it is generally practiced, *i. e.*, as the common punishment for every kind of offense.
5. Compulsory study, inflicted as a punishment. Compulsory study is worse than its own negation in any case, but when imposed as a punishment it is as sure to drive the pupil into a hatred of study, school, and teacher, as forcing an orange into a child's mouth would be to make him resist it. Yet I am aware compulsory study is the common practice in nearly all public schools. The Teachers generally say, "Why, our pupils wouldn't study a particle if we let

them have their own way about it." I reply: This state of feeling with both teacher and pupils is the inevitable result of this terrible malpractice in school management.

6. Any form of physical torture or mental distress beyond the absolute demand of the case, any sudden or violent action, as throwing rulers or slapping the head, are not only highly improper but dangerously criminal.

7. Any punishment whatever beyond the school-yard, or, indeed, any punishment in the school-room, for acts committed beyond the school-yard I consider entirely improper and badly impolitic.

LECTURE ON SCHOOL MANAGEMENT.

LECTURE XVIII.

STRATEGY AND TACTICS.

PRELIMINARY.

---

1. *School Strategy Defined.*

I shall use the term strategy in this discussion more in the sense of contrivance by which an evil can be averted or changed into a good, a difficulty forestalled or converted into an advantage, than in the sense of outwitting by pretended movements.

Strategy means generalship, but generalship does not necessarily signify deceit or over reaching, but rather management by far reaching views and appropriate tactics.

School Work a Training for Life Work.

It requires but little observation to discover that he who rises through difficulties to an eminent position, is stronger in that position than he who is born to it. The training of school life could be no training, were there no difficulties involved in it; but if these difficulties and temptations are not overcome by the pupil and made the means of fortifying him in virtuous action, (and this must be effected by the strategy of the teacher, if at all), the end is lost, perverted, and these difficulties and temptations become inevitably the means of training the pupil to moral delinquency, to self-indulgence in idleness, to the uncontrolled sway of appetites, passions and lusts.

I claim,then,that difficulties and temptations are an indispensable and invaluable part of school training; but it is equally true that unless the teacher has the moral power, enterprise, and skill to convert these difficulties and apply them to their legitimate ends, the school will only contribute to the demoralization of the pupil; and that the teacher only aids in the work of establishing habits of laziness, license and worthlessness. It is with such views that I come to the discussion of this morning's theme.

3. *The Common Idea of Teaching as Derived from Monasticism.*

Monasticism inflicts pains and penances, with no higher end than to mortify the flesh and purify the spirit of the individual—suffering by self-infliction. This is in direct antagonism to the all-diffusive, all-loving spirit of true Christian benevolence. The devoted follower of Jesus has no time to waste in chastising himself, in counting beads, in keeping vigils, in kneeling on bare pavements or on pebbles. His soul is all aglow with desire to bless and save his fellow men. His life is full of generous exertion to this end, and thus is but one continued hymn of praise to his Redeemer. Now the Good Father has not made such a blunder in our constitutions that the training of ourselves and our children to a virtuous life shall necessarily be painful and repulsive; as, for instance, memorizing long pages of meaningless words in any science, or in determining the measure of innumerable Latin words, or in the composition of Latin verses as is still practiced in the schools and universities of England.

No, by no such distressing means are we compelled to work for the attainment for a high degree of mental and moral culture, and power of service in the Master's vineyard. Throwing off the time-worn shackles of the ascetics and the monks, we are permitted to feel and know as teachers that our work is no longer one continued imposition of tasks and enforcing of compulsory labor by floggings, imprisonments and expulsions, but rather the *leading of the lambs* in the paths which the great Shepherd has so kindly provided. For "He knoweth his own and they follow him." It remains for us as teachers to discover these "paths of pleasantness,' to delight in them ourselves, and devise means by which we can lead (not drive) those committed to our guidance. It is true that we have numerous and formidable difficulties to contend with, but nearly all of these are the habits and usages inseparable from the monkish training, still continuing in our families and schools, "Relics of the Dark Ages;" but it is the constant aim of these Normal Methods of school management to drive barbarism and monasticism from the school-room and to introduce the principles of Christianity and the disciplinary usages in accordance with these principles. This is our Strategy.

Normal Strategy and Normal Tactics, then, are but converting the very ideal of discipline from that of the burdensome, the repulsive, the compulsory, into that of the attractive, the winning, the saving; and so making use of the difficulties arising from previous monkish training even, that by contrivance and contrast they shall contribute to the more beautiful attainment of our new ideal. While I claim that this ideal can be maintained through the entire course of school life from the a b c drill to the university graduation, it is only my purpose here to give a few examples of strategy in common school management by which I conceive this ideal has in many cases been measurably attained, hoping thus to afford some succor and encouragement to those of you who have so joyfully labored in the same glad spirit of enthusiasm in all the way in which your teachers have led you, here.

NORMAL STRATEGY.—NORMAL TACTICS.

Teaching the Alphabet.

The 'ts nat method of teaching the alphabet is terrible to contemplate. It is the method in which all of us present were taught. I suppose we have forgotten the dreary days of wearisome weeping, and we ought to be thankful. But I fear many of you have been pushing, scolding, pinching and shaking the little ones through those tearful columns, wondering why children are so dull. Now, Teacher, you have had an opportunity of witnessing the phonic method of our Training Class, and no doubt have said to yourself, "Why was I so dull as to attempt to force and scold children into that which may be made so delightful, so exciting?"

You have seen how this difficulty can be converted, not so much into an advantage as into a joy, a delight. What play or game can keep a phonic pupil away from his reading exercise? But does this Normal phonic method of teaching require more time and labor on the part of the teacher? No, you have well judged that it saves more than three-fourths of the time required by any other method, not excepting the more recently introduced word method, or the other phonic methods so called. But the point I wish to make is that in this case strategy converts repulsive drudgery into attractive and exciting exercise, and that which before made it necessary to force the little fellows off to school, now draws them in spite of themselves. I have known a little boy to run away from home without his dinner in order to read with his class. A little girl who was detained by a sore throat from one exercise making her appearance at the second, I enquired, "How is this, Maggie, I heard you were sick and couldn't come to school to-day." "I be sick, and ma wouldn't let me come, but I cried and cried, and I made her let me come."

Study a Burden. Study a Delight.

I do not believe the human soul so constructed that with all its insatiable thirsting for knowledge, its ever increasing longings after the 'reason why,' and the 'object for which,' there need be any force applied to compel it to gratify these indestructible cravings. On the other hand the use of force is the main 'reason why' *study* is a burden, in spite of these natural inclinations. It is given as a task. The teacher, the Professor in most cases, is little else than a task-master.

It is, then, the office of Normal Strategy and Normal Tactics to take advantage of the means that the "God of nature has put in our power" and change the entire character of the school work. Who does not know that free and cheerful labor is ten times more effective in any direction than slave labor?

I have shown in Lecture XII how a Mental Arithmetic class may be made attractive and exciting, and that pupils properly managed will study their Mental Arithmetic lessons with as much zeal and gusto as if engaged in any game or sport. If a teacher can exercise that degree of strategy, and practice that kind of tactics that will render the study of Mental Arithmetic a success, 'for the love of it,' he can hardly fail in any other branch. All other branches present a wider range for anecdote, a better field for illustration, a more immediate opportunity for useful application, from any or all of which sources the teacher can draw the power to interest his classes, and stimulate them to love study.

In connection with Mental Arithmetic, let me say that difficult problems in Mental Arithmetic, Written Arithmetic or in Algebra are not mastered, nor is any determined effort made to solve them by the *majority* of any class that is managed on the force plan or on the prize plan. This is true enough, I fancy, in the past experience of nearly all of us as pupils. But a still worse method of paralyzing the energy of a class in mathematics, is for the teacher to work all the difficult examples, and give all the explanations and demonstrations. The teacher who does all the work for the class, is not only a lazy teacher himself, but will inevitably make a lazy, listless class, growing more so, until, one by one, they drop off, like gorged ticks not able to hold on longer. Unless a teacher can inspire his class with a love of overcoming difficulties and a pride in doing it, he will come very far short of my ideal. I once heard a teacher in assigning a lesson say something like this, "The fourteenth example is somewhat difficult, I think most of you can work it; the fifteenth is rather knotty, I fear that only a few will be able to master it; the sixteenth and last in the lesson is the most complicated problem of the kind I ever saw, and I doubt whether one in the class can conquer it without help." I overheard a pupil say as she left the room, "I will work it if it breaks my neck." Sure enough, many of the pupils at the next recitation signified that they had solved every example. But suppose no pupil had succeeded the first day, should the teacher have then worked the example for them. By no means. He would rather inquire, "How many would like to try that sixteenth example another day? Just as soon as you 'own up beat' I'll come to the rescue:" and the class would all vote to try it again. A class trained with the kind of tactics of which this example is but an outcropping, can not fail to be enthusiastic; every member of the class will partake of the enthusiasm, and hard study will have more fun in it than any deviltry that can be proposed. Tricks upon teachers are but the necessary result of their want of ability to manage the natural forces of their pupils, and to incite and guide those forces to legitimate and worthy ends. Viewed in this light,are not most college Professors and Presidents, partial or perfect failures?

Parents' Interference Converted.

While teaching and superintending in Marlboro, Ohio, I first introduced the phonic method of teaching the alphabet, using Longley's Phonetic Primer. The Primary teacher informed me that Lizzie Griffith had been kept out of school because her father did not like the new-fashioned phonetic letters in the primer. At the first convenient opportunity, I called to see Mr. Griffith. I found him at a machinist's lathe engaged in turning.

"How do you do, Mr. Griffith?"

"How de do, sir?"

"Miss Dakin says that Lizzie was not in school to-day."

"I thought I wouldn't send her any more at present."

"What is the difficulty?"

"Why—well—ahem—I don't know aoout—I don't understand them new kind of books that the children has to learn to read from."

"Is not Lizzie interested?"

"Yeas, she is interested enough, that ain't no difference; but I'm afraid of them books."

"Why are you afraid of the books?"

"Why, aint them infidel books? I don't find no such letters as them in my testament."

Mr. Griffith was a worthy church member.

"No, sir; these primers have no infidelity in them, as you can readily ascertain by reading them."

"But I can't read 'em."

"Well, it is very easy to read them by the use of the key. But I have a Testament at home in the same kind of type."

"What, is that so? Well, I'd like to see it."

"I'll bring it over."

"Well, I guess you needn't take the trouble. I think Lizzie can go to school again. She's cryin' herself sick, 'cause I wouldn't let her go. I'se afraid there was something wicked 'bout them new fangled letters. But I guess it's all right. I am much obleeged to ye."

"Not at all, sir. Good day, Mr. Griffith."

Parents' Indifference Converted.

We teachers all know that it is immeasurably more difficult to manage the parents and get them interested in their school, and in their children's advancement than it is to manage the children. All sorts of planning and contrivance are required in this direction.

One young lady recently reports that she succeeded so well in interesting her older pupils (that class which generally furnishes the "hard cases,") in Book-keeping, that one of the Directors proposed that she should teach an evening class of "old folks." She consented, adding considerably to her salary; but, better than this, she was enabled, by this means, to enlist the parents in various improvements for the benefit of the school.

Closing exercises, in the form of exhibitions, may be so managed as to be very profitable to the pupils and interesting to the parents. But examinations as they are too often conducted are a sham and a nuisance, and do nothing but evil in every direction.

The exhibitions should consist entirely of original essays and colloquies declaimed, not read; of readings of selected pieces; of scientific experiments and illustrations by the pupils; of reports of the six best pupils in every branch—in decorum, in promptitude, in regular attendance, and the awarding of prizes in penmanship by the committee selected. Not unfrequently will the faithful teacher, on such occasions, be surprised with a present from his pupils. Some teachers are able to sustain monthly exercises in declamation, in composition reading, or in some exercise in the regular branches, which are sufficiently attractive to draw the parents into the school. Thus the enlisting of parents serves to deepen the interest of both parents and pupils in the school and its daily work. As I have shown in Lecture XIII, a suitable interest manifested by the teacher in "getting a good ready" before he commences school is almost an infallible preventive of parental indifference. Here comes in the power and beauty of strategy. I suppose you apprehend, ladies and gentlemen, by this time what I mean by school strategy and school tactics, and that its chief element is an entire consecration to the work of blessing, saving those under your charge. Can this be done by force? Must it not, then, be accomplished by our own devotion to the work, by our own foresight, by our own contrivance and tact in making use of every means within our reach?

False Reporting--How Checked.

In every school, almost, there will be found a class of pupils who think it smart to be mean; who conceive it quite coming down to be decent, and feel very much degraded, if circumstances are such, that they have to submit to the wishes of the teacher.

It is with this class of pupils that self-reporting does not seem to work well at first; and unless some patient strategy, more far-reaching than they are looking for, some adroit tactics sharp enough to flank these unfortunates, can be adopted, it may be possible that they will defeat the plan and make it obnoxious to the old charge, that "it teaches lying."

While teaching a district school in northern Ohio, I had several pupils from families 'squatting' on Granger's lands. Their parents made a livelihood by stealing stave and hoop timber from "Granger's woods," and it is not to be supposed that these overgrown boys of sixteen and seventeen would give up and be decent, without a struggle.

I had adopted the self-reporting system before these squatter children entered school. Soon finding, however, that they were inclined to report falsely and to brag about it, I felt "here's a job to be worked up, not so as to crush out and expel these five or six animals as animals, brutes, but if possible so as to save and win them to love truth, decorum and industry. I tried various expedients, as, for instance, having a private talk with the oldest and worst. This won him to more circumspection, but not to honest reporting, or to any sufficient effort to comply with the rules and improve his time.

One day, at recess, when Ruth, one of my best girls, had reported "imperfect," all these squatters having "gone out" with the rest to enjoy their recess, she came to me saying, with tears in her eyes, "I think it is too bad." "Why so, Ruth?" "Why, Mr. Holbrook, I try to keep the rules—" "I know you do, Ruth." "And there are some of the scholars who report falsely nearly all the time and get their recess, but those of us who try to report correctly often lose our recess." "It *is* too bad, Ruth; I am fully aware of the way the thing works and know perfectly well who are trying to be honest and sustain the rules, and who are not. I shall try to remedy the evil as soon and as well as I can." After much thought I concluded to adopt the following plan, which I brought out next morning in General Exercises, somewhat in this manner:

"My friends, I find this difficulty in our plan of self-reporting: Some pupils report perfect, when others think they are imperfect. Now, it is very possible that those who report perfect think they are right, and those who judge them as reporting falsely may be mistaken. In order to give any who are thus misjudged an opportunity to vindicate themselves, I am going to call on all who think any one has reported improperly, to say so, in order to give him a chance to explain why he reported as he did, and to show that his report was correct. Thus, you see, if you all try to judge charitably, in the first place, and then are desirous to know that every one is trying to do right, and are willing to have the explanation or confession of every one who seems to report incorrectly, we may secure a better state of feeling, and we shall *know* that all are trying to sustain good order and make a good school." "But," says one of the more truthful pupils, "Mr. Holbrook, you don't want us to tell tales on each other, do you?" "No, that is not my object, and if I find any spirit of recrimination or retaliation arising, I shall try to hold it in check. It is my purpose to give every one a chance to vindicate himself when any other pupil thinks he has reported falsely. I want you to learn to have confidence in each other and help each other to do right, and not take satisfaction in blaming any one for doing wrong. I only wish to try the plan a few days; if it does not work well we can lay it aside; and if it does, we shall hardly need to continue it long."

The plan worked, and I had the satisfaction of feeling that the squatter children were just as good pupils as I could desire or expect, considering their home associations.

Hard Cases—How Managed.

In other connections I have given the course of tactics to be pursued with hard cases. The general plan is to provide such employment as shall interest them more than their mischief and wickedness, and, at the same time, let it be distinctly understood that you are able to control them, and are not afraid of them. This is not difficult to accomplish. Either Book Keeping or Physiology as an extra branch can be made an exciting subject of study, and, if once a pupil becomes interested in any study, there is a basis for further action, and the watchful desire on the part of the teacher to approve of every good effort will most surely convert such a hard case into a friend, a docile and assiduous pupil. There is no department of our work, teachers, that demands so much tact in carrying out our plans as this; the salvation of those who seem utterly averse to all good that can come from a school-master.

Mischievous Tricks—How Cured.

A boy who seemed to enjoy more than almost any other one I ever met with, his little tricks and annoyances, still persisting in trying new methods as old ones were checked, came around to paper wads the second or third time. I requested him to make three wads and lay them on a brick which happened to be convenient, telling him that when he had them all made and well made, we would all witness the performance of his lodging them on the ceiling. He demurred. I insisted, saying it was a pity that he should enjoy so much fun all by himself. He ought to let the rest of the school have a share in it. The laughter of the school *at* him, rather than *with* him, as he was throwing the wads seemed to be effectual. Pursuing this plan for a while, viz: compelling him to do whatever he wished to, and depriving him of the privilege occasionally of doing whatever I wished; his preferences seemed to change by degrees, and he learned how to find entertainment in study and decent conduct.

Normal Method of Curing Stammering.

Some time since I received a letter from a teacher, inquiring how to cure a boy of adding the syllable uh to almost every word in reading. The teacher stated that he had tried every plan he could think of, punishing, coaxing, hiring, shaming, and all only made the difficulty worse. I replied, "If you will compel the boy to pronounce the useless syllable after every word in his reading exercise, and persist in it till he is heartily sick of it, I think you will succeed." I soon heard that the plan worked finely. As soon as the boy began to pronounce under compulsion, the whole school began to laugh. It was too much for him. He took hold of the matter himself in good earnest, and, of course, the difficulty soon disappeared.

Evening Parties—How Managed.

It is often the case that the greatest obstacle in the way of a high success in a village graded school is evening parties. Even if but two or three leading pupils are in the practice of attending a party once or twice a week, not only is it impossible to excite any thorough-going interest in their minds, but their influence is a dead weight on the school. But of all kind of parties, dancing parties are the most fascinating, and the pupils that attend them the most uncontrollable. Having taught a graded school about four months, in M. I found that nearly all the older pupils in the high school department, young ladies and gentlemen, were attending dancing parties, frequently. After having requested them several times to abstain from the practice during term time, and yet finding that the practice continued, and realizing that all my efforts to interest and benefit them were in a great measure neutralized, I came to the conclusion that something must be done. I could not longer permit myself to be a party to their self-abuse and waste of opportunity, nor could I feel it right to throw away my time and reputation in such a fruitless work. The young people were always ready to admit the force of my statements, and saw the evil of their course, but some new and unforeseen circumstance arose time after time to seduce them from their purpose; and so the frequency of the parties rather increased than diminished. A day of weariness, listlessness and inattention having passed, in consequence of the young people having been out late at a ball the night previous, the next morning but one after the ball, finding them comparatively rested and cheerful, I made some remarks in this wise, at General Exercises:

"My young friends, I am glad to find you so well recovered from the fatigue and excitement of the ball. It is now, I think, a fit time to state my determination in this matter of balls and parties. You well know that until dancing parties commenced, I enjoyed my position and labor here, that I was well satisfied with your progress and general deportment. Even now, I have nothing to complain of in the want of personal respect, or in your willingness to comply with my wishes in all other respects than that of attending dancing parties. My personal feelings are as kindly towards all of you this morning as ever before, and my desire for your improvement and happiness could not be greater than it is at this moment. But, under the circumstances, I feel compelled to resign my position, and yield it to some other person better calculated to win your respect and confidence, and to whose wishes you will be more willing to defer. My only ground of complaint is in this matter of dancing parties. You are as well aware as myself that your school privileges are almost entirely lost in consequence of attending evening parties, and I do not think you can blame me when I say that I am not willing longer to spend my time and efforts where they can accomplish so little. I shall therefore feel it necessary to ask the Directors to release me from farther connection with the school after this week."

I sat down. One of the older pupils arose and said: "We are sorry we attended the ball against your wishes, and I am willing to promise that I will not attend another ball this winter." "So am I," said another, and so said several. "Well I have no wish to leave here. I came at some sacrifice and considerable expense; I have enjoyed my work exceedingly until these dancing parties commenced. All I wish is to see you as interested in your school as you were, and as earnest for your own improvement:" Said the first speaker, James M.: "We will do whatever you ask of us, and try to give no more trouble, we don't want you to leave us."

"Will you be willing to sign a pledge that you will not attend any dancing party hereafter during term time?" "Yes, I am willing." "Well, let me see how many are willing to sign such a pledge." All hands were raised.

"But such a pledge will not continue in force very long without some penalty for its violation. Some peculiar and unforeseen temptations will arise in all probability when it will be impossible, or next to impossible, to abide by the pledge, and it will thus gradually lose its force, and the evil will then be worse than now, I fear. If you will sign such a pledge as this, which I shall write including a penalty, all of you, I shall be willing to serve you still, and I have no doubt our school will then prove as interesting and attractive as it was during the past term."

I wrote and read the following pledge: "I hereby agree not to attend any dancing party during this or the remaining terms of this school year; and in case I do, to deprive myself of school privileges for the two consecutive school days after the offense."

Some one saying that he thought the privation of one day would be sufficient, I replied that the pupil virtually lost one day any how. He was so tired, jaded and cross, that it would be better for him to remain at home and sleep all day, and that would hardly be any penalty; so I thought the pledge would have to include two days to work well. So all consented and signed their names to the pledge.

We had prosperous times again. The only infraction of of the pledge that occurred was by a young man who spending a Saturday and Sunday with some friends in the country, felt compelled to dance in a party that had been gotten up especially for his benefit, without his knowledge. On Monday, at roll-calling, he rose and stated his case, and left it with me to decide whether the circumstances did not justify his violation of the pledge. My sympathy was aroused for the young man, he was so candid, kind and respectful, and the circumstances seemed so beyond his control; but taking the matter into careful consideration for an hour or so, I then decided that it would be better for the school that the law should take its course rather than that we should begin to take excuses. I admitted that I thought it very severe on him, but assumed that he would be willing to make the sacrifice for the good of the school. He suffered the penalty, and we had no farther difficulty with dancing or evening parties of any kind; in fact, this contest with old habits and usages, this triumph of law and order, was necessary to the highest success of the school. It gave that school more union in effort, more manliness in character, more devotion to school objects, than they could ever have obtained without it. Thus this greatest of all evils, which threatened to ruin the school, was converted by this course of management into the highest positive advantage.

One morning, months after the pledge had been signed, William M., at roll-calling, answered "six." Now "five" was the report which denoted perfect decorum for the day previous.

"Why six, William?"

"Well, sir; I was out to cousin G.'s last Friday night, and they had a dance there. It was just as much as I could do not to 'go in.' But I went off to bed and let them dance. Now, if these scholars in town with no such temptation report 'five,' I think I ought to have six."

"Very well, William, I will give you six this time."

LECTURE ON SCHOOL MANAGEMENT.

LECTURE XIX.

ERRONEOUS OBJECT TEACHING.

Preliminary Remarks.

1. It is charged that I am opposed to object teaching. No charge can be more groundless. I am opposed to the errors, abuses and absurdities of object-*lesson* teaching, and I propose in this lecture to point out some of these errors, abuses and absurdities, together with some others, practiced in other lines of teaching.

As well might it be claimed that I am opposed to the conveniences, comforts and embellishments of my home, because I think it would be absurd for me and my children to confine ourselves in a warehouse an hour or more every day to talk about cooking-stoves, sideboards, bureaus, pianos, pictures and statuary. I prefer to enjoy these comforts in their legitimate uses and applications. So of objects for illustration.

If there is any body of teachers anywhere that makes use of a greater variety of these objects, material and immaterial, real and invented, and in a greater variety of applications, than the corps of Normal teachers here employed I know not where they are to be found. I would travel far to shake hands with them.

2. In order to develop more vividly, what I consider the true method of objective teaching, I shall be compelled to

dwell somewhat at length on the errors and abuses in this direction, now so prevalent in the educational world. Some of these belong more particularly to the object-lesson systems, and are somewhat extensively practiced in the mechanical routine of too many of the *trained* (?) object-lesson teachers found in the primary and secondary departments of several of the city public school systems.

ERROR I. *Book Lessons; no Illustrations; "Thoroughness."*

The teacher who requires memoriter recitations, and makes use of threats and punishments to enforce his requisitions, is a most venerable nuisance; revolutions come and go, in church and state, in home and school; but this oppressive dynasty still holds its sway over millions of innocents. If any extraneous power is ever adjured to consummate and justify this tyranny, it is that of the relentless exactions for examinations, under that baleful watchword, "Thoroughness." The exact letter of the text, in Definitions, Rules, Special Rules, Paradigms, Remarks, Observations, Notes, are extorted by imprisonment and ferule; and this is thoroughness, in the estimation of the force teacher. No explanations, no applications, no illustrations, no objects, but words, fear and force; no apparatus; but the letter of the text, pure and unmixed, and this is the unvarying mandate, the ever present *object*, enforced with conscientious integrity of purpose and rigorous persistence of exaction.

Am I not safe in saying that at least seven-tenths of all children and youth now in our city and village schools are being repressed, disheartened, demoralized, demonized, by just such an infatuated idea of thoroughness, and just such a terrible mode of reaching it?

The present city and village public school systems, with here and there a marked exception, are among the most viciously effective agencies in crushing our children and youth from an eager love of knowledge, and from a hearty good will in their school work, into a positive antagonism to all reasonable requirements, and into the fixed habit of despising and avoiding all remunerative labor. This combination of tyranny and rote, so inseparable in nearly all our graded schools, is the secret, if there is any, of this terrible efficiency.

I ought, in justice, here to say that in many of these tread-mill systems there are one or more subordinate teachers who infuse their own life and inspiration into their own pupils, in spite of the reign of suspicion and tyranny all around them. I have known such a subordinate to modify, if not purify, every department in the building in which she worked.

Again, I have known one of these "lesson grinders" and per cent. extortioners, a principal teacher, of course, to have apparatus, (a pair of globes, and an air pump perhaps,) standing in a glass case, dusty and rusty, exhibited, indeed, to visitors "through a glass darkly;" but he thought it took too much time from the daily lessons, and diverted his pupils' attention too seriously from their regular work, to use this apparatus, if, indeed, he had any idea how it could be used.

I have known another teacher to bring out the apparatus for show in an evening lecture, hoping to win *eclat* in this form of public effort. Singed eyebrows, burnt extremities, stunning explosions, not provided for in the programme, were the most exciting portions of the evening's performance. The apparatus was laid away, charged with being ill constructed, and the manufacturers were denounced as humbugs and swindlers.

ERROR II. *Book Lessons, with Illustrations and no Applications.*

Another class of errorists are those who, using illustrations of various kinds, fail to carry the minds of their pupils beyond the experiment, or the use of the apparatus itself. For example, in illustrating the change of seasons by the use of a tellurian, or globe, such a teacher fails to make the connection with nature, and to carry the mind of the pupil to the grand machinery of the solar system. Too much of objective teaching is of this character, and, falling short of its true aim, is often almost as bad as lesson grinding.

ERROR III. *The Teacher Using Illustrations, but Failing to Arouse the Power of Illustration in the Pupil.*

College professors in natural sciences belong to this class. The result is a most helpless condition of mind on the part of the pupils, the victims of these lecture-spinners and experiment exhibitors. This error can be corrected only by putting the apparatus into the hands of the pupils and permitting them to perform the experiments and to give the necessary explanations and applications.

ERROR IV. *Dealing in Quidities.*

Now and then I have seen an expert in scientific manipulation who took special pride in the curiosities of science, using up the time of his pupils in illustrating far-fetched anomalies, curious and unexplained phenomena, dwelling always with special unction on the "last achievement of scientific research," not realizing that his pupils had failed entirely of the veriest outlines of the science under consideration, and were profoundly ignorant of its fundamental and well established principles.

ERROR V. *Object-Lesson Teaching.*

There is no doubt that object-lesson teaching has among its advocates and practitioners many good and worthy men and women. The system is undergoing constant modifications, and has, in fact, taken to itself many improvements since its introduction into this country; but these are always in the direction of the Normal, or Direct methods, and at the expense of the boasted peculiarities of the object-lesson methods. By these modifications at the hands of some of the leading object-lesson book-makers, several of the absurdities which I shall characterize have been laid aside, and thus, in every instance, a nearer approach has been made to correct practice in teaching, and the object-lesson teaching has become less and less object-*lessonative*, and more and more objective. I may also add that I consider object-lesson teaching, with all its absurdities, a decided improvement on lesson grinding, or "setting on the bench and saying A."

ABSURDITY I. *While Insisting on a Certain "Natural Order of Development,"* the object-lesson teacher ignores the natural fact that the faculties can not be detached from each other. He works on the absurd assumption that the mind is made of parts, and each of these parts can be separately trained. Now, the mind is a unit; the different faculties are only different modes of its activity. Nor can any faculty, or any class of faculties, be well trained, or, in fact, trained at all, without the corresponding activity and training of other faculties. To ignore this fact is as absurd as for a plow-boy to use the beam of his plow in the morning, the share at noon and the handles in the evening; or more closely, perhaps, to use his feet in the spring, his body in summer, and his hands in autumn.

Nor is the intellect the whole of the child. The training of the *will* to determined persistence in right action, the training of the entire individuality to *habits* of eager industry and cheerful self-denial for the attainment of noble ends, are of infinitely more moment in any period of education than the following ot any "natural order of development" that has ever yet been shown to exist.

The best and only worthy training of the memory is by means of relations, and these relations the mind must learn to find for itself, *in fixing the habits* of investigating, systematizing and utilizing all proper subjects and objects of thought or study. Now, the object-lesson method rejects or subordinates the use of the understanding for the first three or five years of the child's training, and thus depends almost entirely on the sensible impressions and the inadequate and feeble inductions called "points," as brought out in the concert exercises of object-lesson drill for training the memory to retain—what? Principles? No. Principles belong to the reasoning faculties, and involve relations; but these exercises train the memory to retain a knowledge of the properties of natural or artificial objects and the technical terms that express them. Is it not obvious that the memory is not thus trained in its legitimate hold on truth, (namely, through relations), but is burdened by a multiplicity of disconnected facts, and their corresponding technical terms?

ABSURDITY II. *Rejecting the use of Books.*—I feel myself safe in asserting that there is no stage in the school life of any pupil in which books judiciously used may not become a marked and effective aid even in the unnatural operations of the object-lesson school room, or yet in accomplishing the ends which the object-lesson teacher professes to have in view. The object-lesson abuse is but the necessary and natural opposite extreme of the lesson-grinding, and per-cent. extorting abuse, so generally cursing our American school system. Men of small calibre, copyists and imitators are prone to absurd extremes in their futile application of valuable principles discovered by original thinkers. Such, undoubtedly, are many of the present advocates and practitioners of object-lessons. I am glad to be able to state in this connection that some leading object-lesson men are gradually falling back from this absurd extreme of "no books in primary teaching" into a more rational use of books than they left; while most of those primary teachers in our graded schools who were compelled to adopt the object-lesson methods are as rapidly as they dare resuming the other extreme and grinding more fearfully than ever in the prison house of books, and per-cents.

ABSURDITY III. *Training children to helpless dependence on their teachers.*—Undoubtedly any true or valuable training tends towards independent and self-propelling activity, and the development of true individuality, but no one of any discernment can witness an object-lesson drill without perceiving that with the majority of object-lesson teachers all individuality is lost in the concert drıl (the almost universal concomitant of object-lessons); the teacher and one or two leading pupils doing all the thinking, while the others are mere echoes in their parrot like repetition of the words of the leaders. This special form of mental abuse, however, so generally practiced by the first object-lesson teachers, is more recently being somewhat corrected in more advanced classes by assigning writing lessons to fix the results of the object-lesson drill. But these writing lessons are relatively open to nearly all the objections which lie against the object-lesson system as a whole.

ABSURDITY IV. *Using Technicalities out of their true Scientific Relations.*—The object-lesson system claims, as its special aim, and advantage that it cultivates the perceptive faculties in the child, without making unreasonable demanps on the reflective or reasoning faculties. But in doing this, beside involving itself in absurdity 1st, it also necessarily brings into use a very considerable variety and extent of scientific technicalities. To have any just understanding of the proper use and application of these technicalities, the true relations of the properties and facts which they legitimateiy express, must be understood; otherwise, as is too generally the case with object-lesson pupils, they fall into very superficial and inadequate, if not absurd uses of these technicalities; and what is worse, fix the *habit* of loose and incoherent use of high sounding words. With the more sensitive class of childern, the ridicule excited by the misapplication of some few object-lesson terms, will generally repress too severely the use of even appropriate language, and drive the child into common-place and slang; while with those less sensitive, the habit of parrot-like use of big words and small, is engendered. This habit, in some cases, seems to be ineradicably fixed for life.

ABSURDITY V. *Ignoring the power of Systematic Relation and Dependence in training the Memory.*—The only plan of mnemonics worth any attention, is that of systematic relations and dependence. Nature, at once, begins to train the memory in generalizing, by the application of names to similar objects; first, material objects and their concepts; then, and almost simultaneously, to abstract objects and their concepts. But nature teaches by the use and application of these objects to the common wants and satisfactions of life, and in these relations, their appropriate terms are obtained and treasured in the memory. Scientific terms, not found within the ordinary range of daily wants and experience, when forced on the memory, out of relations, must be held, if at all, by dint of repetition. But by any correct and comprehensive training in any science as such, the necessary terms, technical, or otherwise, are received with avidity, and retained permanently, without effort, as inseparable from its objects, laws and applications.

To illustrate. How long will it take an ordinarly intelligent class of children to learn the names of the two hundred and forty bones in the human system, saying nothing of their common and peculiar properties, provided these bones are presented in any detached arrangement. But I have often seen a class grasp all the names and relations, and very many of the properties, uses and elements of the entire osseous system in two or three lessons; the teacher depending on the use of the reflective faculties to sharpen the activity of the perceptive faculties, in ascertaining and fixing in memory the names, relations, properties and uses of each of these two hundred and forty bones.

I repeat it then, it is not only an absurdity but a gross abuse of the memory, the understanding, of good sense especially, to force a mass of disconnected and incoherent names and facts upon the minds of children.

Absurdity VI. *That Children can learn to read more readily, intelligently, by the Object-Lesson method than by any other.*—While there is no doubt that the object-lesson method, with all its absurdities and abuses, is, in most cases, an improvement on some other prevalent methods, yet, so far as the object-lessons themselves are concerned, they stand in the way of the pupil's progress to an independent use of his books, in the practice of diligent study, and in acquiring and fixing the *habit* of earnest work for the love of it.

I have seen pupils of less than six years of age, trained in the Normal method, with phonetics, who, in eleven weeks, were able to read, write, and study independently; and in comparing this progress with that of those children who had been trained by the most approved object-lesson teachers, for more than a school year, I was satisfied in every case, that from one-half to two-thirds of the labor, time and expense bestowed by the object-lesson teacher, might have been saved; while the *habits* formed in the first case were good, and in the latter, for the most part, were indifferent or bad—*i. e.* I discerned in the children trained by object-lessons, no positive love of school, or power of independent study, or of individual effort in observation and investigation, or appreciation of the beauty of systematic arrangement and procedure; or any perception of departure from it on the part of the teacher.

Now, all of these I hold as objects of vital moment in the primary department, as well as in every other department of the school work.

The Normal method, aiming, as it does, at these *habits*, will surely be more likely to reach them than the object-lesson method, which ostensibly aims at the development of only the perceptive faculties, and the power of expression, by oral drill, with drawing and writing lessons, as an essential accompaniment.

Besides, if in graded primary schools, there is time enough in the six school hours of a day, for a teacher to give a considerable portion of it to the exercises called object-lessons; in an ungraded school of a country district, in which, by the best classification, twenty different classes at least must be attended to, in order to meet the wants of all the grades of pupils in attendance, where is the propriety of wasting the little time that can be given to the primary class in such indirect and dilatory processes?

ABSURDITY VII. Assuming that any object-lesson book, in

the use of which the teacher is trained, contains, or can contain enough of all the physical sciences to make safe teachers of the technicalities ot these sciences or of any one of these sciences.

There are, perhaps, a dozen different volumes published, each claiming to be a correct and sufficient guide for object-lesson teaching, each embracing lessons involving nearly all the physical sciences. Yet any one of these physical sciences, if but very meagerly presented, must occupy a volume, quite as large as any object-lesson book yet published, the greater part of which is given to matter entirely irrelavent to any science or any scientific course of procedure. To carry out the assumed purpose of object-lesson advocates, and object-lesson book compilers, legitimately, would then require the thorough training of the object-lesson teacher in at least ten different physical sciences but much more in psychology, logic, rhetoric and moral phylosophy. But a person thus trained would never practice the absurdity of attempting to develop one class of faculties the better by ignoring or subordinating the rest.

CONCLUDING REMARKS.

I. These animadversions are directed entirely against the abuses and perversions of object teaching. But these abuses and perversions are practiced by so many of the trained object-*lesson* teachers, that they seem to be inherent in the object-*lesson* system. Still I do not wish to deny that a large minority of object-lesson teachers are doing a good work in the primary school-room, as compared with the other force work almost universal in city schools.

II. I have sometimes thought, in visiting city schools, and in hearing the Principals boast of their success in their exactions; of their rigor in carrying out their laws, so grinding and crushing to all free action and noble aspiration on the part of the pupils, that object-lessons might perform the same office in the force system of instruction as the dancing and revelry of holidays among the former slaves of the Southern plantations; or as the gladiatorial shows in the governments of Nero and Caligula. Object-lessons, by an enthusiastic teacher, do afford some considerable mitigation to the reign of force, and the exactions of tyranny, and seem to make the rote-force management much more tolerable to its subjects; are indeed a kind of safety-valve, the more necessary as the pressure of tyranny is the more severe.

III. There is no desire on my part to deny the validity of the principles which *are said* to underlie the object-lesson system of instrution; but it is the ignoring of these very principles in the object-lesson practice that I complain of. I do deny,however,that all knowledge is acquired through our external senses. This fundamental principle of the object-lesson system, is Comptism, and belongs to the sensational or positive school of infidel thinkers. On the other hand, I am confident that much the greater part of all valuable knowledge, even in childhood, comes through other channels, and the sense perception affords only one basis of intelligence, the other being the internal sense, or conciousness and the intuitions. But all of these are mere bases which, with out communication with other minds in conversation, reading, and study of books, would yet leave their possessor a savage or an idiot. And right here I wish to reiterate that knowledge is not education, through what ever channels it may be obtained. *Education is the established working of good habits*; and it does seem to me that the object-lesson system as generally practiced, is not designed, nor is it expected by its advocates to establish such habits as a love for work, a love for investigation, a love of self-mastery, a love of thoroughness, a love of noble and benevolent activity.

IV. The question arises, if there are so many objections lying against object-lesson teaching, why has it been received with so much favor in many of our city school systems?

I have virtually answered this before, but will again give my solution of the problem.

I have observed that the more grinding the despotism in any system of schools the more ready was the Superintendent to accept the object-lesson palliation.

Again I have noticed, and in fact it has been confessed by some politic Superintendents that the object-lesson sensation, in its ad captandum features, enables Superintendents to introduce other modifications which are really needed and which could not be obtained from their Boards of Education by any other means, as soon, if at all; and it must be admitted by those who have watched the movements of affairs, that Superintendents are not unwilling to avail themselves of the exciting exhibitions of infantile wordiness to enhance the value of their own services, even though their better judgment may condemn many features in the workings of the object-lesson system of primary instruction.

V. If the object-lesson exercises are recognized then as an amusement, necessary to while away the time and relieve the evils of six hours' daily confinement of the children in the primary departments of graded schools, perhaps their true place is found. Or if it be asserted that they are a kind of compensation in the force system for the iniquitous stripes and imprisonments inseparable from a government of force and fear, I am willing to grant the fairness of the statement.

VI. So far, then, as object-lesson teaching is introducing true objects or ends into the school work; so far as it is calculated to relieve the children of the spirit of tyrannical rule, and the grinding of intolerable rote; so far, I am in favor of object-lesson teaching. I have no doubt but that there are trained object-lesson teachers who work with sufficient enthusiasm to make their departments attractive, and they do some thing to counteract the baleful influence of their respective school systems which drives so many of the children from their only school privileges into the marble-gambling crowds of young ruffians that infest nearly all our towns and villages.

Now, I know, and have seen it accomplished, that the

change of objects, from "thoroughness," to *good habits;* the change of spirit, from that of oppressive control by means of stripes and imprisonment, to a spirit of enthusiasm and encouragement; a change of school work from that of memorizing book formularies, to that of studying subjects, and with the aid of suitable illustrations or "objects," will revolutionize, not the school only, but the moral aspect of the town.

Why, think of it once; on the one hand children are *compelled* to attend school, and avail themselves of every opportunity to escape school drudgery; they rejoice in holidays, and brag of any success in eluding or evading the scrutiny and exactions of their teachers; exult especially in "playing hookey," and not getting caught in it. Is it any wonder with such a condition of things that from one-third to one-half the enumerated children are not regularly in school with such worthless parents as many have? On the other hand if the school is managed on Normal principles and by Normal practices the children will have to be compelled to stay away from school, and every school day is better than a holiday. They brag, if at all, on the superiority of their own teachers, and discover that there is a thousand times more fun in right than in wrong. Will not such a change work a revolution in a school; in a community? Nay, will it not almost of necessity build up each pupil in a new and true life? instead of driving him into a continued practice of deceit and evasion; of shirking and shamming, of hating every thing that is good and loving every thing that is evil?

VIII. In my next lecture I shall endeavor to present very briefly—what I consider TRUE OBJECT TEACHING. 1st. The True Objects and Ends. 2d. The True Spirit in working for those Objects. 3d. The True Processes in carrying out that Spirit. 4th. The True Forms of Objective Illustrations in conducting those Processes. 5th. The True Methods of using those Forms of illustrations to reach the true Ends in view.

LECTURE ON SCHOOL MANAGEMENT.

LECTURE XX.

TRUE OBJECT-TEACHING.

PRELIMINARY REMARKS.

Ladies and Gentlemen :

Having in my last lecture considered some of the prevalent errors practiced in schools and colleges, with reference to the use of objects and methods of illustration, I shall now as briefly as possible present some of the points in what I consider the true use of objects, both as ends and means—in other words, I shall try to present what I understand to be the true system of object-teaching.

As I conceive the Normal Method of instruction to be broader in its scope and more far-reaching in its outlook than any of the methods which I have characterized as erroneous, or than any method which tolerates such abuses and absurdities, I shall feel compelled to present a condensed synopsis of the general scheme of Normal Instruction, as given in Lectures X, XI, and XII, but in the reverse order. In giving this general view, I shall take occasion to show, as I proceed, some of the points of difference existing between the Normal or Direct Methods, and Object-Lesson Methods on the one side, and the Rote or College Methods on the other.

The True Objects in any Course of Instruction.

In Lecture XII these were given in the natural order, thus: Immediate, Mediate, Ultimate. I shall here reverse the order, and first consider the Ultimate objects or ends which should be aimed at by every teacher and every pupil in every department of education, primary or advanced, theoretical or practical, in school-room or work-shop. Nay, these are the true ends of life; and any education, or department of education, which does not harmonize with them, is abnormal and vicious.

The True Objects of True Object-Teaching.

(1.) The highest of these is *to glorify God* and win his approbation. Any line of instruction or any process of school drill which leaves this object out, or holds it in the remote future, or commits it to other spiritual guides, is so far abortive, and must in a measure defeat the first and highest of all objects in *true object-teaching.* I abhor sectarianism, but the teacher who is not all aglow with the love of the Father, who is not working in the communicated energy of His Son, falls far short of his own true inspiration; and how can he hope to inspire his pupils with that which he does not possess?

(2.) The next true ultimate object in the school work, in the descending order, is *to bless mankind,* and win the approbation of good men. It may be said, and is, that the school work is but preparatory; it should look to the acquisition of knowledge, for future use, and the teacher should be fully absorbed in his present aim. To this I reply, that by so limiting himself in his views he cripples himself, and paralyzes the nobler energies of his pupils, and thus in a great measure defeats the attainment of even his own meager end. By the way, I consider that end, or object, relatively absurd and practically abortive, as I do many other of the aims and processes of the rote or college system of instruction, whether practiced in school or in college. Again, it may be said, and is, that the training of the senses and development of the mental faculties should be the chief or only object of the school work; and these, together with the cultivation of the power of expression, should command the exclusive attention and interest of the object-lesson teacher, at least for the first two or three years of primary instruction. Such short-sighted views, however, object-lesson teachers themselves will deny when alleged against their system; however much they may urge them in their books and training lectures. Now, I claim, and I have no fear that any one will dispute it, that these true and highest objects will, far more than any other, energize and sanctify the labor of every teacher for every pupil, and more effectually aid him in reaching any of the lower objects or ends desirable in any course or department of instruction. Not only so, but the love of God and the love of man, or Faith, Hope, and Charity, may, and do in many cases, neutralize in some measure the abnormal practices and vicious tendencies of the present rote-force system in many school-rooms, giving a gleam of spiritual light and warmth, all the more cheery in the surrounding moral darkness and winter of death, too generally pervading the rote-force systems of school discipline and instruction.

(3.) The remaining ultimate objects, or ends, in the school work, still following the descending scale, are *position in society* and *success in business*. I call all these objects ultimate, because they are ends which give fruition in themselves, and do not look to others for this end, viz., happiness or personal enjoyment. Now, my complaint still is, that even these lower ultimate objects are too generally left out of sight, both in the object-lesson drills and in the rote-force methods of school and college management, including both instruction and government. The application of force in the absurd attempt to compel children and youth to study and be virtuous, necessitates the use of improper objects, as the avoiding of disgrace and bodily pain, the attainment of school or college honors or prizes. As every clear and candid observer must admit, these vicious objects poison the entire moral atmosphere, and vitiate, more or less, all the spiritual energies of both teachers and pupils, in whatever school or college the rote-force is in operation.

But the Normal Methods, using these legitimate objects or ends, and rejecting rote and rant, suspicion and force, relies on the natural constitution of "human nature" in children and youth, as being able to be incited in the spirit of *Liberty* and trust for the attainment of these ever-present ultimate ends by the use of the appropriate Normal processes in each of the consecutive stages of the school work.

True Mediate Objects.

These I have given somewhat at length in Lectures X and XI. They are the *Habits*, Established Habits, controlling and energizing all mental, moral, social, and religious activity, vitalizing these higher objects, and making them the very substance and essence of the entire life. But these habits, to be worked for and established, if possible, in the very nature of every pupil, are the love of work, as if by a matchless inspiration; the love of mastery, or thoroughness, as if by a dauntless enthusiasm; the love of order and system, as if by the spirit of beauty; the love of utilization, as if by the power of a benevolent and loving heart. What less dare I aim at in my efforts to prepare you for your work? What less can you strive for, my friends, in calling forth the soul energies of your pupils, and in giving them direction for life; nay, for eternity?

These habits well established, I affirm, are an education; and without them there is no education, though there may be, and too often is, in place of them, effectual *training* in these vicious habits, viz., repugnance to all continuous labor, perfunctory accomplishment of every school task and life duty, a dilettante cultivation for general uselessness, often called culture, and yet all this under the popular idea that these habits are compatible with, if not the most distinguishing characteristics of, a polished gentleman or of an accomplished lady.

True Immediate Objects or Ends in the School Work.

(1.) These are not what the rote-force system assumes—(*a*) "perfect memoriter lessons for high per cents."; nor are they what the object-lesson system assumes—(*b*) "the development of the perceptive faculties and of the power of expression." Such immediate objects or ends are comparatively futile and ineffectual in establishing the habits before mentioned. The rote-force object necessitates processes and methods which establish habits of laziness and deceit. The object-lesson objects are reached with vastly more directness and certainty by the *true immediate objects* of Normal management, while the vicious habits of depending on the teacher for excitement, and of the parrot-like use of language, are avoided.

(2.) These true immediate objects of class management I have already given in Lecture XII. I will only recapitulate them here:

(*a*) Earnest and interested attention and independent activity of *every* pupil in every class, during every moment of a recitation or drill.

(*b*) Enthusiastic and spontaneous study in preparation for every recitation.

(*c*) Self-reliance in continued and coherent speech; and this may be, normally, worked for in primary and secondary departments, as I have shown in Lecture XII.

(*d*) Quickness of apprehension and grasp of memory. These,

as I understand them, are virtually identical, as objects in class management.

(*e*) Power of independent investigation and self-propelling analysis in the thorough mastery of every *subject* assigned for study.

(*f*) Entire familiarity with the principles and processes of the particular branch under consideration, and ready and constant application of these principles to the affairs of life, or to the explanation of natural phenomena.

(*g*) Orderly self-control, with a manly or ladylike bearing toward the teacher and fellow-pupils.

These, in my estimation, are the true objects (immediate, mediate, and ultimate), ever present and ever operative, in the daily, hourly work of every true object-teacher. Not one of them can for a moment be lost sight of in *true object-teaching*. They most effectually preclude all the rote force methods, while they include all that is valuable in the object-lesson methods, vitalizing and intensifying them.

It may be objected, that children in the primary stage can not study lessons, hence some of these objects would be out of place with a primary teacher. To this I reply, (1.) that in the proper management of primary pupils, a brief time in school each day is required; (2.) that appropriate exercises on slates and with blocks, or with such natural objects as minerals and plants, can be furnished, in connection with the phonetic drill, as to occupy their attention, and, as far as desirable, accomplish all the objects proposed; (3.) that children will learn to read and study in from three to six weeks, when properly trained by a *true object-teacher;* so that study, good, earnest, independent study, may enter even a primary department, and hold and interest the children just so far as is desirable for them.

The True Spirit of True Object-Teaching.

(1.) The system of Pestalozzi is often assumed as the basis of all modern improvements in teaching. Now, there is no doubt that Pestalozzi was a success, in his way, and that he possessed much of the true spirit of true object-teaching; but I apprehend that if he should witness much that assumes to bear his name in the training schools of America, and much more in the schools of the trained, he would hardly know why his name were assumed, unless to cover practices which he worked all his life to eradicate. These are, mechanical routine, coercive government, suspicions, censoriousness, and compulsory study. These elements are no part of Pestalozzianism, as I understand it; and yet, so far as I know, they are some or all of them retained in all object-lesson schools, inasmuch as object-lesson teaching has scarcely been introduced elsewhere than into the treadmill systems of education existing in our larger villages or cities; and in every case, so far as I know, it is used to mitigate but not to eradicate the rote-force evils of these schools.

I would look higher than Pestalozzi, even to the Great Teacher, for my inspiration; and partaking of His Spirit, I would before, beyond, and above all forms and methods, work in the spirit of love, and hopefulness, and trust.

(2.) It is not unfrequently the case, however, that the spirit of some teacher engaged in the rote-force work of a system of schools, or working in an isolated position, is vastly superior to his own or her own theory; and while he or she may maintain the frame-work of compulsory labor and the machinery of coercive rules, the spirit of enthusiasm and gentleness that pervades the school-room renders this frame-work and machinery almost entirely inoperative, and thus, of course, they do little harm. I have even found teachers of this character contending for the force system of government, and appealing to Solomon for wisdom. Why, I should as soon think of asking Solomon for instruction on matrimonial affairs as in school teaching—at least, unless he has been very badly misunderstood. Teachers, you may always feel in your school-room, "A greater than Solomon is here." "Suffer little children to come unto me," and "Put up the sword," are to me mandates of higher authority than "Spare the rod and spoil the child."

(3.) While the spirit of Pestalozzi or of Jesus does not necessarily dwell in any *objective* or *subjective* forms or methods, I do feel that it is impossible for any one of you to gain any clear conception of these true objects as I have tried to present them, and not imbibe somewhat of the spirit necessary to teach them; at least, you can not fail of a better spirit, a higher tone, and a more vigorous effort, in the prosecution of your daily work.

(4.) But what is this true spirit of the teacher's work? I answer, first and always,

1. The spirit of liberty. Force in the direction of right is oppression, is absurd, is abominable. It makes right hateful; beauty, hideous; and truth, a lie. If coercion must be used, let it be applied only to prevent wrong, never to compel right action or right feeling. But the true teacher will sooner or later grow out of even the necessity of using force to prevent wrong action; for this necessity is manifestly only his want of power. This lack of moral, personal power has to be made up by the use of physical force; and the true teacher will, by ex-

perience and daily improvement on himself, obtain this power. Again, is it not perfectly obvious that right can not be compelled? Moral rectitude belongs only to *free* agents. How, then, can there be any morally right action or right feeling as the result of coercion? If any of you hear the wisdom of Solomon in answer, listen only to the higher wisdom, not of Pestalozzi, but of Jesus.

2. The true spirit is a spirit of ENTHUSIASM, that can no more be restrained by any particular forms or methods than can an eager traveler by the laziness or fatigue of his horse. If one horse does n't suit, he takes another; if none can, he seizes the mane of steam, or rushes forward on foot. This spirit of enthusiasm is contagious in the school-room. This was the secret of Pestalozzi's power and success, in spite of his many errors and much short-sightedness. This spirit abominates rote, supersedes coercion, wins respect, if not admiration, reaches its objects by dint of its own essential vim. Impossibilities?—it knows none; none which it does not convert into higher possibilities, nobler achievements, and sweeter conquests—victories of love, how sweet, how uplifting!

3. This true spirit is the spirit of CHARITY, of SYMPATHY; it believes against belief, it hopes against hope, it loves the meanness all out of a boy. Woman, thy sphere is here, where man fails. Where man is compelled to fall back on his muscle and apply the rod to crush rebellion or insolence, thy tender spirit has disarmed or converted it. A perfect teacher demanded? No. The more imperfect, the more filled with the consciousness of infirmities, the more effectively will this spirit work, and the more speedy and certain its victories.

Teachers, let us sit at the feet of Jesus; he is touched with the feeling of *our* infirmities, else he is not our Savior or Deliverer.

REMARK.—I have been led to compare the enthusiastic spirit of pupil teachers in training here, with that exhibited in training schools elsewhere. The almost universal promptitude, regularity, and energy of every pupil teacher in attendance here, where the spirit of freedom reigns, is, I apprehend, quite in contrast, if reports are at all reliable, with the spirit of perfunctory compliance with rules, and frequent evasions of school duties, in those training schools where rules are held to be necessary, and "submission to authority is considered essential in the training of teachers." While pupils here, of their own spontaneity, not unfrequently establish additional class recitations at five o'clock in the morning, I am told that at the annual training exercises in the Cincinnati schools, conducted mostly by object-lesson advocates and practitioners, it is necessary to call the roll in the respective training rooms four times daily, in order to secure the continuous attendance of the pupil teachers. And even this is found inoperative without cutting down, for absence, *the wages paid to these same pupil teachers* for attending these training exercises in the annual City Normal Institute.

True Forms of Illustration.

1. Rhetorical Illustrations. Instead of the rhetorical forms, the object-lesson teacher would place real objects first in the list. In teaching addition, he would use such articles as pen-holders, pencils, or, perhaps, the balls on a numeral frame. It is my opinion that the child is trained into ideas of number, or, rather, acquires the power to grasp and combine numbers, much more rapidly and surely without these objects before his eyes, and that the use of them retards his development in the clear conception of numbers, and the power of combining them and computing with them. It is better, then, to concrete the ideas of number by using rhetorical illustrations, and arousing the imagination of the children by using the ideas of these objects, and multitudes of others which can not be brought into the school-room, rather than the objects themselves; and yet, when such objects are seen to be necessary or desirable, I would not fail to use them. Right here, the assumed end, the development of the perceptive faculties, stands plainly in the way of the true end, that of securing earnest and interested study during the study hour.

I would, then, make use of rhetorical illustrations, *chiefly*, in teaching primary arithmetic, instead of any kind of real objects whatever. The idea of number can thus be concreted more rapidly and certainly with any primary class; and ideas of abstract numbers, and their abstract relations, can be conveyed to the minds of children with much more facility and interest by means of rhetorical or invented illustrations, than by counting beans or shoving red and black balls on an arithmometer.

It is a sad mistake to assume that no correct primary teaching can be done in number without real objects; and again, that these can be entirely laid aside in higher classes. The truth is, the more advanced classes need the objective illustrations the most; and the farther those classes advance, the more necessary do real objects become, especially in the combination of form with number, as in squares and cubes, with their roots, or in the more obscure relations necessary to be understood in demonstrating the computation of the contents of curved surfaces and curved solids.

To illustrate rhetorical illustration by a rhetorical illustration, I will assume that I am combating the definition given in many of our grammars, that "Case is the condition of a noun or pronoun." I would state to my class that "Case is the external form which the noun or pronoun assumes to indicate its relation to the verb or other words in a sentence, and thus to give a clear idea of the use it is intended to accomplish in the expression of a thought.

"So the case on a bag of feathers, giving it a certain form and appearance, will indicate whether it is to be used as a cushion or a pillow. The case is virtually its external form. So the cases on meat may indicate the kind or condition of the meat, whether ham or sausage. But the external form is not the condition, or the quality, or the use; it is the result of that condition, quality, or use intended, and thus can be safely taken to indicate it.

"Just so with the forms of nouns, but more distinctively with those of pronouns; they assume one form when used as the subjects of a verb, and another when used as the objects of a verb or of a preposition. For example, *He* helps *me*, *I* will reward *him*. *I* and *he* are used as subjects, but *me* and *him* are used as objects."

2. SCIENTIFIC ILLUSTRATIONS. It is hardly necessary to detain you with any continued remarks on scientific illustrations. These are for the most part objective, that is, the real objects are presented and used by the pupils. These consist of the apparatus and materials appropriate for every science. Geography demands its globes, maps, and charts; but the true object-teacher will make more frequent use of such real objects as his own town, township, and county, with whatever physical features they present, as rivers, lakes, plains, hills, etc.; and by means of these object illustrations he will convey clear and correct conceptions of physical geography to his pupils.

In chemistry, the true object-teacher will not only make use of the appropriate apparatus and materials, but he will incite his pupils to make apparatus for themselves; as you know it is the constant practice in our classes here for the pupils to construct a considerable part of their apparatus for themselves, from such common utensils and articles as can be obtained in the boarding-houses, or at the groceries, or hardware stores, or tin-shops. This is done by our pupil teachers here, that they may be able to teach this science objectively in their own schools.

Thus, we see, every science has its own objective forms of illustration, and that every true object-teacher will not limit himself or his class to purchased apparatus; but that, in every science, the best part of objective illustrations are those obtained by the pupils from the every-day operations of life.

So in mineralogy, botany, and zoölogy, the true forms of object illustrations are not so much those found in extensive collections of museums and cabinets, as those which the pupils can collect for themselves in their rambles and journeys, classifying and labeling them under the direction of their teacher, or by the aid of such books or other authorities as can be reached without too much labor or expense.

3. Artistic Illustrations. Under this head of illustration in true object-teaching, I would include chiefly those efforts in drawing, which it is the special endeavor of every true object-teacher to encourage. In geography, map drawing and somewhat of natural scenery and architecture; in natural history, the drawing of vegetable and animal forms; in natural philosophy, the drawing of apparatus as arranged for special experiments. All of these, in exhaustless variety, are some of the appliances by which these subjects are made inviting, and study is converted from a burden and a task into a pleasure and a triumph.

Especially in the primary and secondary departments in a graded school, or with the primary class in an ungraded school, is drawing indispensible as a means of interesting the children, advancing them in reading, spelling, and writing, and giving them more interesting employment than mischief; last, not least, in the normal method of school management.

To these results in drawing, in all of the departments, the true object-teacher will add such pictures, drawings, casts, and other artistic productions as he or she may be able; all of which increase the attractiveness of a school-room, and of the normal teacher himself, or herself, in making his or her school the cynosure of every child that enters there.

Besides the illustrations already mentioned, suitable for all classes, I would furnish for the primary and secondary departments a considerable quantity and variety of blocks; some of the shape of bricks, four inches long; some one-inch and two-inch cubes; also, connecting blocks, sawed with grooves and tongues for dove-tailing; also, a variety of blocks for pillars and turrets. These, with a set of geometrical solids, would furnish interesting employment and valuable self-instruction. I would also have the teacher trained in drawing from real objects, and thus able to guide and incite the children in their first efforts at linear and perspective drawing of real objects, on their slates and on paper. These bricks, cubes, pyramids, etc., before mentioned, are as good as any simple objects to commence drawing from. Soon it will be found, if children are *permitted*, not *required*, to draw, that drawing any real objects in the school-room, as tables, chairs, stoves, hats, buckets, will be the amusement and excitement of the children at the times assigned for this exercise in the programme.

Thus, drawing from real objects on slates, building blocks

into architectural and mechanical forms, using the blackboards (which boards should extend to the floor all around the primary school-room), may, with some little contrivance and tact, some real sympathy and interest, occupy the time of the children when not under the direct drill of the teacher in phonetic teaching and phonetic reading.

But in a few days—at most, in a few weeks—by phonetic training, a primary class of children will be able to begin to study and prepare exercises in mental arithmetic, or primary geography, or primary physiology. It is preposterous that children should be kept in the primary department one year, learning to read in the first reader; and in the secondary, another, in conning over a second reader; and so on through eight or ten departments in as many years; learning nothing that in any measure counterbalances the bad habits of hatred for school and repugnance for labor, which they must inevitably get thoroughly established under any method that makes their progress so slow, and their continuance in school so useless and irksome. So far as my judgment could decide, I would not have a child in school at all till eight or ten years of age. But, as a teacher in charge of children who are legally entitled to school privileges when six years old, I would introduce such employments and such apparatus and appliances as would make the children happy, and just as far independent of the teacher during study hours as possible.

This is all the more necessary in an ungraded school, under the care of one teacher with at least twenty classes to attend to, besides all other business.

I shall dwell more at length on the methods of accomplishing these ends, in speaking of the true processes of using these objects and materials of illustration for amusement and instruction. I pass now to speak of

4. Practical Illustrations. I shall only be able to give a few examples of this class of illustrations. They may more properly, perhaps, be called applications. In geography, I would have the children measure the school-room, the school-yard, the distance of a mile in some one direction, and for this purpose a foot rule and a measuring tape would be necessary apparatus.

In studying weights and measures, I would have the actual weights and measures used in the school, in weighing and measuring water and other substances. Scales, weights, and measures might be borrowed or bought for this purpose.

In studying the mechanical powers, or the steam-engine, I would take the class, or the school, to visit the machine shop, or the steam saw-mill or grist-mill, and examine the machinery in operation; and I would ask the proprietor for a full opportunity to examine the machinery in all its details, and relations, and particular uses.

In teaching surveying, I would train the pupils in the reality of surveying; in the use, adjustment, and repair of the instruments; in plotting their own surveys, and computing them.

In chemistry, I would not fail to give the student opportunity to examine the substances described, and to familiarize him with the use of the apparatus in preparing experiments, and performing the various operations of the laboratory. A good working laboratory can be fitted up by any teacher who "has a heart to it," with comparatively little expense.

These are only a few of the numberless varieties of practical illustrations, which I consider essential to good teaching in every branch. Is it then asked, what practical illustrations could be used in studying English grammar? I answer, the true study of grammar is conducted entirely by practical illustration, and less by memoriter book lessons than almost any other science or art, not excepting the common trades of shoemaking, tailoring, blacksmithing, etc. If our children were *permitted* to study the language practically, instead of being *compelled* to learn some grammar by heart, the study would become the most exciting and valuable in the school drill, instead of the most repulsive and useless, as is now too often the case in many schools. The *writing of letters, essays, and reports* are practical illustrations of mental power and its development, as well as of the principles of spelling, syntax, and rhetoric.

But the *collection of cabinets* of minerals for the school, and each pupil for himself, can in many localities be made a very interesting and useful exercise. Besides the mineral cabinet, the collection of animal and vegetable curiosities, and the proper display of them in the school-room, can be made exceedingly useful in elevating the school in the opinion of the children, and changing the idea of school life from that of hateful, prison drill, to that of a really free and happy employment, immeasurably more attractive and exciting than any villainous games or sports that boys playing hookey can engage in.

But walks, short journeys even, with a class or school, as affording opportunity for observation in geography, study in geology, mineralogy, botany, and natural history, will be found full of practical illustrations in these sciences and others, and in many of the useful arts.

By the means of all of these illustrations, and the processes which I propose to describe in connection with them, not only is every worthy object, whether in the rote-force system or in the object-lesson system, attained, with greater rapidity and certainty than in those systems, but what is of infinitely more value than any thing which either of these systems seems to contemplate in its drill or outlook—the *habits* of cheerful, joyous occupation for worthy and remunerative ends is fixed; the *habit* of thoroughness and mastery in whatever the child or youth engages is established; the *habit* of promptitude, systematic action and dispatch, becomes itself a success in giving success to every work and enterprise engaged in; the *habit* of real enjoyment in doing good (rather than in doing evil) is vitalized, *energized*, and becomes the working power of the life. These habits make the boy or the girl just what the God of Nature and of Grace designed that he or she should be, in His great scheme of agencies for the redemption of our fallen race.

REMARK.—The briefest statement possible of the means of illustration has occupied so much time and space, I shall be compelled to devote another hour to the description of some of the processes necessary to make these different classes of illustration available in *True Object-teaching*.

THE OBJECTS AND AIMS

OF THE

SUCCEEDING TWELVE LECTURES ON SCHOOL MANAGEMENT IN VOLUME II, NATIONAL NORMAL.

They will demonstrate that the entire school management, as based on the "principles avowed" and exemplified in the twelve lectures already published, in volume I, can be carried out in the spirit and power of truth and love; and they will give such methods for school organization, sustaining order, inciting diligence, arousing ambition, sustaining cheerful, earnest effort, and FIXING GOOD HABITS, as will overcome all difficulties, and such as have, in a multitude of cases' converted the school room from a prison into a paradise, from an incipient hell, where the most favorable state of affairs, resulting from suspicious domination and wearisome routine, is treacherons eye-service, cringing servility, compulsory toil and repressed antagonism, into a brotherhood, where mutual confidence begets earnest endeavor, where **increasing** daily success incites higher aspiration and more determined effort, where the teacher finds his every faculty, every susceptibility, exercised to its utmost in guiding and blessing those so eager to appropriate every suggestion, so anxious to comply with, or forestall, every request. Such is the power, the success of truth and right in the Normal Methods of School Management as these Lectures will demonstrate.

XIII LECTURE	Preliminaries to organization. Contracting with directors. Most important items generally neglected.
XIV LECTURE.	Organization; a definite mode of procedure; the beginning of a noble success.
XV LECTURE.	Normal methods of sustaining order and exciting diligence. Rules? how enforced without corporal punishment.
XVI LECTURE.	Discipline; incentives, proper and improper.
XVII LECTURE.	Discipline; penalties, proper and improper.
XVIII LECTURE.	Strategy, how to convert difficulties into advantages.
XIX LECTURE.	Illustrations; or true object teaching.
XX LECTURE.	General exercises, how made attractive.
XXI LECTURE.	Superintendency, with six hours' teaching, and no time for examinations.
XXII LECTURE.	Superintendency, with sufficient time for examination of classes.
XXIII LECTURE.	Declamation and composition; how introduced and ustained without compulsion.
XXIV LECTURE.	Professional improvement, self-culture.

SYNOPSIS OF FIRST TWELVE LECTURES ON SCHOOL MANAGEMENT, IN VOL I NATIONAL NORMAL.

In order to present the general scope of this course of lectures on School Management, we present here a very brief outline of the twelve lectures in Volume I., NATIONAL NORMAL. Also, of the twelve lectures, yet to come, in Volume II.

I LECTURE. QUALIFICATION 1st, Common Sense.

II LECTURE. QUALIFICATION 2d, Knowledge of The Branches.

III LECTURE. QUALIFICATION 3d, Teaching Power.

IV LECTURE. QUALIFICATION 4th, Governing Power.

V LECTURE. QUALIFICATION 5th, Love of the Work.

VI LECTURE.

DIFFICULTIES IN SCHOOL ROOM. How to overcome them.

1. Insubordination from bad predecessors.
2. Insubordination from good predecessors.
3. General prejudice against novelties.
4. Bad habits in school room.
5. Interference of parents.
6. Amount of labor to be performed.
7. Irregularity in attendance.

VII LECTURE.

DIFFICULTIES IN SCHOOL ROOM. How to overcome them.

8. Tardiness.
9. Indifference of parents.
10. Want of uniformity and sufficiency of books.
11. Want of sufficient accommodations.
12. Want of properly prepared fuel.
13. Hard cases.
14. Low wages.

VIII LECTURE.

SELF-DIFFICULTIES. How to overcome them.

1. Bad grammar, pedantry, dogmatism.
2. Use of tobacco, and what comes of it.
3. Want of self-control, seven specifications.
4. Want of social power, the reason and remedy.
5. Want of confidence in one's self, how to obtain it.
6. Want of confidence in human nature, why.
7. Want of confidence in God.

IX LECTURE. Human constitution as the material for training. School training defined and exemplified.

X LECTURE. School management in class management.
Education the formation of habits.
The habits to be aimed at in the school work:

1. Cheerful, earnest industry. Love of work
2. Careful, thorough investigation. Promptitude and energy.
3. Systematic arrangement and methodic action. Good order

XI LECTURE.

4. Useful and benevolent activity. A noble and virtuous life

XII LECTURE. School management in class management. Exemplified and explained in the management of a Mental Arithmetic class.

LECTURE ON SCHOOL MANAGEMENT.

LECTURE XXI.

PROCESSES OF TRUE OBJECT-TEACHING IN THE HIGH SCHOOL.

PRELIMINARY REMARKS.

1. In attempting to *describe* the processes of true object teaching, two difficulties present themselves: (1) the description is unnecessary to those present, who have been trained here, more or less, in these very processes; (2) they can hardly be made intelligible to those who have not used them, or, at least, witnessed their operation and enjoyed their results in the school work; nevertheless, in order to give a somewhat complete view in this course of lectures of the system of Normal School management as here wrought out and taught, I shall venture on the description of these processes, with the hope that the statements and details may hereafter prove valuable by way of reference or suggestion in your several fields of labor.

2. I would like, if possible, to make these statements, so that they may be applicable both to graded and unclassified schools, saving the time and space necessary for a re-arrangement and restatement for either purpose. I shall attempt this double work as one; and in order to bring the description within the least limits consistent with perspicuity, shall give

the processes only for five departments in a graded school, viz: The High, Grammar, Intermediate, Secondary, and Primary Departments. These four last, it will be noticed, correspond respectively, as near as may be, to the four grades in a well organized unclassified country school.

3. It must be kept in mind at every step, as we proceed, that in every effort you make in carrying these processes into practice, that the same true objects of True Object Teaching are ever present; the same spirit of *Liberty*, of *Enthusiasm*, of *Charity*, of *Benevolence* is ever operative and controlling both teacher and pupil; and that the noble and precious results of a true manhood, a beautiful womanhood, working in cheerful industry, with vigorous enterprise, for eminent attainments in a pure, honorable, and useful life, are constantly foreshadowed, with more and more promise day by day, in every pupil's character engaged in these processes and their concomitant exercises.

4. In order to make these descriptions intelligible to the uninitiated, and at the same time to bring them within the limit of a lecture, I shall be compelled to select one or two exercises in one or two branches in each of five departments, more to *illustrate* the nature and drift of these forms of instruction, than to give any connected and available guide to their development and practice. These can only be obtained by a consecutive and protracted course of training.

I. Objective Teaching in the High School.

1. Rhetoric.—In this branch, in contradistinction from the ordinary rote method of requiring memorized recitations from one text-book, we make use of a variety of text-books in a class, using them more for the purpose of training our pupils in the processes of *finding* what they desire to know in the development of a given theme, than as text-books. The real work in the study of rhetoric, with us, is most purely objective; making text-books our servants, or mere tools, collateral or subordinate aids, in the prosecution of the class work. From first to last, the teacher lays out the work in the hour of recitation for the class to perform during the study hours assigned to them. He also gives such preliminary drill as is necessary to the understanding of the work to be performed, and such as will excite an interest in this work, so that, while it shall be done intelligently, it shall be done with all cheerfulness, in the spirit of true enterprise and of noble emulation. The only difficulty in this plan is, that pupils can hardly restrain themselves to the prescribed hours,

and too often give more time to these themes than is consistent with other duties.

Now, such a class, managed by this objective method, with these Normal objects in view, enumerated and explained in my last lecture, never fail to rouse themselves to their highest effort, in the preparation of their daily assigned work. Day by day, as the result of such earnest labor in the spirit of liberty and enthusiasm, a higher power is evoked in each soul, and a better habit of strenuous exertion for noble ends is fixed in every life. And just this is what we work for, and what we consider the True Object System of teaching. And we accomplish what we work for; that 's the beauty of the thing.

I have shown, in another lecture (Lect. , p.), how the higher objects, good-will to man and reverence for God, are reached in the spirit of charity, benevolence, and devotion. Success in attaining these higher objects, as also the others, must depend on the peculiar character of the teacher. He can not fail, in the Normal method of Object-Teaching, to impress his own spirit into the very life and soul of every pupil.

Now, I claim that, while a knowledge of Rhetoric, as a science and art, is held as very subordinate in this objective method of treating the subject, yet a more than ten-fold power is obtained by this method over that obtained by any other method which I have ever known used in the college drills. Work that is work, in the spirit of enthusiasm and liberty, accomplishes miracles, when compared with work which is drudgery in the spirit of toil and submission to exacting requiistions for such mere temporary and inadequate ends as good recitations, in expectation of reward, or avoiding censure, and in preparation for a quarterly or annual examination. How hateful and burdensome, comparatively, is such work; and how much of shirking, deceit and shamming necessarily enters into all this line of what is called instruction, education, preparation for life! If there is any vim or juice in it, it is all in the wrong direction—establishing bad habits, and fixing the supremacy of bad inclinations, passions, and practices in the school work for the life outfit.

To make this objective method as intelligible as possible, I will ask your attention for a moment to some specimen points in the management of a Rhetoric Class, conducted in the method that I consider Normal, or that, for the time being, I denominate "The True Object Method." No object-*lesson* taint can be found in it. Instead of assigning lessons by the page or chapter in one text-book, according to the college method, the teacher gives a drill in partitioning some theme involving some common and interesting *object*—as "The Watch." The class is led on to consider and suggest the subordinate topics contained under the general theme, such as the history, construction, materials, classes, movements, modes of manufacture, uses, abuses, etc. While the hour of recitation is thus mostly spent in developing this theme in subordinate themes, by arousing the thinking and observing energies of the class, at the close of the exercise another theme is given for the class to study out, each pupil by himself, during his study hour. The steam engine, for instance, would be an appropriate theme, provided the class could visit one, or more, in the village or neighborhood.

At the next recitation the prepared outlines are received, examined, commented on by the teacher and pupils; and, possibly, it may be best to give another day to study the same theme, *objectively*, in this same general manner; probably not.

The logical or natural order of arrangement of these subordinate themes now receives attention. Each pupil is requested to pin or tack his paper to the wall, that every other pupil may have opportunity to aid himself by examining the work of every other in completing his arrangement of subordinate topics in the general outline. When this is done, each pupil is requested to arrange the entire list of subordinate topics in that order which seems to him the most natural and appropriate for their consecutive discussion. The several arrangements are then examined by the teacher, the merits or demerits of one or two discussed by the class, and the place of each topic decided by a vote of the class, so far as time will permit. The *object* of this part of the drill is to interest the class in the power of relations, beauty of systematic arrangement, and to confirm the *habit of systematizing whatever they take in hand*, and to establish the love of good order everywhere.

Then a subordinate topic is assigned to each, for him or her to partition in preparation for elaboration in a brief and yet exhaustive essay, giving a description or discussion appropriate to the particular theme assigned. The partitioning of some of these subordinate topics may be necessary in the class, and by the whole class, under the guidance of the teacher, in order to secure earnest work at this step, and prevent discouragement on the part of any pupil. These outlines of subordinate topics are received at the next recitation, and examined by the teacher, or they may be pinned or tacked to the wall, as before, for general examination. It may be well to propose to grade these consecutive papers in three particulars, viz.: neatness, exhaustiveness, logical arrangement, on a scale from 1 to 5 in each particular.

The pupils, in making out these outlines, have been encouraged to get information from every reliable source, first, and best always, by using their own powers of observation on the object itself; secondly, by conversation with those who are most familiar with the article or object under consideration; and, lastly, by consulting any books that will give any pertinent information.

The subordinate topics are then elaborated and read by the several pupils, for the general interest and instruction of the class. The teacher often finds himself as much instructed as any other member of the class. These papers are then taken and examined by the teacher, and returned to the pupils, with the errors noted by figures given on the scale of criticism—from 1 to 20. The pupils are then requested to correct the errors thus indicated, and another hour or more is occupied in receiving from the pupils the correction of their own errors, as they give them aloud before the class. As soon as the work on the first general theme is completed by any of the pupils, another general theme of similar character is assigned. It is necessary, in this class, as elsewhere, to furnish work, a plenty of work, for every pupil, or the result is dissatisfaction, laziness, or mischief.

But, after having assigned two or three themes of these visible and tangible objects, the ends for using them are attained, and a higher class of themes is then assigned—as photography, telegraphy, or some other useful art. These being treated in a more vigorous manner—as the pupils can bear it—are laid aside, and a more abstract class of themes is gradually reached, and more thoroughly canvassed, and more elaborately discussed by our young writers. The development of power by this process is so rapid, and the accumulation of energy is so great, that no unprejudiced observer will say I exaggerate when I affirm that ten times as much is accomplished by this "True Object Method," as by any of the musty, lazy, slavish book-lesson methods pursued in the academies or colleges. Rather, he would say, I opine, that these same college methods, handed down from the dark ages, are a positive waste of time, and a terrible abuse of mind and character, when compared with the True Normal Method of Objective teaching in this branch of study.

The enthusiasm aroused is so intense that the laziest are reached, and the most actively mischievous and vicious are controlled and converted, for the most part, into noble and pure workers. These vicious ones, made so by bad school management in previous schools; from being the curse of the community and the dread of the teacher, become the pride of the school, and the leaders in all good works in the community at large. But these are only the necessary and legitimate results of true teaching; and the true teacher expects such things. He is satisfied with nothing less. It is his mission to do what the pulpit can not—to reach even further, with his schemes of active benevolence, than the Sabbath-school or the colporteur.

To those of you who have participated in just such exercises in our Normal classes here, I am sure my description of these processes will seem meager, and my statements, as to the results obtained in this kind of normal objective drill, very tame; but I trust you feel energized by your experience as pupils here to carry these same processes, improved by your own ingenuity and enthusiasm, into your own schools wherever you go.

2. Chemistry.—I shall now, as time and space may permit, develop the objective method of treating one of the natural sciences, chemistry, for instance. It would be supposed that college professors, with a good supply of materials and apparatus, would, at least, in the natural sciences, prove to be objective teachers. But, I am sorry to say that I consider them only object-*lesson* teachers; they do too much of the work in handling the apparatus and materials, and nearly all the thinking in lecturing before the classes, thus making their pupils more helpless, lazy, and mischievous than if helplessness, laziness, and mischief were the *objects* for which they were working.

It is true that many professors in colleges, and many college teachers in academies, require memoriter recitations from text-books in the natural sciences; and I am at loss to determine which of the two methods is the most effective in establishing bad habits in the pupils—the lecturing plan or the memoriter plan. Much evil inevitably results from both; and some good, undoubtedly, in spite of their general and baneful tendency. You know very well, my friends, how these things are managed here. We permit our pupils to do the work, the thinking, the lecturing; and a more enthusiastic crowd was never witnessed, than that which assemble daily to *work out* a thorough mastery of chemistry. Laziness, where can it lodge? Mischief, who has any time for it? The only trouble is, there is not time enough to do one-tenth of what each pupil desires to do.

It is asserted by some college gentlemen that, by such methods as these, the pupils fail to get a *thorough* knowledge of the science or art studied, because they do not prepare themselves to be examined in some text-book on that science or art. My reply is, that, by such objective processes as are practiced here, the pupil obtains a ten-fold more practical and valuable knowledge of any subject, than by any amount of mental labor bestowed in memorizing one text-book, or in preparing for any examination, however rigid. In the one case, the labor is bestowed directly and objectively on the substances and facts involved, also to their applications in business or in science; and these real and objective processes, if managed with any skill on the part of the teacher, can not fail to arouse every energy the pupil possesses. In the other, the mental labor is given indirectly to the words and ideas of the text-book, looking more to the marks of censure and approbation in the recitation, than to the applications and relations of the truths contained in the text-book. In fact, not one in a thousand gets any clear apprehension of the ideas contained in a text-book without the objective work to aid the mind and heart in the effort.

The Objective or Normal Method is full of enthusiasm and fruitful in results for good, both in the school life and in after life, through the habits established and the power obtained. The college or rote-force method is a paralysis to all voluntary effort, and is fruitful in results for evil, both in college or school life, and after life, through the vicious habits established and the utter lack of personal power, energy, and enterprise engendered, whether by the memoriter processes, or by the object-*lesson* processes connected with the lecturing method of instruction as now pursued in nearly all colleges and universities.

THE MANAGEMENT OF A CHEMISTRY CLASS.

Instead of assigning a lesson of some six or eight pages at the beginning of the book, to be memorized by the class, for the first recitation, according to the rote-force method; instead of delivering a learned introductory lecture, desiring the pupils to take notes in preparation for an examination on the subject-matter of the lecture, according to the most approved college method; which method, as it proceeds, develops itself as being the veritable object-lesson method imported from Germany into our colleges, and into our primary and secondary schools by the way of Oswego; instead of any rote-force method, or any object-lesson, however modified, I would strive, in my first exercise, by the use of objects, to arouse an interest in the subject; such an interest as would stimulate my pupils at once to *apply themselves to work*, for the love of it; to thorough-going, self-propelling work. This I would strive to accomplish by processes like these which I shall attempt to describe. I would, in the first place, direct the attention of pupils to the iron rust on the stove, stove-pipe, or other iron surface in the room, noticing the difference between the iron and iron rust. I would also ask the class to mention other kinds of rust; and I would then ask the class to open their text-books (of which there would better be several different kinds in the hands of different pupils) to the chapter on oxygen. I would ask them to find the article on oxides, and from that, if possible, discover the true nature of rust, whether of iron or other metals. I would then ask my class to discover, if possible, from their books where else oxygen could be found beside in rust. The leading facts in regard to the presence of oxygen would thus be drawn out of the text-book by the class, in connection with the objects; rust, air, water, etc. I would then inquire if any one in the class can ascertain the process by which oxygen can be obtained in a separate and pure state. Yes. The description of the process is read. Now, who would like to step forward and perform the experiment, as described in the book, of "making oxygen?" "Here is the apparatus; here is the material given; here is every thing you need for the purpose." I shall, probably, have a dozen volunteers for the work. I accept of two to work under my eye, and in the presence of the class, in the manufacture of oxygen.

All are watching eagerly the process of preparation, and when the oxygen begins to "come over," expressions of satisfaction or delight burst from members of the class. Several jars or glass fruit-cans are filled with the gas. By this time, perhaps, the hour of recitation is nearly gone, and time must be taken to assign the lesson, and to explain the method of study. A topic list, previously written on the blackboard, is now presented and explained as the means by which they can study the substance and the subject, oxygen. Pupils are requested to copy this topic list, and to prepare themselves to discuss any topic contained in the list, in its relation to oxygen, at the next recitation. It is also stated that some of these topics will be found more fully treated in some books and some in others. It will be desirable for every pupil to have the use of more than one text or reference book in preparing the lesson. If this is not practicable, each must do the best he can with one book. If the teacher can possibly find time and strength, he will do well to ask two or three pupils to meet him, at some time, outside the regular school hours, to prepare experiments for exhibition before the class at the next recitation. The proper conducting of any class in natural science needs an extra hour with a part or the whole of the class in the preparation of materials and the arrangement of apparatus for successful experimenting during the hour of recitation. This hour of drill in manipulation is worth more to the pupils who engage in it, vastly more, than all the rest without it.

At the next recitation, then, the experiments are performed by those who have enjoyed the previous drill during the extra hour; and, possibly, some others are permitted to repeat the same experiments for the sake of general practice, and giving greater familiarity to the whole class with the experiments, their manipulations and explanations.

It will be borne in mind that, as each pupil performs an experiment, he is expected to give an explanation of its details and results, and make its applications and connections with the general line of discussion in the development of the general subject. It may be necessary, at first, for the teacher to aid the pupil in his efforts at explanation by some suggestions or questions; and if the pupil fails, the class is called upon for the elucidation of the point under consideration, and some volunteer is requested to give his view in regard to the matter in hand.

Oxygen being the first substance examined, it may be necessary to detain the class on it, as a subject of study and manipulation, for three or four days, before hydrogen shall be assigned as the next substance to be examined in the light of the same "topic list." A similar but more rapid course will be pursued in the management of hydrogen, and other simples and compounds, the teacher always selecting such as, in his judgment, will be best calculated to sustain and increase the interest and working power of the class.

I have only attempted, here, to give a description of the introductory work for a class in chemistry. It is sufficient, however, I apprehend, to give some idea of the processes involved in TRUE OBJECT TEACHING, as applied to the natural sciences.

As the class progress, on the same general plan, new devices are introduced at every step, to secure the grand OBJECTS set forth in order in lecture XIX.

Can it be supposed that, with such processes, carried out in the spirit of liberty, enthusiasm, and kindness, that there can be any possibility that any pupil should continue in habits of laziness and mischief, shirking and shamming?

It will be perceived that no memorizing of definitions, processes, or explanations is tolerated, much less required. Nothing so repulsive and hateful, so useless and abominable, is permitted to neutralize the interest and power of True Object Teaching. It will also be noticed that the lecturing is done almost entirely by the students, and that the manipulations and experimenting are given into their hands and hearts, as a means of arousing the highest possible interest and energy, as the true *working* power of the class.

It has not unfrequently been the case that pupils managed in this way originate apparatus of their own in their own rooms, homes, or elsewhere, to practice still more than the possibility of class drill will permit. Sometimes, indeed, the teacher calls for volunteers to get up a certain experiment with apparatus of their own construction; and, in a class properly managed, there will be no lack of volunteers for this or any other good purpose. Such experiments and apparatus are generally exhibited before the class, and commented upon by the class in due order, after the explanation or lecture by the exhibitor.

Now, if some good, honest, hard-working rote-force teacher objects to this method of teaching chemistry, natural philosophy, or physiology, by saying that "I can teach the lessons as they are given in the book well enough for me; but as for the experimenting, I have n't any apparatus, and if I had, I would not know how to use it; in fact, it would only keep the scholars from getting good lessons," I reply, that your teaching any one of the natural sciences by book lessons alone is just as sensible and useful as it would be for the architect or surgeon to teach his pupils the "art and mystery" of his profession by book lessons alone. No; the book teacher, the rote-force teacher, is a quack and a nuisance. He makes his pupils wicked, and, in the main, defeats the true OBJECTS of school life, and too often of the entire life, by making school work burdensome and hateful. But what shall we say of the object-*lesson* lecturers, with their most approved courses of instruction after the manner of the German Universities? I am free to say that, comparatively, they belittle and paralyze their pupils, by failing to arouse that spirit and enthusiasm of independent investigation, of self-propelling work, of thorough mastery of subjects, of systematic arrangement of their labor and acquisitions, of a ready, coherent, and apt expression of their own thoughts; by failing to draw out of their pupils that self-sacrificing energy for the good of a class, which the True Object method of teaching is sure to accomplish, as its necessary and legitimate result.

[See Next Page.]

HOLBROOK'S IMPROVED GYROSCOPE.

No. 17, Ex., having 3 rings. No. 18, having 2, and No. 19, having 1 ring. A very wonderful piece of mechanism, explaining the centrifugal and centripetal forces in mechanics, and the motions of the heavenly bodies.

NUMERAL FRAMES.

No. 21, nicely made and varnished havging 144 colored balls.
No. 22, " " " " " 100 " "

This frame is used in Primary, Intermediate and Grammar Schools. It greatly assists in teaching to count, add, subtract, multiply and divide, and is especially useful in *illustrating fractions.*

HOLBROOK'S GEARED TELLURIAN.

No. 8, brass mounted, with day circle and compass.
No. 9, " " " " next best.
No. 10, " " " " " "
No. 11, " " " " " "

THE TELLURIAN is an instrument designed to illustrate all the phenomenon resulting from the relations of Sun, Earth and Moon to each other, and showing the causes of the following: 1st. Succession of day and night, and difference in length. 2d. Changes of the Seasons. 3d Changes of the Moon. 4th. Solar and Lunar Eclipses. 5th. Philosophy of the tides. 6th. Precession of the equinoxes. 7th. Differences of solar and sidereal time, etc., etc.

HOLBROOK'S ORRERY, OR PLANETARIUM.

No. 12, brass standard like No. 8, highest finish. No. 13, brass standards, like No. 8, next best. No. 14, wood standard, next best.

THE ORRERY is an instrument which shows the proportional size and relative position of the planets, and times of their revolution. An illustration with this machine brings out our vast system of sun, planets and moon into so perfect and tangible a shape, and so small a compass, that the *young* even can easily comprehend it. For teaching Astronomy and Geography.

HOLBROOK'S CELESTIAL SPHERE.

No. 15, brass mounted, highest finish. No. 16, brass mounted, next best.

THE CELESTIAL SPHERE is designed for classes in Astronomy, or Geography of the Heavens. The celestial meridians, equator and poles of the Heavens, and zodiac, divided into signs and degrees, are represented as they are imagined to exist.

CUBE ROOT BLOCKS.

No. 25, double, for carrying illustrations to three or more places. No. 26, single, for carrying illustrations to two or more places. No. 27, sixty-four inch cubes, for same purpose. The question of Square and Cube Root can be solved in no other way so easily as by illustrating with blocks of this kind.

CONIC SECTIONS.

No. 28, Dissected Cone, with pins, showing the Circle, Eclipse, Parabola and Hyperbola, colored sections. No. 29, ditto, Smaller. No. 32, Blackboard Rubbers with handle, made of best sheep's wool. Two styles and four sizes. No. 33, Pointing Rods, hickory, best jointed.

HOLBROOK'S OBJECT-TEACHING FORMS AND SOLIDS.

No. 20. Thirty-four forms in neat wood box.

GEOMETRICAL FORMS.

No. 23, large size, very nice, neatly boxed. No. 24, smaller size, with Arithmetical Solids. Forms and Solids are indispensable in teaching square and cubic measure.

MAGNETS.

No. 30, Horse Shoe, or U Magnets, of all sizes, with armature.

Every School and Teacher should be provided with one, furnishing as does a means of illustrating the law of attraction, besides endless amusement to the children.

JOSIAH HOLBROOK, Lebanon, O.,
Or 117 West Fourth St., Cincinnati.

www.ingramcontent.com/pod-product-compliance
Lightning Source LLC
LaVergne TN
LVHW010232110826
845151LV00004B/1267

* 9 7 8 1 4 2 5 5 2 5 0 7 1 *